LOW & SLOW

MASTER THE ART OF BARBECUE
IN 5 EASY LESSONS

BY GARY WIVIOTT
AND COLLEEN RUSH

Running Press
PHILADELPHIA · LONDON

Published by Running Press,
A Member of the Perseus Books Group

Books published by Running Press are available at special discounts for bulk purchases
in the United States by corporations, institutions, and other organizations. For more
information, please contact the Special Markets Department at the Perseus Books Group,
2300 Chestnut Street, Suite 200, Philadelphia, PA 19103, or call (800) 810-4145, ext. 5000,
or e-mail special.markets@perseusbooks.com.

ISBN 978-0-7624-3609-5
Library of Congress Control Number: 2008943526

E-book ISBN 978-0-7624-5107-5

20   19   18   17   16   15   14
Digit on the right indicates the number of this printing

Cover and Interior design by Amanda Richmond
Edited by Geoffrey Stone
Food Stylist: Carrie Purcell
Prop Stylist: Megan Hedgpeth
Typography: Berkeley, Downcome, Hawksmoor,
and Helvetica Neue

Running Press Book Publishers
2300 Chestnut Street
Philadelphia, PA 19103-4371

Visit us on the web!
www.offthemenublog.com

TABLE OF CONTENTS

ACKNOWLEDGMENTS

FROM GARY WIVIOTT

TO MY SWEET, PATIENT AND BEAUTIFUL BRIDE ELLEN, you make my heart grow a little each day.

Longtime friend Andy Bloom gets credit as idea man behind gifting me my first smoker.

Thanks to Colleen Rush—writer, friend, drinking buddy, and GPS to my low and slow wandering.

Because one must learn before he can teach, a tip of my hat is in order to Bob in Georgia, Big Jim in Central Florida, Kit Anderson, Bill Ackerman, Dan Gill, Danny Gaulden, Garry Howard, Dave Linebeck, and the participants on the BBQ Porch.

To the many friends, LTHForum members, and Wiviott.com users who completed the original 5-Step program, your willingness to follow, learn and question was critical in helping me refine the program.

Thanks to Scott B. Orr, nephew and friend, whose simple statement "thanks for the gift, now what do I do with it" signaled the start of this journey.

To friend and 5-Step program graduate Subha Das, your brilliant input on chapter 8 demonstrates a clear commitment to barbecue.

To Cooper's in Llano Texas, where god goes when she is in the mood for Texas-style brisket. One small taste nudged me down the true path of BBQ enlightenment.

Finally, a thank-you to my parents, Howard and Joanne—always encouraging and supportive even when they are not quite sure what they're encouraging and supporting.

FROM COLLEEN RUSH

FOR MY MAMA—you may have been Miss Mansura High, but you'll always be the Pig Queen to me. *Vive le cochon!*

To Gary, my barbecue sensei—you have an uncanny ability to incite aggro-ness, but also to ease it. I can't imagine working on a project like this with anyone else. This book was meant to be.

INTRODUCTION

DEAR STUDENT,

MORE THAN TEN YEARS AGO, MY WIFE, ELLEN, GAVE ME A WEBER SMOKEY Mountain (WSM) cooker for my birthday, thinking I'd make smoked salmon or maybe the occasional rack of ribs. She never anticipated that it would inspire a complete obsession with low and slow barbecue.

How did it happen? I went through many phases while learning this form of cookery. It started out innocently—I made some chicken or ribs for dinner, and they were just fine. Then I did a little research and learned a few more things. So I bought some new tools and experimented with wood flavoring and vent closures. Next, I started making different types of sauces and rubs. Finally, looking for a magic bullet to make my barbecue better, I bought another cooker. And another one. Pretty soon, I was parking on the street. My garage was stuffed with barbecue equipment and bags of charcoal. I was also reading and participating in a few of the major barbecue Web sites and newsgroups, swapping ideas with and learning from the other barbecue-obsessed out there.

My point? I've gone overboard in every possible direction—learned everything I *never* needed to know about barbecue, made every mistake (at least twice), and got suckered into buying all the bells and whistles—so you don't have to. I'm not the guy who learned how to barbecue and decided to join the competition circuit to win a few trophies or bragging rights for an award-winning sauce. Nothing gives me greater pride or pleasure than teaching someone the simple art of low and slow.

This program started out as an e-mail to a nephew who wanted to learn how to use a WSM, and it is still guided by the same K.I.S.S. (Keep It Simple, Stupid) philosophy I preached to him. Do exactly as I say, and you will be able to make better barbecue than 95 percent of the so-called barbecue restaurants out there. More than anything, this program is about gaining confidence in your instincts—learning to trust the senses you were born with to create tasty barbecue.

The techniques and instructions for the five dinners are designed to gradually build your understanding of low and slow. You'll learn how to set up and use three different types of charcoal cookers for low and slow barbecue. You'll learn the single most important element of barbecue: how to build and maintain a clean-burning fire. As you make the five dinners, you'll build faith in your cooker's ability to burn for hours without you constantly fiddling with vents and thermometers. And let's not forget about the food. You'll learn how to impart pure, clean smoke flavor and make tender, delicious barbecue. You'll also learn valuable kitchen skills along the way, from the basics of making your own marinade to how to toast and grind spices for signature rubs.

Now, for a stern lecture. It is strictly an issue of publishing limitations that there isn't a system of locks attached to this book. If I had it my way, you would have to sign a legal document swearing you had successfully completed each dinner before moving on to the next. Then I'd give you a key to access the next lesson, and another, and another, until you had followed my instructions to the letter through the last dinner. I can't stress enough how essential it is for you to turn off your brain and simply follow the instructions exactly as I outline them. And they are simian-simple instructions—the product of years of my own trial and error with backyard low and slow barbecue. You will take no short-cuts. You will not borrow tips from some Hawaiian shirt–wearing fool on the Food Network or your half-wit uncle, Pete. You will not invite all of your friends over the first time you attempt a dinner (because there will be failures along the way). Rest assured, the path to great barbecue is yours in just five dinners. But until you successfully complete the Five Easy Lessons Program, you are mine. Do you swear to do as I say, no questions asked? Good. Pupil, prepare to begin your journey.

Sincerely,

Gary Wiviott

★ 1. ★

GEARING UP FOR
LOW &
SLOW

WHAT IS BARBECUE?

THE WORD BARBECUE MOST LIKELY evolved from one of three origins: the Caribbean word *barabicu*, the Spanish *barbacoa*, or the French *de barbe et queue* ("beard to tail"), all methods of drying or roasting meat and whole animals on a platform over a wood-burning fire. Today barbecue has become a catchall word covering everything from grilling hot dogs or drowning chicken in a slow-cooker full of sauce to any gathering where outdoor cookery takes place. But for the purpose of this program, and if you want to sound like you know what you're talking about, barbecue is a method. It's a noun. Barbecue is not a verb or a sauce. It's a cooking technique that requires the interaction of wood, charcoal, fire, and meat. If there's no smoke and fire involved, it's not barbecue. (Some hardcore barbecue traditionalists would even argue that point and insist that you have to burn down your own wood to make charcoal. I'm not going that far.)

You'll probably notice how strongly I feel about this issue throughout the book, but it's important to make the distinction because too many people have the wrong idea about what constitutes barbecue. Ribs, chicken, and pulled pork cooked on gas or electric grills or smokers or steamed or baked in ovens is not barbecue. Just because it's covered in a sticky, sweet sauce or has grill marks on it doesn't make it barbecue. Don't even get me started on liquid smoke. Generically calling this style of cooking "barbecue" ignores (and, in my opinion, is an insult to) the rich tradition of real barbecue. At its best, meat cooked by gas or electric heat is only evocative of real barbecue—it simply hints at the possibilities. It tastes grilled, roasted, or baked, which is fine. Just don't call it barbecue.

Although my definition of barbecue may seem narrow or limiting, within this strict definition, barbecue is infinitely diverse. Regional barbecue is a whole category of its own, with the variations loosely defined by the type of meat used, the method of cooking it, and the sauce used to dress it. Famous regional forms of barbecue include Memphis, Kansas City, Texas, and North and South Carolina.

No matter how knowledgeable you become about techniques or styles of barbecue, it is still nothing more than the alchemy of wood, smoke, and meat. Don't try to complicate it. In my experience, people typically follow an arc of barbecue knowledge when they're learning low and slow. After the simple, initial principles are understood, you'll want to make barbecue more difficult—with sauces and rubs, exact times and temperatures, bigger equipment, and accessories and other stuff. Before long, you're relying on all of these tools and secret sauces, which actually dull your barbecue instincts.

DON'T BE JOHN D. FROM OKLAHOMA

HE'S A GOOD GUY. A NICE GUY. But this guy has been cooking barbecue for quite a few years now, and he's still searching for that magic bullet. He's the kind of guy who's always in love with the one he's with—in this case, whatever new method, idea, or piece of equipment is the hottest thing in barbecue at the moment. He keeps messing with sauce recipes and buys new gear as it hits the market. He's forever trying new techniques he reads about on online barbecue forums. To him, everything seems like a good idea. The problem is, he doesn't stop to think about how some methods and equipment might clash. Having collected all of this information and stuff over the years, he incorporates a little bit of every-thing he's learned into his cooks. But he has yet to develop his own natural instincts for barbecue.

You can learn barbecue from a variety of people, but you can't mix and match techniques. You can't take parts of Five Easy Lessons and incorporate them with tips you picked up online or from the winner of your city's annual rib fest. This is why I'm so adamant about using the prescribed tools and following the directions to a T. Once you learn the basics, you're free to futz around. But as a newbie, you don't have the ability to know which techniques and methods go with each other, so you just have to follow along and trust me.

DON'T USE IT OR BUY IT. GET RID OF IT!

IN BARBECUE, LESS IS MORE. It is much simpler, and requires much less equipment and expertise than you might believe. When it comes to great barbecue cooks, I say, beware the man with one gun. Here's a list of gear you don't need. This is the stuff many first-time barbecuers and even some seasoned veterans use, thinking it will make the cooking easier. In fact, these items can ruin a low and slow cook, and they should be avoided at all costs.

LIGHTER FLUID

If you want meat to taste like gasoline, why not pour the gas directly into the marinade? Charcoal soaked in lighter fluid may ignite faster initially, but once it has burned off, the lighter fluid residue overwhelms the barbecue's subtle smokiness and infuses your food with an unpleasant flavor. Once you learn how fast and easy it is to fire up a chimney starter with three sheets of newspaper (page 28), you'll never go back.

CHARCOAL BRIQUETTES

These noxious nuggets contain more filler than government cheese. Anthracite coal, borax, sodium nitrate, and the other unsavory gunk makes them burn slower, hotter, and more evenly, but these additives give barbecue the Exxon Valdez of flavors. Don't even try to use up the leftover bag in your garage on your first few cooks. Give it to your neighbor if you want to follow the path to true low and slow mastery. Hardwood charcoal (see Buy It, Use It, or Quit the Program, page 14) is essential for a clean, controllable fire.

L*QU*D SM@KE

These are the dirtiest words of all in the low and slow lexicon. And it's phony-tasting crap. Never use it, or for that matter, any sauce, rub, marinade, or flavored wood with ingredients that defy the natural laws of physics. Smoke is, by definition, not liquid.

HALF-BURNED COALS FROM YOUR LAST COOKOUT

Don't be penny-wise and ten-pounds-of-ribs foolish. Reusing coals makes for an unpredictable fire, and the ashes that fall to the bottom of your grill or smoker can block the vents and obstruct airflow. Also, there's a reason charcoal is used as a filter. Charcoal absorbs moisture and other miscellaneous tidbits and odors from the air, which will make old charcoal smolder and give off musty flavors when sparked up again. Always start with a clean cooker.

SOAKED WOOD

Curse the fool who started the myth that water-soaked wood burns more slowly and is therefore ideal for low and slow cooking. Wet wood thrown on burning charcoal will indeed burn slowly, but it also causes a drop in temperature in the cooker, smothers the fire, and makes the wood and charcoal smolder. Smoldering wood releases tar and other chemical byproducts that are not good flavoring agents.

WOOD CHIPS OR PELLETS

Small bits of wood burn up too fast on live charcoal. To get the right amount of smoke, you'll have to replenish the wood chips frequently, which requires opening and closing the cooker. This causes the temperature in the cooker to fluctuate. This is a bad idea.

TEMPERATURE GAUGE

Most cookers come equipped with built-in temperature gauges, and 99 percent of them don't work. They're welded onto the lid, which means they can't give an accurate reading of the grate temperature, which is the only temperature you need to be concerned with. Analog meat thermometers can also be unreliable, and new barbecuers tend to misuse them, namely by dropping the thermometer spike into the vent of the smoker or grill. Not only does this block the airflow, but these thermometers are not designed to read air temperature. They're meant for sticking into meat.

HIGHLY SPECIALIZED BARBECUE TOOLS

Do not buy an electric charcoal starter, a telescoping digital meat fork, a basting mop, a stainless steel smoker box, a rib rack, or any other shiny, "time-saving" barbecue accessory ensconced in a velvet-lined attaché case and marketed to the masses. It's a well-known phenomenon that once you have the reputation of being a serious barbecuer, people who know nothing about barbecue will begin giving you books, celebrity-endorsed tools, and accessories that you should never use. My motto: Accept graciously, re-gift rapidly.

CAMPFIRE GIRL TRAINING

You won't be holding hands or singing songs around your cooker, so please just forget everything you ever learned elsewhere about starting and tending a fire or cooking over an open flame.

BUY IT, USE IT, OR QUIT THE PROGRAM

CHANCES ARE, you already have most of the gear you need for all five lessons. If you're starting from scratch or restocking your barbecue equipment, the following products are not optional. This is the stuff you must have for a successful cook. Don't ask questions. Just get it.

HARDWOOD LUMP CHARCOAL

This is natural charcoal made by burning wood. Unlike briquettes, it is not ground up, blended with filler, and reformed into neat little squares. It actually looks like burned pieces of wood. Lump charcoal burns clean, has no chemical additives, and produces less ash and residue—all of which adds up to cleaner smoke and better barbecue.

You'll find lump charcoal at many grocery stores and most national retailers that sell grilling supplies, including Home Depot, Lowe's, and Wal-Mart. It's bagged under brand names like Royal Oak, Lazzari, Holland, Cowboy, and Nature-Glo. Because lump charcoal is a natural product, the type of wood used to make it, the size of the pieces, and how it burns will vary from brand to brand and even bag to bag. Experiment with different brands, find one you like, and stick with it to get the most consistent cook.

Nakedwhiz.com tests and rates dozens of brands and is a good resource for learning about lump charcoal. (Don't order lump charcoal online. The cost is prohibitive, and the extra pounding the charcoal takes during shipping breaks it into smaller pieces.)

WIRE GRATE BRUSH

Nobody wants to taste the leftover crispy burned bits from your last cookout. Clean, well-scrubbed grates are a must, as is a wire grate brush with a long, sturdy handle made from a durable material.

WOOD CHUNKS

Notice the word *chunks*. Not chips. Not shavings. Chunks. Chunks are approximately fist-sized pieces of wood. Because they burn more slowly than chips, you won't have to replenish the wood as often during a cook, which means you won't have to keep opening and closing the lid of your cooker. You're free to use whatever type of wood you prefer (see Smoking Wood, page 30), but hickory is synonymous with barbecue and most hardware and grocery stores stock it. If you have an offset smoker, use splits of wood—longer pieces that are split from logs.

EXTRA CHARCOAL GRATE

Natural lump charcoal is irregularly shaped. With the second round grate set crosswise over the original charcoal grate in a Weber Smokey Mountain (WSM) or kettle grill, less charcoal will fall through the grates, so you'll get a longer, better burn from the charcoal with less waste. For an offset, buy a piece of expandable metal grating cut to fit over the charcoal grate.

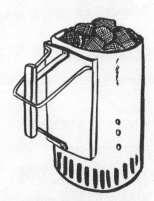

WEBER CHIMNEY STARTER

Plenty of companies make a workable chimney starter, but the Weber has a larger charcoal canister and is simply engineered better for starting a fire cleanly and quickly. It's also my reference guide for measuring out the right amount of charcoal for each of the cooks.

ALUMINUM LOAF PANS

These rectangular 12½ x 6½-inch containers are ad hoc water pans for the kettle grill and the offset smoker and will help moderate the temperature inside your cooker. (The WSM has a built-in water pan.)

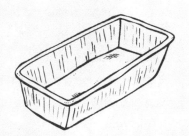

NEWSPAPER

Not glossy circulars or cardboard or perfumed magazine inserts. Just three sheets of plain old newspaper for each chimney of charcoal you ignite. Why? Because I said so.

TONGS AND PAPER TOWELS

I saved the most important gear for last. These two items illustrate just how low-tech and simple barbecue can be, if you let it. Tongs and paper towels can be used in place of nearly every fancy barbecue tool or accessory on the market, for tasks from flipping meat and moving grates to picking up stray pieces of charcoal. As a home barbecuer, you don't need lots of specialized equipment for the volume of cooking you'll be doing.

BELLS AND WHISTLES

Beyond the essential tools, there are a handful of other items and ingredients that can help you achieve barbecue nirvana.

ROASTING RACK

There's no point in buying a special rib rack because you probably already have one. Just flip over the big V-rack you use to roast turkeys and you've got a rib rack.

PLASTIC CONDIMENT BOTTLE

A shot of seasoned liquid, like the Tart Wash (page 115), over meat in a cooker can add a needed dash of moisture or tang to the barbecue. A squirt bottle is fast and clean, unlike a stringy basting mop or a spray bottle, which gets clogged.

OVEN THERMOMETER

A simple stainless steel analog thermometer is about $5. The digital probes with remote display are expensive, and aren't as accurate when it comes to reading grate temperature. By the end of the program, you'll be able to read your cooker using only your senses, but this basic thermometer will help you get a feel for the grate temperature throughout the first few cooks.

INSTANT-READ THERMOMETER

Please do not open and close your cooker seventeen times to poke the meat and check the temperature. For food safety reasons it's a good idea to have an instant-read thermometer to check the meat in the last stages of the cook. And, during Lesson #5, you'll use it to learn more about how meat temperature plateaus and spikes during a long low and slow cook.

SUGARCANE KNIFE

This inexpensive tool is multi-functional. The small hook on the blade makes moving hot grates easier. The business end of the blade shears through bones and big pieces of meat, and the long, flat side can be used as spatula to rotate meat or scoop charcoal back into place. It's also handy for intimidating anyone who tries to peek inside your cooker. (Credit goes to Big Jim in Central Florida for demonstrating the usefulness of this tool.)

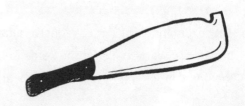

SPICE GRINDER

The only secret to making any great sauce or rub is using freshly ground whole spices, which requires a grinding device. A mortar and pestle, an electric grinder (like one used to grind coffee beans), or a hand mill (think pepper mill) will do just fine.

TIP: If you use your coffee grinder to grind spices, run a few batches of uncooked rice through it to clean out residual powder before you use it again to grind beans.

WHOLE HERBS AND SPICES

Processed, pre-ground bottles of herbs and spices have a shelf life of about six to twelve months before they start tasting musty. Using whole, toasted, and freshly ground spices or herbs, like peppercorns or dried chiles, makes a huge difference in the flavor of any recipe. Whole herbs and spices have a longer shelf life—up to three years—and are also far less expensive than the bottles in a supermarket spice aisle, particularly if you buy in bulk. Ethnic markets often have the best bulk price and a better selection of both typical and unusual whole herbs and spices.

BARBECUE MISE EN PLACE

SAY IT WITH ME: MEEZ AHN PLAHS. IT'S French for "all of your ingredients are washed, chopped, diced, or otherwise prepared, and in place for cooking." Or something like that. Having a few key low and slow ingredients always at the ready not only saves time, but over time it also improves your creative and intuitive seasoning skills in the kitchen. With a pinch of this or that at hand, you can start to make your own rubs or marinades by sense instead of being a slave to recipes. I keep these non-perishable ingredients in small, half-cup bowls on my counter:

- Kosher salt
- Black pepper
- White pepper
- Crushed red pepper, finely ground

KOSHER SALT 101

ALWAYS USE KOSHER SALT FOR THE recipes in this program. This coarse-grained salt has no additives, like iodine or anti-caking agents, and has a better flavor and texture than common table salt. The two most popular brands, Morton and Diamond Crystal, are shaped differently and have different volumes compared to table salt. I prefer the flakier texture of Morton kosher salt, but Diamond Crystal kosher salt works, too. All of the measurements in this book are for Morton's, so be sure to adjust accordingly.

1 tablespoon table salt =

1½ tablespoons Morton kosher salt =

2 tablespoons Diamond Crystal kosher salt

TOASTING HERBS AND SPICES

FOR THE BEST FLAVOR, herbs and spices should be toasted and ground from whole. However, toasted herbs and spices deteriorate quickly because of the volatile oils released during heating. Only toast and grind as much as you need for the recipe you're making.

To toast, preheat a heavy-bottomed pan until the surface is medium-hot—not smoking but almost too hot to touch. Pour the ingredient to be toasted into the hot pan and swirl the pan constantly; this keeps the ingredient from sticking or burning. When the herb or spice becomes fragrant, it's toasted. If the pan starts to smoke or the herb or spice burns, start over with a fresh batch. The bitter flavor of a burned herb or spice will ruin a dish.

TOASTED MEXICAN PEPPER BLEND

This is the blend I use on a regular basis and reference throughout the book. Feel free to customize it, using more or less of the same chiles, to suit your taste. I recommend making a double or triple batch so you have a supply on hand.

MAKES ABOUT ½ CUP

4 or 5 dried guajillo chiles

2 dried ancho chiles

2 dried pasilla chiles

2 dried morita chiles

10 dried pequín chiles

Stem, seed, and roughly tear the dried chiles. Toast the chiles in a preheated skillet until they're fragrant. Pour the toasted chile pieces into a spice grinder and grind to a coarse powder.

MEET YOUR COOKER

THERE ARE HUNDREDS OF DIFFERENT TYPES OF smokers and grills out there, but I've focused this program on only three: the Weber Smokey Mountain (WSM), the offset smoker, and the kettle-style grill. My personal favorite is the WSM. It's the equipment that turned me into the barbecue-obsessed man that I am today, and it's the cooker I used to develop this program. But all three are fine cookers for backyard low and slow. Each cooker can also be re-configured for direct-heat grilling. I think of them as ideal urban cookers because they're compact and inexpensive compared to gas grills, and relatively easy to operate. They represent the most popular styles of charcoal cookers on the market today.

DECKS, BALCONIES, AND SMALL BACKYARDS

Wooden decks and small spaces can create problems for the charcoal cooker (landlords and condo associations, too). Be sure that your cooker is properly safeguarded before you start messing around with live charcoal. If the surface your cooker sits on is flammable, look into buying a fireproof mat, concrete pavers, or cement backer board. My good friend Steve Z. went to a metal fabrication shop and purchased a large sheet of aluminum, which acts as a "blast shield" under his WSM. Water heater pads work well too.

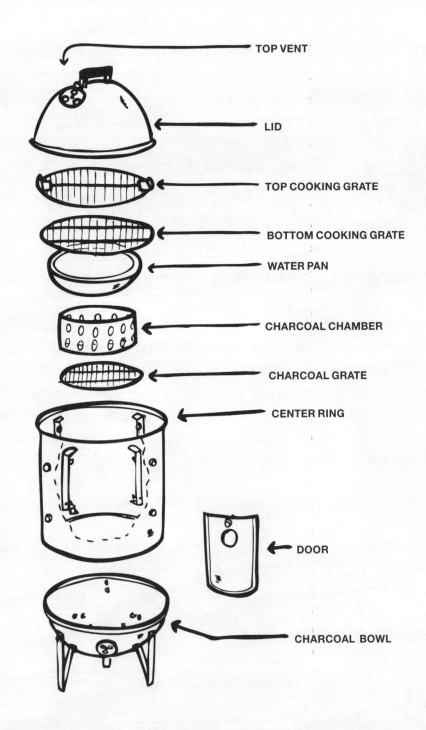

TOP VENT

LID

TOP COOKING GRATE

BOTTOM COOKING GRATE

WATER PAN

CHARCOAL CHAMBER

CHARCOAL GRATE

CENTER RING

DOOR

CHARCOAL BOWL

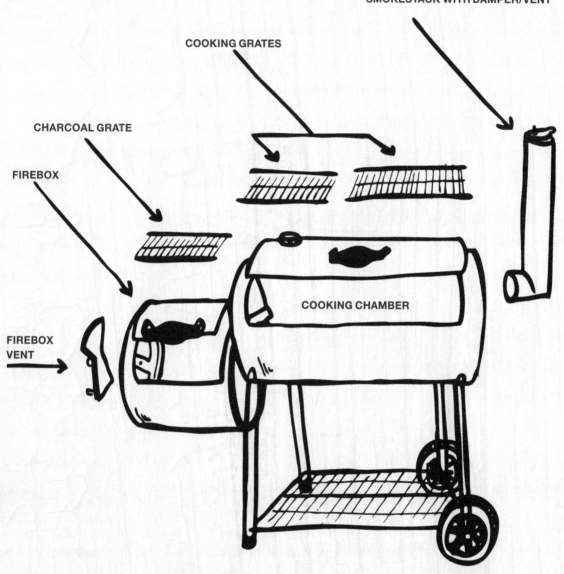

SMOKESTACK WITH DAMPER/VENT

COOKING GRATES

CHARCOAL GRATE

FIREBOX

FIREBOX VENT

COOKING CHAMBER

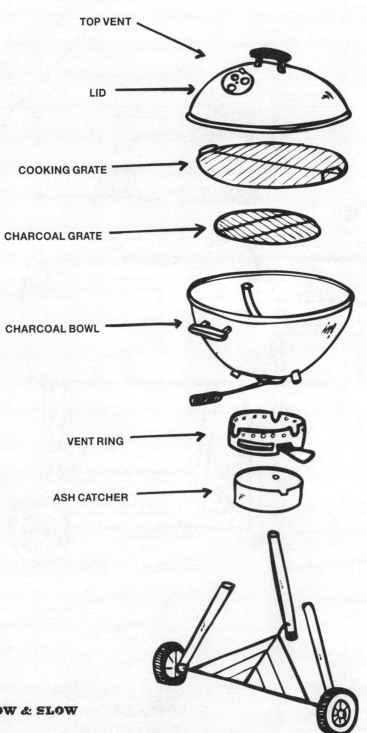

TOP VENT

LID

COOKING GRATE

CHARCOAL GRATE

CHARCOAL BOWL

VENT RING

ASH CATCHER

CLEANING YOUR COOKER

THERE'S REALLY NO WAY TO GET AROUND THE MESS THAT GOES ALONG WITH cooking with charcoal, but these tips should make the process a little easier.

- **IF YOU HAVE A WSM,** foil the water pan (page 31). Instead of scrubbing the oily drippings out of the water pan after a cook, you can toss the foil.

- **AT THE END OF A COOK,** open all of the vents on your cooker to allow the charcoal to burn through. Closing the vents will smother the charcoal before it burns out, so you'll have more big pieces of half-burned charcoal to get rid of.

- **CLEAN THE GRATES WHILE THEY'RE STILL HOT.** Charred food bits are easier to remove when they're hot and crispy.

- **DON'T USE SIMPLE GREEN,** oven cleaner, or any other industrial chemical to clean any part of your cooker. It's not only unnecessary (fire cooks off all gunk), but these products deteriorate the grate's metal and any leftover residue could taint the fire or the food from your next cook.

- **BUY A FIVE-GALLON PAINT BUCKET.** This container is big enough to hold the detritus—cooled charcoal and ash, water pan liquid, tin foil—of five to ten cooks.

- **STORE YOUR COOKER WITH THE LID AND VENTS OPEN** to keep moisture and mold down.

2.

LIGHTING THE LOW & SLOW ✶✶✶ FIRE

DEAR STUDENT,

IF THERE IS ANY POINT WHEN THE POTENTIAL FOR OVERCOMPLICATING AND ruining a low and slow cook happens, it is the moment when fire enters the picture. People go to great lengths to try to micromanage and predict every aspect of cooking with fire, but that's a little bit like trying to predict tomorrow's winning horse race. If you could, you'd be rich.

As I see it, the biggest problem people have with lighting and maintaining a clean, happy fire is the overabundance of ideas and instructions floating around about the best way to do it. Over the last thirty years or so, the primal, instinctive skill of cooking with fire has been lost to gadgetry and the yen for instant perfection, which leaves no room for error or true learning. Instead of relying on the senses we were born with, it's all about remote digital thermometers and counting briquettes. Web sites powered by well-meaning barbecue enthusiasts grind on about closing vents an eighth of an inch if the temperature outside drops by seven degrees, adjustments based on the direction the wind is blowing, and other tedious information that stops just short of tracking lunar phases. It's barbecue for engineers, and although I have nothing against engineers, per se, that kind of tinkering and precision is counterproductive. It'll drive the average person nuts and scare you off of making barbecue forever.

Cooking barbecue should be fun. That's why I am so adamant about sticking to the program and not futzing around with my method. I want you to learn to rely on your instincts instead of numbers and to enjoy the process instead of turning it into an engineering project. There are normal temperature fluctuations throughout the cook, and I give you slight tweaks to make along the way based on what your senses are telling you. There is no reason to obsessively monitor and adjust. In fact, the frequency with which you check, open, close, and poke at your cooker is directly proportional to the likelihood that you will screw things up and inversely proportional to the amount of fun you will have making barbecue. Or, the more you mess with the cooker, the more it messes with you. Forget flowchart cooking. Go with the flow.

This is barbecue, not rocket science. Keep It Simple, Stupid.

Gary Wiviott

BARBECUE DEGREES

THE TEMPERATURE RANGE in this program runs higher than what most barbecue "engineers" would deem acceptable. Ask what the ideal grate temperature range is for low and slow, and they'll say 200°F to 225°F, or 250°F tops. Stay away from these people. They are the ones who fiddle with digital probes and fret about the temperature outside.

As far as you need to know, 250°F to 275°F is a perfectly good range, and drops or spikes in the temperature are no big deal. Why? Because those fluctuations are what give good barbecue its distinct character, and trying to compensate for those inevitable fluctuations will drive you crazy. When you work so hard at keeping a constant, stable temperature in the cooker, you mess up the environment that gives barbecue its delectable, unique qualities. The caramelized bark and crunchy, fatty bites on a rack of ribs don't come about because you hovered over the cooker and adjusted the vents every time the temperature moved five degrees. The flavor and texture are there because the temperature jumped to 300°F and dropped below 250°F at some point during the cook. Of course, you don't want the cooker to sit at 300°F for hours, but if you follow your senses (and my directions), you'll get the kind of easy ebb and flow that makes for great barbecue and a stress-free cook.

HOW MUCH CHARCOAL?

UNLIKE MOST BARBECUE EXPERTS, I won't give you precise briquette counts because 1) you're not using briquettes (are you?) and 2) the irregular shape and size of natural lump charcoal makes it harder to give an exact count. That's why we're using the chimney starter as a measure.

For the first few cooks, you'll use about four chimney starters full of charcoal (or, if you're using a kettle grill, about two chimneys), which is far more than you actually need for these cooks. (Don't cry over $5 in lump charcoal. The point of using so much is to help you get familiar with how long the charcoal will burn in these cookers.) One chimney of lump charcoal will burn approximately forty-five minutes to one hour if the vents on your cooker are opened according to the instructions. You'll get at least four to five hours of cooking time out of one complete batch of K.I.S.S. method charcoal in a WSM, one to two hours on an offset smoker, or up to one hour of cooking time on a kettle. For the longer cooks required for spare ribs and pork shoulder, you will restock the charcoal to extend the capacity to nine or ten hours of cooking time.

STARTING YOUR CHIMNEY

IF YOU'VE MADE IT THIS FAR and are still thinking about hosing down slow-burning "charcoal" briquettes with lighter fluid to start your cook, please use this book to light the pile. I can't help you.

You will never touch a bottle of lighter fluid once you learn this simple setup for starting a chimney. It's not only easier than firing up lighter fluid–soaked briquettes, it's safer (no flare-ups), cleaner (no harsh chemicals), and less expensive (just three sheets of newspaper). The most important reason of all? Flavor. Your barbecue will never taste like it passed through the exhaust pipe of an eighteen-wheeler. Here's the foolproof, lighter fluid–free method for sparking up a chimney full of charcoals.

STEP 1. Roll three sheets of newspaper into loosely crumpled, concentric circles. Place the paper rings in the bottom of the charcoal chimney, leaving enough space and looseness between the sheets to allow air to flow around the paper.

STEP 2. Set the chimney on a grate or any other fireproof surface that allows air to flow under the starter.

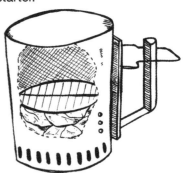

STEP 3. Fill the chimney almost to the rim with lump charcoal. (If you're cooking on a kettle grill, only fill the chimney halfway.)

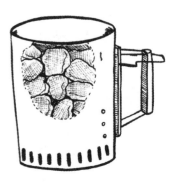

TIP: Air will not circulate around twisted or tightly packed paper. Without adequate airflow, the paper will smolder instead of flaming up and catching the charcoal.

STEP 4. Light the newspaper in two or three places at the bottom of the chimney.

STEP 5. Stare at the chimney for five to ten minutes. At first, thick swells of dirty, white smoke from the lit newspaper will pour out of the top, sides, and bottom of the chimney. Lump charcoal also crackles and pops as it engages. It's common for ashes from the burned paper to blow around, too. In about ten minutes (five minutes for the smaller, kettle-bound batch of charcoal), the charcoal should be fully engaged and burning brightly.

STEP 6. When you see red-hot coals glowing from the holes in the side of the chimney, clear flames shooting from the top, and a gray-white ash edging the charcoal in the top of the starter, the charcoal is ready to pour into the chamber (WSM), or into the fire-box (offset), or onto the grate (kettle).

SMOKING WOOD

VOLUMES HAVE BEEN WRITTEN about the various flavors and qualities of the wood used in low and slow barbecue, but frankly, it's all in the mouth of the beholder. Telling you which wood goes best with which meat is just the kind of distracting filler information that obscures the real lessons to be learned. For the five lessons in this book, I recommend using hickory because many hardware and grocery stores stock it, and the flavor of hickory is a common one in barbecue. Starting with hickory also gives you a good point of reference for gauging the strength of other wood flavors when you start using other types.

Once you get the hang of using wood chunks (remember: chunks, not chips), feel free to experiment with different combinations of wood. The most common woods for smoking are mesquite, hickory, oak, pecan, cherry, and apple. Often, the type of wood people use in a smoke varies with what's available in the region. In Texas and other southern states, post oak, pecan, hickory, and mesquite are common. In the Midwest, hickory, apple, and cherry are popular. Alder is used—mostly for smoking fish—in the Pacific Northwest.

There's no point in describing the ethereal and effervescent qualities of each type of wood. You just have to taste them for yourself. However, it's worth noting that mesquite has a very strong, distinct flavor that can be over-powering or acrid if it's not used in moderation. It's best to mix mesquite with a more neutral wood, like oak, or to use it very sparingly in a cook. And cherry tends to produce a darker smoke, so meat smoked with cherry will have a darker tint.

WOOD TLC

UNLESS YOU HAVE EASY ACCESS to cut, dried, aged wood, you'll probably end up buying bags of wood chunks at your local hardware or grocery store. This is perfectly acceptable, as long as you use a hand ax to carefully chop or shave off any remaining bark on the chunks. The bark is where critters, mold, and other impurities reside, and these elements produce off flavors that can penetrate your food.

After shaving the wood, give it a sniff. It should have a clean, woody smell. Moldy wood is a common issue with bagged wood chunks. If, after trimming the wood, it still smells musty or damp, toss it. You'll probably end up throwing away a few chunks of wood out of every bag.

This mantra also bears repeating: wet wood is no good. Despite the fact that nearly every chef on TV and barbecue cookbook on the shelves advises you to soak wood to make it burn slower and longer, I beseech you: do not soak the wood chunks in water, wine, beer, or any other liquid. Initially, you'll just have to trust me on this one. But as you progress through the cooks, you will begin to understand intuitively that adding wet wood to hot coals causes unsavory reactions in the cooker, including a spew of ashy steam or a drop in temperature. If you insist on using wet wood chunks to test the theory, you'll also get a taste of the tarry substance smoldering wood produces. "Flavored" wood falls in the same category of no-nos, but for a different reason. Wood soaked in any unnatural flavoring or twenty-year-old bourbon is a waste of money (and of good bourbon).

FOILING THE WATER PAN

REMOVE THE WATER PAN FROM THE WSM. Tear off a two-foot sheet of extra-wide, heavy-duty aluminum foil—enough to cover the bottom of the bowl and over the lip of the water pan. Smooth the foil against the bottom of the water pan and up the sides, then gently crimp the edges of the foil around the lip of the water pan. (Do not wrap the entire pan—just the inside and outer rim.) If the foil rips or doesn't cover the complete surface of the water pan, start over. This tight layer of foil holds the water, but also keeps the fat drippings from dirtying the water pan. Foiling the water pan isn't essential because it doesn't affect the cook, but it does make cleanup easier.

K.I.S.S. ON A WSM

THIS METHOD OF LAYERING CHARCOAL and wood in your WSM is very specific, but there is good, solid reasoning behind each step. If you stray from the methodology to incorporate techniques you picked up in the Girl Scouts, I can't guarantee the outcome. Follow the steps—exactly as I outline them—and you will have a consistent, clean-burning, 250°F to 275°F low and slow fire in your WSM for about five hours.

TO GET STARTED, YOU NEED:

- Charcoal chimney starter
- Natural lump charcoal
- Six wood chunks
- Three sheets of newspaper (not glossy)
- Extra-wide, heavy-duty aluminum foil
- Metal tongs

> **TIP:** Use your tongs to pick up stray pieces of charcoal that fall outside of the chamber to keep charcoal from blocking the bottom vents on the WSM. Blocked vents choke off your fire.

1. Open the top and bottom vents. The top vent should remain open at all times throughout the cook.

2. Remove the center ring and the lid of the WSM. Fill the charcoal chamber halfway with unlit charcoal—about two chimney starters full of charcoal.

3. Lay three clean, debarked wood chunks on top of the unlit charcoal in the chamber.

4. Fill the chimney starter halfway with unlit charcoal. Spread this charcoal over the wood chunks and unlit charcoal already in the chamber. The charcoal level should be just below the top edge of the chamber.

5. Prepare the chimney starter for lighting charcoal (see Starting Your Chimney, page 28): Roll three sheets of newspaper into loose concentric rings. Fit the paper rings inside the bottom of the chimney. Fill the starter to the top with unlit charcoal. Set the chimney on a grate or other fireproof surface that allows air to flow underneath. Light the paper in two or three places.

6. After about ten minutes, when the charcoal in the chimney is fully engaged—you should see glowing red coals, clear flames shooting from the top of the chimney, and a gray-white ash edging the top layer of coals—gently pour the lit charcoal in an even layer over the unlit charcoal and wood in the chamber. As you're topping the unlit charcoal, pieces of charcoal may spill out of the chamber and into the bowl. Use the tongs to pick up and return the strays to the charcoal chamber.

7. When the charcoal stops billowing white smoke (about five minutes after you pour the lit charcoal into the chamber), add three debarked wood chunks to the pile.

8. Return the center ring (empty water pan and grates in place) to the top of the charcoal bowl.

9. Using a slow-running garden hose or a watering can, pour water through the grates to fill the water pan to within one inch of the top edge. Avoid splashing water into or down the sides of the cooker.

10. The cooker will continue to billow white smoke for about five minutes. When the smoke dies down to steady, lighter puffs, arrange your meat on the top grate.

11. Return the lid to the WSM with the top vent at 1 o'clock and the small metal door at 6 o'clock. It's time to cook.

K.I.S.S. ON AN OFFSET SMOKER

I GENERALLY PREFER TO COOK ON THE WSM—particularly in the confines of a city dwelling's back yard—but the offset does offer some conveniences. Restocking charcoal and wood in the side firebox is simple, and the single-grate surface makes cooking in quantity and rotating meat easier.

However, there is a slight glitch in the engineering of most horizontal offsets that can create problems: the opening between the firebox and the cooking chamber allows too much hot air to flow into the cooker and directly across the grate. This problem is easily fixed with a cheap aluminum loaf pan filled with water. Place it an inch or two from the firebox vent on the cooking grate, and this impromptu water pan will improve heat circulation by directing heat downward, below the grate, and act as a heat shield between the food on the grate and the hot stream of air flowing out of the firebox. Instead of direct, radiant heat, it creates a flow of indirect, convective heat. (Some people modify the cooker by inserting a small metal heat shield into the vent opening inside the cooking chamber, but the aluminum loaf pan works just fine for this program. If you have the tools and inclination, instructions for the more permanent modification are easily found online.)

TO GET STARTED, YOU NEED:

- Charcoal chimney starter
- Natural lump charcoal
- One split of wood
- Aluminum loaf pan
- Three sheets of newspaper (not glossy)
- Metal tongs

TIP: Place the splits of wood next to the firebox to preheat. The wood ignites faster when it is hot. Use your tongs to pick up the wood. It's hot—remember?

1. Open all of the vents on the offset.

2. Pour two chimneys full of unlit charcoal onto the grate inside the firebox.

3. Fill the aluminum loaf pan three-quarters full with water. Place the pan on the grate in the cooking chamber, about one inch from the firebox vent.

4. Prepare the chimney starter for lighting charcoal (see Starting Your Chimney, page 28): Roll three sheets of newspaper into loose concentric rings. Fit the paper rings inside the bottom of the chimney. Fill the starter with unlit charcoal. Set the chimney on the cooking grate or another fireproof surface that allows air to flow underneath. Light the paper in two or three places.

5. When the charcoal is fully engaged—after about ten minutes, you should see glowing red coals, clear flames shooting from the top of the chimney, and a gray-white ash edging the top layer of coals—gently pour the lit coals over the unlit charcoal in the firebox.

6. Place one clean, debarked split of wood on top of the lit charcoal in the firebox. In about ten minutes, when the charcoal stops billowing white smoke and the wood begins to blacken or ignites, close the lid on the firebox.

7. Arrange the meat on the grate in the cooking chamber with the most heat-sensitive side of the cut (the breast on chicken, the meat end of the rib) facing away from the firebox. Close the lid. It's time to cook.

K.I.S.S. ON A KETTLE GRILL

DON'T GET ME WRONG: I love the kettle-style grill—for grilling. And with some guided instruction, you can use this equipment to make some fine low and slow barbecue. But of the cookers in this book, the kettle requires the most vigilance by far. You have to build a two-zone fire on the charcoal grate to cook by indirect heat. This setup means you will use less charcoal and sacrifice some space on the grate to an aluminum water pan, which sits over the charcoals and deflects the heat down and under the meat. (Without the water pan modification, the grate temperature would be too hot for low and slow barbecue.) Because you have less cooking space and use a smaller batch of charcoal, you will need to check and restock the cooker about every forty-five minutes.

TIP: Grilling is a form of "direct heat" cooking—exposing meat directly to a flame or live charcoal. Grilling cooks fast and hot, which makes it ideal for cooking smaller, tender cuts of meat like steaks, chops, and fish. Indirect heat is best for large, tough cuts, like ribs, pork shoulder, and brisket. The lower temperature and longer cook slowly tenderizes the meat by rendering the fat and breaking down the tough connective tissue. Direct heat would turn these cuts into shoe leather.

To get started, you need:
- Charcoal chimney starter
- Natural lump charcoal
- Metal tongs
- Two wood chunks
- Two aluminum loaf pans
- Three sheets of newspaper (not glossy)

1. Open the top and bottom vents on the kettle.

2. Fill the chimney three-quarters full with unlit charcoal.

3. Remove the top grate and pour the unlit charcoal on one side of the charcoal grate, using your tongs to "bank" the charcoal in a slight slope against one side of the kettle.

4. Lay one clean, debarked wood chunk in the middle of the unlit charcoal.

5. Set one empty aluminum loaf pan on the opposite side of the charcoal grate. Return the top grate to the cooker.

6. Prepare the chimney starter for lighting charcoal (see Starting Your Chimney, page 28): Roll three sheets of newspaper into loose concentric rings. Fit the paper rings inside the bottom of the chimney. Fill the chimney halfway with unlit charcoal. Set the chimney on a grate or other fireproof surface that allows air to flow underneath. Light the paper in two or three places.

7. When the charcoal is fully engaged—after about five minutes, you should see glowing red coals, clear flames shooting from the top of the chimney, and a gray-white ash edging the top layer of coals—lift the top grate and gently pour the lit coals over the pile of unlit charcoal. Use your tongs to retrieve any charcoal that spills off of the pile.

8. When the charcoal stops billowing white smoke, about five minutes later, place one more clean, debarked wood chunk on top of the lit charcoal. Replace the top grate.

9. Fill the second aluminum loaf pan three-quarters full with water. Set the pan on the top grate over the lit charcoal and wood.

10. Lay the meat on the opposite side of the grate, as close to the outer edge of the grate as possible without touching the side. Face the most heat-resistant side of the cut (the thighs/legs on a chicken, the chine bone on ribs) toward the fire.

11. Set the lid in place with the vent positioned over the meat. It's time to cook.

RESTOCKING THE COOKER

THE FIRST THREE LESSONS—CHICKEN
Mojo Criollo, Brined Chicken, and Baby Back Ribs— are relatively short cooks that do not require additional wood or charcoal if you're using a WSM or offset. Because you're only using half the grate for charcoal on a kettle, you will need to add more unlit or lit charcoals to the pile about every thirty to forty-five minutes throughout all kettle cooks.

WSM

If all is set and running according to the master plan—vents are unblocked and opened to the right degree, you're using the right kind and quantity of charcoal—the initial KISS batch of charcoals should last at least four to five hours without any meddling. The only thing you'll have to keep an eye on is the water pan: check it about every hour and a half, and refill it any time it's less than half full.

A stern warning: As you learn to restock water and charcoal, you will be tempted to flip open the flimsy side door on the center ring to refill the water pan or the charcoal chamber. It will seem like an efficient way to get the job done. It is not. If I had my say, Weber would remove these doors from all future WSMs. If I thought you would actually do it, I'd instruct you to weld the door shut because its alluring presence invites unnecessary peeking and futzing. If it isn't latched properly, the door can fall open. The blast of air across the coals will overheat the cooker and screw up your lesson. If that's not enough to convince you, consider this: poking a rubber hose through the door over glowing-hot charcoal to refill the water pan is dangerous and dumb.

REFILLING THE WSM WATER PAN

1. Remove the lid and set it on the ground.

2. With oven mitts on to protect your hands, remove the top grate from the center ring and set it on a heat-safe surface, like a pair of clean bricks.

3. Refill the water pan within one inch of the top, being careful not to splash down the sides of the cooker. (Once you get the hang of refilling the water pan this way, try your hand at pouring the water through the grates.)

4. Reassemble and close the cooker.

RESTOCKING THE WSM CHARCOAL CHAMBER

1. At the four- or five-hour mark, when half to three-quarters of the initial batch of charcoal has burned through, fill the chimney starter with charcoal and light it (see Starting Your Chimney, page 28).

2. When the charcoal in the chimney is fully engaged, put on a pair of heatproof gloves and carefully remove the center ring and lid together from the charcoal bowl—using extra caution to keep the water in the pan from sloshing out.

3. Set the center ring on the ground, but leave the lid on to retain as much heat as possible.

4. Pour fresh, unlit charcoal over the burning coals, filling the chamber to the top edge.

5. Pour the chimney full of lit charcoal into the charcoal chamber over the unlit charcoal and wood. Remember to check the bottom vents and remove any stray pieces of charcoal blocking the vents.

6. After five or ten minutes, when the initial clouds of charcoal smoke stop billowing, reassemble the cooker.

> **TIP:** After refreshing the charcoal on any of the cookers, leave the lid of the firebox or cooker open for five to ten minutes, until the charcoal fully engages and stops billowing smoke. This initial smoke from the charcoal can give your meat a bitter, acrid flavor.

OFFSET

When it's time to replenish the charcoal or refill the water pan in an offset smoker, you will no doubt understand why this style of cooker is popular among the bourbon-drinking set. When the initial batch of charcoal is half to three-quarters burned through—plenty of time to sip a few fingers of whiskey—loading in new charcoal takes no more effort than lifting the lid of the firebox and pouring in a fresh batch.

RESTOCKING THE OFFSET FIREBOX

1. If the charcoal grate is less than half full of glowing hot coals, pour a chimney starter half full of unlit charcoal onto the grate. (If the grate is more than half full of hot coals, pour a chimney full of unlit charcoal directly onto the lit coals and skip steps 2 and 3).

2. Fill the chimney starter with charcoal and light it (see Starting Your Chimney, page 28).

3. When the charcoal in the chimney is fully engaged, scatter the lit charcoal on the grate in the firebox.

4. Add one clean, debarked split of wood to the pile of lit charcoal.

5. Wait five to ten minutes, until the initial smoke from the new charcoal and wood stops billowing; then close the firebox.

> **TIP:** Check the water pan every time you refresh the charcoal and wood. A low water pan will cause the coals to burn hotter and faster. The water pan should be at least half full at all times.

KETTLE

Using a kettle for low and slow barbecuing requires more maintenance throughout the cook. You're using less charcoal in a smaller cooker that tends to run hotter, all of which means you'll need to check the water pan and charcoal every thirty to forty-five minutes. The hinged cooking grate on most large kettle-style grills makes replenishing the charcoal easier. If your kettle does not have a hinged grate, look into buying one.

REFILLING THE KETTLE WATER PAN

1. Lift the lid and carefully pour clean water into the aluminum loaf pan if it is less than half full.

RESTOCKING THE KETTLE TWO-ZONE FIRE

1. Ten minutes before you need to re-stock, fill the chimney starter halfway with unlit charcoal and light it (see Starting Your Chimney, page 28).

2. When the charcoal is fully engaged, remove the lid of the grill and lift the handle on the hinged cooking grate with a pair of tongs. (If the grate is not hinged, use a pair of heatproof oven mitts to remove the cooking grate.)

3. Add one clean, debarked wood chunk to the burning charcoal on the grate.

4. Carefully pour in the new batch of lit charcoal. Use your tongs to corral any stray pieces and maintain the bank of charcoal over half of the charcoal grate.

5. Wait five minutes, until the initial smoke from the new charcoal stops billowing, then close or return the cooking grate and the lid to the kettle.

STOP, OR I'LL KICK YOUR ASH

THROUGHOUT YOUR EDUCATION IN LOW AND SLOW BARBECUE, you will make mistakes. Meat will overcook. Fires will burn out. It's inevitable. Even with the very detailed and simple instructions I've given you, things can go wrong. I can't change the future, but I can help you make it taste better with these fixes for common problems with heat, fire, and smoke in a low and slow cook.

ISSUE Nº1:
THE CHARCOAL IN THE CHIMNEY WON'T CATCH ON FIRE.

Did you get nervous and shove four or five balls of paper in the bottom of the chimney? Lack of airflow around the paper is the most common reason a chimney won't light. If the paper only smolders and singes around the edges, but doesn't go up in full flames, you've used too much paper or packed the paper in too tightly. If the paper flares up but dies out quickly, perhaps you're not using enough paper. You need three full sheets of newspaper to fuel the kind of flames it takes to completely light that bottom layer of charcoal. Also, check the charcoal. Is it wet or does it smell musty? You will have trouble lighting wet charcoal.

ISSUE Nº2:
THICK, DIRTY SMOKE IS BLOWING OUT OF THE TOP VENT.

Surely you're not using the *verboten* briquettes. If you are, shame on you. If not, maybe you closed the lid of the firebox or cooker too soon. When you mix lit and unlit natural lump charcoal, the batch needs five or ten minutes to fully catch before that heavy, darker smoke stops billowing. If you close the lid while it's still catching, two things happen: 1) you choke off the airflow that feeds the initial high heat and gets the charcoal to the clean burning phase and 2) you trap the smoky smolder inside the cooker. If that's not the case, check your vents to make sure that they are all fully opened. Something is causing the fire to smolder, and it's probably a blocked vent.

ISSUE Nº3:
I CHECKED MY CHEAP OVEN THERMOMETER, AND THE GRATE TEMPERATURE IS TOO HOT.

Check your water pan. Usually when the temperature spikes above 275°F, the water level has dipped too low. Refill the water pan, and check it every hour or so—particularly in the kettle and offset cookers, as the aluminum loaf pans are smaller. The pan should be at least half full at all times. The temperature in a cooker will also spike immediately after fresh wood is added to the fire, but this is temporary and should stabilize. Next, check your vents. If it's a windy day and air is blowing directly into the vents over the charcoal, you may need to create a wind block. Turn the cooker so the vent is not facing into the wind, or partially close the vent.

ISSUE Nº4:
THE COOKER ISN'T AS HOT AS IT SHOULD BE.

If the cooker is dropping in temperature, your fire is choked or you don't have enough charcoal burning. Check your vents. Sometimes small fragments of lump charcoal and the dust from the bottom of a bag clog the vents and block airflow. Remove any charcoal pieces from the vent area with a pair of tongs. If there is an excess of charcoal dust, gently stir the charcoal with the tongs to redistribute it. If any vents are partially closed, slide them completely open. Check your charcoal supply, as well. If it's running low, restock with a full chimney (or half, if you're on a kettle) of lit charcoal.

ISSUE Nº5:
WHILE REFILLING THE WATER PAN, I DUMPED WATER ON THE HOT COALS AND NOW THEY'RE SMOLDERING.

If you dumped a considerable amount of water on the charcoal and the coals are barely lit, you'll need to reignite the fire. Fire up another chimney starter of charcoal. When the charcoal is fully engaged and burning hot and red, pour the lit charcoal over the smoldering batch. While a small amount of water is not good for the fire, if it's just a splash and most of the charcoal is still burning bright, leave it alone. Or if the damp charcoal is all in one area, use your tongs to pick up a few chunks of burning charcoal and lay them over the smoldering pieces.

THE NO-PEEKING POLICY

THERE'S NO DENYING IT: a cooker at work is irresistible. You will want to touch it. You will want to open the lid to check the temperature or to gaze at that glorious slow-cooking barbecue. You will tell yourself you need to check the water pan—for the fifth time in the last half hour. Low and slow student, you must resist these temptations. Unless instructed or unless something is going terribly wrong—flames are shooting out of the sides or you get a whiff of burning meat—leave your cooker alone. Wrap barbed wire around the handle of the lid, or better yet, just wire the lid shut, so opening and closing it becomes a tedious chore and a reminder of the strict no-peeking policy. Every time you open your cooker, the blast of air burns the charcoal hotter and that precious, stabilized heat is lost. The temperature drops, and you extend the cooking time by about fifteen minutes.

LOW AND SLOW INTUITION

IT SHOULD BE OBVIOUS BY NOW that this is a really low-tech program. A cheap oven thermometer and metal tongs are as fancy as it gets. Anyone who relies on gauges and gadgets or exact temperatures and times will always be disappointed because there are too many variables in low and slow. Everything from the temperature outside and the marbling in the meat to the orneriness of the animal and the condition of your lump charcoal affects the outcome of a cook. That's why it's important to stay low-tech and hone your barbecue reflexes. You want to be able to sit in your chair with a beer in your hand and a dog at your feet, knowing that some instinctive response will tell you when everything is right or when something has gone wrong. Like any skill, this takes time. These are some of the cues that will help you read a cook with your senses.

SIGHT: Yes, you're smoking, but you really don't want to see a lot of thick smoke billowing out of your cooker. It's counterintuitive, but a proper, clean-burning fire doesn't produce much superfluous smoke. If the cooker is running right, you should see only the occasional wisp of thin, blue smoke coming out of the top vent. The smoke will be heavy for the first ten minutes after the charcoal is added to the firebox or grate—which is why you should leave the lid open until it dies down. But if the smoke is heavy and cloudy at a later point in the cook, something is wrong.

SOUND: The crackling sound of lump charcoal burning is normal. It usually happens when smaller pieces and the dust from the bottom of the bag ignite in the chimney starter. You'll also hear the occasional pop in the cooker. What don't you want to hear? The hissing sound of water hitting hot charcoal. It could be an accidental sloshing of the water pan, or it might mean water is bubbling out— a sign that the fire is too hot, the water level is too high, or the water has seeped under the foil (if you foiled the WSM water pan).

SMELL: You know when it smells good. That's easy enough. So pay attention when it smells bad, like right after you light a chimney starter or pour charcoal in the firebox or on the grate. That smell shouldn't last long. When the cooker is closed, waft your hand up from the top vent and take a sniff. Does it smell warm, lightly smoky, and meaty? Or is there a sooty, dark quality to the aroma? If you smell something off mid-cook, there's a problem with the fire.

TOUCH: Your hand is a good tool for gauging how high the cooker is running. Please do not put your hand directly on a hot cooker or grate. When you open the lid to check the water pan or restock the charcoal, hold your hand about five inches above the cooking grate. If you can only hold your hand over the grate for two to four seconds, the fire is in the 450°F to 550°F range and far too hot. If you can hold it there for five to seven seconds, it's about 350°F to 450°F. The ideal range is 250°F to 300°F, and you should be able to hold your hand near the grate for eight to ten seconds at that temperature.

3.

LESSON №1

CHICKEN MOJO CRIOLLO

DEAR STUDENT,

NATURALLY, YOU WANT TO MAKE RIBS, NOT CHICKEN. POULTRY ISN'T WHAT MOST of us are hungry for when we fire up the smoker, but this first cook isn't about the meat. It's about learning how to operate your equipment as a low and slow cooker and, more importantly, starting to trust what these cookers can do when you leave them alone. Besides, do you know how many chickens a chucklehead like me had to cook to begin to know what I'm teaching you? Hundreds of chickens have been sacrificed so you can do it perfectly the first time. You shouldn't be able to screw up this lesson no matter how hard you try, but just in case, that's why you're cooking eight dollars worth of chicken instead of fifty dollars worth of ribs.

You'll notice this program is not structured like most cookbooks. Following the list of ingredients for each dinner, the instructions are laid out in a timeline based on when you want to eat. For example, if dinner is at 6:00 p.m., the instructions are to prep the chicken and marinate it about eight to ten hours before dinnertime, or around 8:00 a.m. This allows for four to six hours of marinating time and two hours of cooking time. If there's one idea I want to get across with this format, it's that you can't rely on exact times for low and slow. Times will vary. Be flexible. You'll also find that this format helps you stay organized and serve on time when you're feeding a crowd. But before you even think of risking embarrassment and inviting all of your friends over to celebrate your mastery of low and slow, you need to do each lesson at least two or three times to get the hang of it.

Sincerely,

Gary Wiviott

CHICKEN MOJO CRIOLLO

Mojo criollo [MOH-hoh kree-OH-yoh] is a simple Cuban marinade made with garlic, onion, and citrus. As simple as it is to make, you're buying a bottle of it from the store for the first cook. Purists might balk at using a commercial marinade, but I'm telling you to use it for the same reason we're using chicken for your first lesson. It's cheap, predictable, and readily available. (You'll find mojo criollo in the ethnic foods section of most supermarkets and in grocery stores catering to a Latino population.) After your first cook, feel free to use any of the other marinades (including my recipe for homemade mojo criollo) included at the end of the chapter.

WSM AND OFFSET

SERVES 4 TO 6

2 whole fryers (3- to 4-pound chickens),
    split in half, legs disjointed (page 50)

1 (32-ounce) bottle *mojo criollo*,
    Goya or other brand

$\frac{1}{2}$ cup olive oil

1 lemon, cut in half

Kosher salt and freshly ground
    black pepper, to taste

KETTLE

SERVES 2 TO 4

1 whole fryer (3- to 4-pound chicken),
    split in half, legs disjointed (page 50)

2 cups mojo criollo, Goya or other brand

$\frac{1}{4}$ cup olive oil

$\frac{1}{2}$ lemon

Kosher salt and freshly ground
    black pepper, to taste

6 TO 8 HOURS BEFORE DINNER

Divide the chicken halves between two one-gallon zip-top bags so that there are two chicken halves per bag (Use one zip-top bag if using the kettle cooker.) Vigorously shake the bottle of mojo criollo, and pour two cups of the marinade into each bag. Pour $\frac{1}{4}$ cup of the olive oil into each bag and squeeze half a lemon into each bag. Place the bags in a large bowl or on a rimmed baking sheet to catch drips. Put the bags in the refrigerator and allow the chicken to marinate for 4 to 6 hours, turning the bags once or twice to redistribute the marinade.

2 HOURS BEFORE DINNER

Start a KISS method fire according to the instructions for your WSM (page 32), offset (page 34), or kettle (page 36). While you're waiting for the charcoal in the chimney to engage, remove the chicken halves from the bags and pat them dry with paper towels. Brush the chicken with olive oil and season lightly with salt and pepper. When the lit charcoal and wood are ready for cooking, arrange the chicken on the grate.

HOW TO SPLIT A CHICKEN

Ask the butcher in your grocery store to remove the backbone and split a whole chicken in half, or do it yourself. Here's how.

1. Lay the chicken breast-side down on a cutting board. Using heavy-duty kitchen shears or a sharp knife, cut down both sides of the backbone. You're cutting through skin, flesh, and small bones, so it'll take some effort.

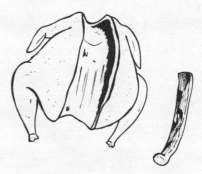

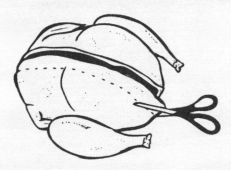

3. Grip the thigh firmly, then bend or twist the legs on both halves to bust the joint between the thigh and leg. (For atmosphere, I recommend shouting "You're two weeks behind on the vig!" while snapping the leg joints.)

2. Flip the chicken over. With the palm of your hands, push against the breast to crack open the chicken. Using kitchen shears or a knife, cut through the middle of the breasts to split the chicken completely in half.

PLACE THE CHICKEN HALVES IN A circle, breast-side in, on the top grate, as close to the middle as possible without crowding. Use your tongs to nudge the thigh/leg portion higher onto the breast. (If you must know why, see sidebar on page 54.) Place the lid on the cooker, with the top vent positioned on the side of the cooker opposite the side door.

TOP/BOTTOM VENTS:

Open. Don't touch the lid for 1½ hours. Seriously No peeking.

1½ HOURS INTO THE COOK

Open the lid of the cooker and puncture the thickest part of the breast with a fork. If the juice running out of the chicken is clear, it's done. Most food types tell you to stick an instant-read thermometer into the chicken at this point. I don't recommend using a meat or oven thermometer the first few cooks because you learn to rely on numbers instead of trusting your instincts. However, if you must, the meat is done when the breast reads 155°F and the thigh reads 165°F.

If the juice is still pinkish, or the meat isn't registering the correct doneness, leave the chicken on the cooker. To improve the likelihood of crisping the skin, squirt the chicken skin with cooking spray or olive oil and flip the chicken over, skin-side down.

Check the water level in the water pan. Refill it if it's low.

Replace the lid and fork-test the chicken every 10 to 15 minutes until the juices run clear.

PLACE THE CHICKEN HALVES ON the grate. Place the first chicken half in the middle of the grate with the wing/leg side facing the firebox. Lay the remaining chicken halves away from the firebox. Use your tongs to nudge the thigh/leg portion higher onto the breast. Don't touch the lid for 1½ hours.

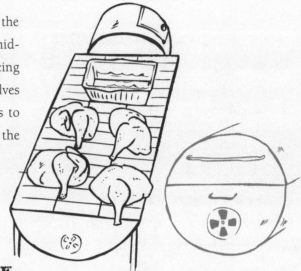

TOP/BOTTOM VENTS:

Open

1½ HOURS INTO THE COOK

Open the lid of the cooker and puncture the thickest part of the breast with a fork. If the juice running out of the chicken is clear, it's done. Most food types tell you to stick an instant-read thermometer into the chicken at this point. I don't recommend using a meat or oven thermometer the first few cooks because you learn to rely on numbers instead of trusting your instincts. However, if you must, the meat is done when the breast reads 155°F and the thigh reads 165°F.

If the juice is still pinkish, or the meat isn't registering the correct doneness, leave the chicken on the cooker. To improve the likelihood of crisping the skin, squirt the chicken skin with cooking spray or olive oil and flip the chicken over, skin-side down.

Check the water level in the water pan. Refill it if it's low.

Replace the lid and fork-test the chicken every 10 to 15 minutes until the juices run clear.

TUCK EACH WING UNDER THE BREAST and place the chicken halves on the grate, with the breast-side close to the edge of the grate without touching the side of the cooker. The breast should not face the water pan and bank of charcoal. Use your tongs to nudge the thigh/leg portion higher onto the breast. Place the lid on the cooker with the top vent positioned directly above the chicken.

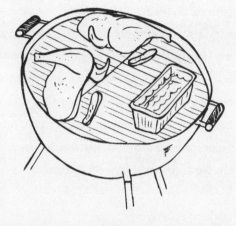

TOP/BOTTOM VENTS:

Open

30 MINUTES INTO THE COOK

Check the charcoal. If more than half of the charcoal has burned to ash, top the charcoal with one-third chimney of lit charcoal. Check the water level in the water pan. If it is less than half full, add water.

BOTTOM VENT:

Close the bottom vent by one-third.

1 HOUR INTO THE COOK

Remove the lid of the cooker and puncture the thickest part of the breast with a fork. If the juice running out of the chicken is clear, it's done. If the juice is still pinkish, or the meat isn't registering the correct doneness. I don't recommend using a meat or oven thermometer the first few cooks because you learn to rely on numbers instead of trusting your instincts. However, if you must, the meat is done when the breast reads 155°F and the thigh reads 165°F. To improve the likelihood of crisping the skin, squirt the chicken skin with cooking spray or canola oil and flip the chicken over, skin-side down.

Check the water level in the water pan. Refill it if it's low.

Replace the lid and fork-test the chicken every 10 minutes until the juices run clear.

★ IF YOU MUST KNOW WHY... ★

WHY CAN'T I JUST THROW THE CHICKEN ON THE GRATE? you ask. Because the breast is more susceptible to drying out. Arranging the chicken on the grate with the breast away from the hottest zone on the grate protects the breast, and the meat cooks more evenly. On a WSM, the perimeter of the grate is hotter because heat flows around the water pan and up the sides. The chicken breasts should face the middle of the grate on the WSM. On a kettle grill set up with a two-zone fire, the heat is more intense at the center of the grate. The chicken breasts should face "out" on a kettle. Offset smokers are hottest closest to the firebox, so the chicken breasts should face away from the firebox.

Incidentally, we're off to a bad start if you're already thinking of and asking these types of questions. Just follow the directions and you'll have your barbecue epiphany soon enough.

★ THE SMOKE RING ★

IN BARBECUE, THE SMOKE RING—the bright pink layer just under the surface of the meat—is one of the signs of a successful low and slow cook. But some people get nervous when their chicken is pink. If you fall into this category of people, rest assured, this pink does not mean your chicken is undercooked. The smoke ring is the result of a chemical reaction between the wood smoke and the meat, and you want it there.

DEAR STUDENT,

CONGRATULATIONS! YOU SHOULD HAVE A PLATTER OF TASTY, PERFECTLY SMOKED Chicken Mojo Criollo in your hands. Now, do a little victory dance around your cooker in the backyard. Because you followed the instructions exactly, didn't you?

What's that? You incorporated some tips you saw on the Virtual Weber site? You had a half bag of leftover charcoal briquettes and figured, Why not use it up? You smoked bologna instead of chicken?

I have a stock letter for transgressors of my program. It goes like this:

Dear [Name of the Damned Withheld],

Stop reading the Virtual Weber site. It's a great resource, but if you pick up techniques and methods from Web sites and try to incorporate them into the program, things get confusing and don't work well. Virtual Weber and I have very different philosophies on barbecue. The site is populated by engineers who tend to put too much emphasis on things like time charts and ambient temperature. My program cares about none of that. Start the fire, put the meat in the cooker, and leave it the hell alone.

Now, go take that damn thermometer out of the vent. Not only is the thermometer blocking airflow, which causes smoldering (which leads to creosote-flavored food), but these thermometers are meant to be inserted in food. They don't measure the air temperature in your cooker, so you'll never get an accurate reading. Repeat after me: we don't care about no stinking temperature. Remember, you're learning to read fires and meat, not thermometers.

Also, do not reuse charcoal. Ever. Charcoal is an absorbent. It drinks moisture and odor from the air, which is why it's often used as a filter. Moist charcoal cooks slow and transfers off flavors to your food. And let me guess: you used regular briquettes instead of natural lump charcoal? Do I have to remind you that briquettes contain a witch's brew of chemicals, while lump charcoal is a natural product?

Okay, now try Lesson #1 again, but ditch the thermometer and the briquettes and buy some natural lump charcoal. If you are still interested in continuing this program . . . great. If I come on too strong and you think I'm full of soot, and you wish to discontinue, that's perfectly understandable. No hard feelings. But the deal is this: please follow instructions exactly or drop out of the program.

Cordially but firmly,

Gary Wiviott

CONTINUING EDUCATION

TO TRULY MASTER THE SKILLS YOU'VE LEARNED IN LESSON #1 and hone your expertise, I recommend practicing the cook over and over again. However, you'll soon learn that eating Chicken Mojo Criollo over and over again is a drag, and likely to discourage you from perfecting the techniques you need in order to move on to the next lesson. To keep you in the program, here are some simple marinades to expand your flavor repertoire. Or check the index for more recipes that incorporate your delicious, soon-to-be-legendary (in your neighborhood, at least) smoked chicken.

MARINADE 101

MANY PEOPLE WOULD enthusiastically skip this part of the tutorial, buy commercial marinades for the rest of their lives, and be none the wiser. But you, student, have already proven your desire to know more—to elevate your understanding of barbecue cookery—by committing to this program.

If you're not used to making your own marinade, the following recipes might seem like a lot of work for food that picks up most of its flavor from wood smoke. Instead of relying on garlic or onion powder and salt for flavor, the recipes call for real ingredients—freshly squeezed citrus juice, toasted and ground dried chile peppers, garlic cloves, onion, and more. This extra step is what will separate you from every other person who cracks open a bottle of sauce and calls himself or herself a "good cook." Those preservative-laden concoctions can't touch the flavor of a marinade made with fresh ingredients.

I am not as strict about the ingredients in a marinade, however, as I am about following instructions for the cooks. You won't get kicked out of the Program if you use store-bought OJ because you don't have eight oranges lying around the kitchen. A few short-cuts here and there are more like culinary improv than cheating. The beauty is that learning the simple fundamentals of making a marinade will serve you well. If you're taking the time to learn the art of barbecue, using the freshest available ingredients in your marinades not only makes for better barbecue—but it also makes you a better cook.

HOT SAUCE

IN THIS PROGRAM, there are two types of hot sauce: Louisiana-style and Mexican-style. Although Tabasco is the hot sauce most associated with Louisiana, I rarely use it because it is a one-note sauce. It contains a higher ratio of vinegar—too much, in my opinion—which brightens the flavor of the hot sauce, but you lose some of the characteristic heat of the peppers. My preferred Louisiana-style hot sauces—Crystal, Louisiana and Texas Pete—aren't as punchy as Tabasco. These hot sauces have the perfect balance of vinegar and heat. It's an accent flavor. It enhances without overpowering. Mexican-style hot sauce, like Cholula, Búfalo and El Yucateco, has a broader spectrum of flavors because most brands use a mix of chiles. The consistency of the hot sauce also tends to be thicker, and some are even gritty.

★ MARINADE MUST-HAVES ★

Shortcuts are tempting, but not tasty.

- Always use real, fresh-squeezed juice from citrus fruits, not "juice" that comes out of fruit-shaped plastic.
- Use canola or inexpensive olive oil.
- If your spices have been collecting dust for more than eight months, buy a fresh batch. For the best flavor, toast and grind whole spices (page 18) from sources like The Spice House (www.thespicehouse.com) or Penzeys (www.penzeys.com).

MOJO CRIOLLO II

This is a marinade-making baby step: tweaking your store-bought, bottled mojo criollo. You slightly doctored the mojo criollo in the first cook with olive oil and lemon—a simple twist that freshens the flavor of a commercial product. Here, you have a list of optional ingredients to customize the marinade to your taste. Pick one or two. Or three. Adding in seasonings like fresh jalapeño or whole garlic cloves brings another level of flavor to the bottled marinade. The WSM and offset recipe makes enough for four chicken halves and the kettle recipe for two chicken halves.

WSM AND OFFSET

MAKES 4½ CUPS

1 lemon

½ cup olive oil

1 (32-ounce) bottle mojo criollo, Goya or other brand

Kosher salt and freshly ground black pepper to taste

KETTLE

MAKES 2¼ CUPS

½ lemon

¼ cup olive oil

2 cups mojo criollo, Goya or other brand

Kosher salt and freshly ground black pepper to taste

OPTIONAL ADD-INS

½ medium white onion, quartered

1 to 2 jalapeños, quartered (plus seeds if you want more heat)

½ tablespoon grated citrus (lemon, lime, or orange) rind

1 teaspoon Louisiana-style or Mexican-style hot sauce, such as Texas Pete, Louisiana, or Búfalo

½ tablespoon Toasted Mexican Pepper Blend (page 18)

2 unpeeled garlic cloves, smashed

½ chipotle in adobo, pureed

Squeeze the juice from the lemon into a large bowl and add the rind. Add the olive oil and mojo criollo. Add one or more of the optional add-ins to amp up the flavor profile.

For the WSM or offset, divide the marinade between two one-gallon zip-top bags.

For the kettle, pour all the marinade into one zip-top bag.

Add two chicken halves to each bag and press the air out of the bags and seal. Place the bags in a large bowl or on a rimmed baking sheet. Allow the chicken to marinate for 4 to 6 hours in the refrigerator, turning the bags once or twice to redistribute the marinade.

DIY MOJO CRIOLLO

Using a commercial mojo criollo *is easier—which is what you want for the first cook—but you'll never go back to the bottle once you've used this homemade version. Look for sour orange juice (a.k.a. bitter orange, Seville orange, or bigarade orange juice) in Mexican markets. It's called* naranja ácida, naranja agria, *or* naranja amarga. *In season, you might find fresh sour oranges in Southeast Asian markets. The WSM and offset recipe makes enough for four chicken halves and the kettle recipe for two chicken halves.*

WSM AND OFFSET

MAKES ABOUT 4 CUPS

$2^1/_2$ cups canola oil

2 garlic heads, peeled and crushed

2 medium white onions, sliced

$^3/_4$ cup sour orange juice (or $^1/_2$ cup orange juice plus $^1/_4$ cup lime juice)

$^1/_4$ cup water

$^1/_4$ cup white vinegar

1 tablespoon kosher salt

2 teaspoons freshly ground black pepper

1 teaspoon cumin

1 teaspoon oregano

1 teaspoon crushed red pepper (optional)

1 teaspoon grated orange rind (optional)

KETTLE

MAKES ABOUT 2 CUPS

$1^1/_4$ cups canola oil

1 garlic head, peeled and crushed

1 medium white onion, sliced

$^1/_4$ cup plus 2 tablespoons sour orange juice (or $^1/_4$ cup orange juice + 2 tablespoons lime juice)

2 tablespoons water

2 tablespoons white vinegar

$^1/_2$ tablespoon kosher salt

1 teaspoon freshly ground black pepper

$^1/_2$ teaspoon cumin

$^1/_2$ teaspoon oregano

$^1/_2$ teaspoon crushed red pepper (optional)

$^1/_2$ teaspoon grated orange rind (optional)

Heat the canola oil over medium heat in a saucepan. When the oil is warmed, approximately 2 minutes, add the garlic and onion to the saucepan. Cook until fragrant (not browned), about 30 seconds. Remove the saucepan from the heat and allow the oil to cool, 5 minutes. Stir in the juice, water, vinegar, and spices. Bring the mixture to a boil over medium-high heat and allow it to boil for 1 minute. Remove the saucepan from the heat and let the marinade cool to room temperature. Pour the mixture into a blender. Blend until smooth.

For the WSM or offset, divide the marinade between two one-gallon zip-top bags.

For the kettle, pour all the marinade into one zip-top bag. Add two chicken halves to each bag and press the air out of the bags and seal. Place the bags in a large bowl or on a rimmed baking sheet to catch drips. Allow the chicken to marinate for 4 to 6 hours in the refrigerator, turning the bags once or twice to redistribute the marinade.

★ ACHIOTE MARINADE ★

Kurt, King of Kurtopia, a barbecue man of some note, created this punchy marinade. It works very well in low and slow cooks, but is also quite delicious on regular grilled chicken. The ingredients are very flexible. As long as you have achiote paste and citrus—there's no need to measure the exact amount or type of citrus juice—all of the other ingredients are flexible and can be added to your taste. The WSM and offset recipe makes enough for four chicken halves and the kettle recipe for two chicken halves.

WSM AND OFFSET

MAKES ABOUT 4 CUPS

1 (3½-ounce) block achiote paste

3 limes, juiced (6 tablespoons)

3 lemons, juiced (9 tablespoons)

2 oranges, juiced (½ cup)

1 grapefruit, juiced (½ cup)

1 cup beer

½ cup canola oil

8 green onions, sliced

1 cup cilantro, chopped

4 jalapeño peppers, seeded and sliced

4 garlic cloves, peeled and sliced

3 tablespoons cumin, ground

2 tablespoons freshly ground black pepper

2 tablespoons kosher salt

3 tablespoons paprika

3 tablespoons Toasted Mexican Pepper
  Blend (page 18)

KETTLE

MAKES ABOUT 2 CUPS

½ (3½-ounce) block achiote paste

2 limes, juiced (about 3 tablespoons juice)

2 lemons, juiced (about 5 tablespoons juice)

1 orange, juiced (about ¼ cup juice)

½ grapefruit, juiced (about ¼ cup juice)

½ cup beer

¼ cup canola oil

4 green onions, sliced

½ cup cilantro, chopped

2 jalapeño peppers, seeded and sliced

2 garlic cloves, peeled and sliced

1½ tablespoons cumin, ground

1 tablespoon freshly ground black pepper

1 tablespoon kosher salt

1½ tablespoons paprika

1½ tablespoons dried Toasted Mexican
  Pepper Blend (page 18)

Place the brick (or half brick, if you're using the kettle recipe) of achiote paste in a large mixing bowl. Pour the juices, beer, and canola oil over the paste. Stir the mixture until the paste dissolves in the liquid. Add the onion, cilantro, jalapeño, garlic, and spices. Whisk the mixture until it is blended.

For the WSM or offset, divide the marinade between two (1-gallon) zip-top bags.

For the kettle, pour all the marinade into one zip-top bag.

Add two chicken halves to each bag and press the air out of the bags and seal. Place the bags in a large bowl or on a rimmed baking sheet to catch drips. Allow the chicken to marinate for 4 to 6 hours in the refrigerator, turning the bags once or twice to redistribute the marinade.

INGREDIENT FINDER
ACHIOTE

[ah-chee-OH-tay], a.k.a. annatto or *pimentão doce*, is a thick, deep-red paste made with the dried, ground seeds of the achiote tree, plus garlic, cumin, and other spices. It has a subtle earthy, tangy flavor. It also imparts a vibrant yellow, orange, or red hue to food, which is why some people call it "poor man's saffron." Although it sounds exotic, many grocery stores stock it.

ITALIAN MARINADE

Smoked chicken gets an added bump of flavor if you pile red peppers and capers on top of the chicken as it cooks. The WSM and offset recipe makes enough for four chicken halves and the kettle recipe for two chicken halves.

WSM AND OFFSET

MAKES ABOUT 4 CUPS

2$^1/_2$ cups canola oil

1$^1/_4$ cups red wine vinegar, white wine vinegar, or tarragon vinegar

4 tablespoons minced fresh oregano or 4 teaspoons dried oregano

2 tablespoons Dijon mustard

4 garlic cloves, peeled and chopped

2 teaspoons kosher salt

2 teaspoons freshly ground black pepper

$^1/_2$ cup marinated roasted red peppers, drained and chopped (optional)

2 tablespoons capers (optional)

KETTLE

MAKES ABOUT 2 CUPS

1$^1/_4$ cups canola oil

$^1/_2$ cup plus 2 tablespoons red wine vinegar, white wine vinegar, or tarragon vinegar

2 tablespoons minced fresh oregano or 2 teaspoons dried oregano

1 tablespoon Dijon mustard

2 garlic cloves, peeled and chopped

1 teaspoon kosher salt

1 teaspoon freshly ground black pepper

$^1/_4$ cup marinated roasted red peppers, drained and chopped (optional)

1 tablespoon capers (optional)

In a medium bowl, whisk all of the ingredients together until the mixture is blended.

For the WSM or Offset, divide the marinade between two one-gallon zip-top bags.

For the kettle, pour all the marinade into one zip-top bag.

Add two chicken halves to each bag and press the air out of the bags and seal. Place the bags in a large bowl or on a rimmed baking sheet to catch drips. Allow the chicken to marinate for 4 to 6 hours in the refrigerator, turning the bags once or twice to redistribute the marinade.

CAJUN MARINADE

The word Cajun gets slapped on a lot of recipes, but this marinade passes the authenticity test with the addition of fresh onion, celery, and bell pepper—the "holy trinity" seasoning of Cajun cuisine. This marinated smoked chicken is perfect for using in Chicken and Sausage Gumbo (page 240). The WSM and offset recipe makes enough for four chicken halves and the kettle recipe for two chicken halves.

WSM AND OFFSET

MAKES ABOUT 4 CUPS

2$\frac{1}{2}$ cups canola oil

6 lemons, juiced (1$\frac{1}{4}$ cups)

2 medium white onions, quartered

2 ribs celery, sliced

1 bell pepper, seeded and sliced

2 tablespoons Louisiana-style or Mexican-style hot sauce, such as Texas Pete, Louisiana, or Búfalo

2 teaspoons Cajun seasoning, such as Tony's Chachere's

$\frac{1}{2}$ teaspoon cayenne pepper (optional)

KETTLE

MAKES ABOUT 2 CUPS

1$\frac{1}{4}$ cups canola oil

3 lemons, juiced ($\frac{1}{2}$ cup plus 2 tablespoons)

1 medium white onion, quartered

1 rib celery, sliced

$\frac{1}{2}$ bell pepper, seeded and sliced

1 tablespoon Louisiana-style or Mexican-style hot sauce

1 teaspoon Cajun seasoning, such as Tony's Chachere's

$\frac{1}{4}$ teaspoon cayenne pepper (optional)

In a medium bowl, whisk all of the ingredients together until the mixture is blended.

For the WSM or offset, divide the marinade between two one-gallon zip-top bags.

For the kettle, pour all the marinade into one zip-top bag.

Add two chicken halves to each bag and press the air out of the bags and seal. Place the bags in a large bowl or on a rimmed baking sheet to catch drips. Allow the chicken to marinate for 4 to 6 hours in the refrigerator, turning the bags once or twice to redistribute the marinade.

SOUTHWEST MARINADE

The chiles in this marinade—poblanos or Anaheim—are very mild compared to jalapeños or habañeros. If you can't find fresh poblanos, substitute one tablespoon of freshly ground dried ancho chile powder. (Ancho chiles are dried poblanos.) Any type of mild to medium-hot New Mexican chile can substitute for Anaheims. Chicken Enchiladas (page 234) with Tomatillo Sauce (page 235) is excellent made with leftover Southwest marinated smoked chicken. For extra flavor, lay the pepper strips on top of your chicken during the cook. The WSM and offset recipe makes enough for four chicken halves and the kettle recipe for two chicken halves.

WSM AND OFFSET

MAKES ABOUT 4 CUPS

2½ cups canola oil

10 to 12 limes, juiced (1 cup)

¼ cup white vinegar

4 fresh poblano or Anaheim chiles, cut into strips

2 teaspoons cumin powder or 1 teaspoon whole cumin seeds, toasted and ground

1 bunch cilantro, washed and coarsely chopped

KETTLE

MAKES ABOUT 2 CUPS

1¼ cups canola oil

5 to 6 limes, juiced (½ cup)

2 tablespoons white vinegar

2 fresh poblano or Anaheim chiles, cut into strips

1 teaspoon cumin powder or ½ teaspoon whole cumin seeds, toasted and ground

½ bunch cilantro, washed and coarsely chopped

In a medium bowl, whisk all of the ingredients together until the mixture is blended.

For the WSM or offset, divide the marinade between two one-gallon zip-top bags.

For the kettle, pour all the marinade into one zip-top bag.

Add two chicken halves to each bag and press the air out of the bags and seal. Place the bags in a large bowl or on a rimmed baking sheet to catch drips. Allow the chicken to marinate for 4 to 6 hours in the refrigerator, turning the bags once or twice to redistribute the marinade.

ASIAN MARINADE

The quintessential flavors in Asian cuisine—soy, rice vinegar, sesame, and ginger—make one of the best marinade pairings for smoked foods. Perhaps it's because soy is "umami," the somewhat controversial "fifth taste" that is attributed to savory, protein-rich foods like meat and cheese. The WSM and offset recipe makes enough for four chicken halves and the kettle recipe for two chicken halves.

WSM AND OFFSET

MAKES ABOUT 4 CUPS

$2\frac{1}{4}$ cups canola oil

1 cup rice wine vinegar

$\frac{1}{4}$ cup soy sauce

2 tablespoons sesame oil

2 tablespoons sesame seeds

10 green onions, chopped

1 (1-inch) piece fresh ginger, peeled and chopped

KETTLE

MAKES ABOUT 2 CUPS

1 cup plus 2 tablespoons canola oil

$\frac{1}{2}$ cup rice wine vinegar

2 tablespoons soy sauce

1 tablespoon sesame oil

1 tablespoon sesame seeds

5 green onions, chopped

$1\frac{1}{2}$-inch piece fresh ginger, peeled and chopped

In a medium bowl, whisk all of the ingredients together until the mixture is blended.

For the WSM or offset, divide the marinade between two one-gallon zip-top bags.

For the kettle, pour all the marinade into one zip-top bag.

Add two chicken halves to each bag and press the air out of the bags and seal. Place the bags in a large bowl or on a rimmed baking sheet to catch drips. Allow the chicken to marinate for 4 to 6 hours in the refrigerator, turning the bags once or twice to redistribute the marinade.

CARIBBEAN MARINADE

This marinade makes a mild, fruity-sweet blend of easy-going island flavors—a friendly match for eaters who are spice-sensitive or for using in Jerk Chicken (page 237). If you like the burn of a hotter marinade, add the habañero to the mix. For subtle heat, split the whole habañero in half and put one half of the pepper in each bag. For a more aggressive flavor, coarsely chop the pepper and split the amount between the two bags. The WSM and offset recipe makes enough for four chicken halves and the kettle recipe for two chicken halves.

WSM AND OFFSET

MAKES ABOUT 4 CUPS

2$\frac{1}{2}$ cups canola oil

$\frac{3}{4}$ cup freshly squeezed orange juice (about 2 oranges)

$\frac{1}{4}$ cup freshly squeezed lime juice (about 2 limes)

$\frac{1}{4}$ cup puréed fresh or canned pineapple chunks

1 teaspoon kosher salt

10 green onions, coarsely chopped

1 habañero pepper (optional)

KETTLE

MAKES ABOUT 2 CUPS

1$\frac{1}{4}$ cups canola oil

$\frac{1}{4}$ cup plus 2 tablespoons freshly squeezed orange juice (1 to 2 oranges)

2 tablespoons freshly squeezed lime juice (1 to 2 limes)

2 tablespoons puréed fresh or canned pineapple chunks

$\frac{1}{2}$ teaspoon kosher salt

5 green onions, coarsely chopped

$\frac{1}{2}$ habañero pepper (optional)

In a medium bowl, whisk all of the ingredients together until the mixture is blended.

For the WSM or offset, divide the marinade between two one-gallon zip-top bags.

For the kettle, pour all the marinade into one zip-top bag.

Add two chicken halves to each bag and press the air out of the bags and seal. Place the bags in a large bowl or on a rimmed baking sheet to catch drips. Allow the chicken to marinate for 4 to 6 hours in the refrigerator, turning the bags once or twice to redistribute the marinade.

TIP: Always wear rubber gloves when handling hot chile peppers like habañeros and jalapeños. The plant compound that gives these peppers their heat will burn your hands, and your eyes.

★ THAI MARINADE ★

Gai yang issan, *or Thai barbecued chicken, is one of my favorites in Thai restaurants. This recipe is adapted slightly for the long, slow cook. Serve this with one or both of the Thai dipping sauces in Lesson #2: Sweet and Spicy Garlic Sauce (page 107) or Chile Dipping Sauce (page 107). The WSM and offset recipe makes enough for four chicken halves and the kettle recipe for two chicken halves.*

WSM AND OFFSET

MAKES ABOUT 4 CUPS

2½ cups canola oil

1 cup freshly squeezed lime juice (8 to 10 limes)

1 cup chopped fresh cilantro

4 garlic cloves, peeled and chopped

1 (2-inch) piece fresh ginger, peeled and chopped

2 tablespoons freshly ground black pepper

2 tablespoons fish sauce

1 teaspoon ground coriander

KETTLE

MAKES ABOUT 2 CUPS

1¼ cups canola oil

½ cup freshly squeezed lime juice (about 4 limes)

½ cup chopped fresh cilantro

2 garlic cloves, peeled and chopped

1 (1-inch) piece fresh ginger, peeled and chopped

1 tablespoon freshly ground black pepper

1 tablespoon fish sauce

½ teaspoon ground coriander

In a medium bowl, whisk all of the ingredients together until the mixture is blended.

For the WSM or offset, divide the marinade between two one-gallon zip-top bags.

For the kettle, pour all the marinade into one zip-top bag.

Add two chicken halves to each bag and press the air out of the bags and seal. Place the bags in a large bowl or on a rimmed baking sheet to catch drips. Allow the chicken to marinate for 4 to 6 hours in the refrigerator, turning the bags once or twice to redistribute the marinade.

MISO MARINADE

Renowned chef Nobuyuki Matsuhisa's famously delectable black cod with miso was the inspiration for this marinade. The subtle flavor of a light miso is a lovely complement to wood-smoked chicken; red miso can be used, but because it has a stronger flavor, cut the amount in half. Miso can be found in any Asian market and at most gourmet grocery stores. The WSM and offset recipe makes enough for four chicken halves and the kettle recipe for two chicken halves.

WSM AND OFFSET	**KETTLE**
MAKES ABOUT 4 CUPS	MAKES ABOUT 2 CUPS
1 1/2 cups cold water	3/4 cups cold water
1/2 cup white or yellow miso paste	1/4 cup white or yellow miso paste
1/3 cup tamari (Japanese soy sauce)	2 1/2 tablespoons tamari (Japanese soy sauce)
1/4 cup rice wine or dry sherry	2 tablespoons cup rice wine or dry sherry
1/4 cup chopped green onion	2 tablespoons chopped green onion
2 tablespoons brown sugar	1 tablespoon brown sugar
1 tablespoon sesame oil	1/2 tablespoon sesame oil

In a medium bowl, whisk all of the ingredients together until the mixture is blended.

For the WSM or offset, divide the marinade between two one-gallon zip-top bags.

For the kettle, pour all the marinade into one zip-top bag.

Add two chicken halves to each bag and press the air out of the bags and seal. Place the bags in a large bowl or on a rimmed baking sheet to catch drips. Allow the chicken to marinate for 4 to 6 hours in the refrigerator, turning the bags once or twice to redistribute the marinade.

★ PARSLEY MARINADE ★

This is one of those recipes where fresh ingredients are not an option—they're a requirement if you want the punchy, herbal flavor to come through in the dish. Curly-leaf parsley works fine if you can't find flat-leaf, but do not use the musty dried parsley debris shaking around in your spice cabinet. The WSM and offset recipe makes enough for four chicken halves and the kettle recipe for two chicken halves.

WSM AND OFFSET

MAKES ABOUT 4 CUPS

2 cups olive oil

$^{3}/_{4}$ cups red wine vinegar

12 garlic cloves, peeled and cut in half

2 medium onions, cut in half

1 cup Italian flat-leaf parsley, stemmed, and chopped

$^{1}/_{2}$ cup freshly squeezed lemon juice (about 3 lemons)

2 teaspoons dry mustard

2 teaspoons kosher salt

KETTLE

MAKES ABOUT 2 CUPS

1 cup olive oil

$^{1}/_{4}$ cup plus 2 tablespoons red wine vinegar

6 garlic cloves, peeled and chopped

1 medium onion, chopped

$^{1}/_{2}$ cup Italian flat-leaf parsley, stemmed and chopped

$^{1}/_{4}$ cup freshly squeezed lemon juice (about 2 lemons)

1 teaspoon dry mustard

1 teaspoon kosher salt

In a medium bowl, whisk all of the ingredients together until the mixture is blended.

For the WSM or offset, divide the marinade between two one-gallon zip-top bags.

For the kettle, pour all the marinade into one zip-top bag.

Add two chicken halves to each bag and press the air out of the bags anseal. Place the bags in a large bowl or on a rimmed baking sheet to catch drips. Allow the chicken to marinate for 4 to 6 hours in the refrigerator, turning the bags once or twice to redistribute the marinade.

CURRY MARINADE

There's a rich tradition of tandoor-barbecued meats in Indian cuisine, so it seems only natural to fuse low and slow chicken with classic Indian spices. For a good visual presentation, add the optional achiote paste (page 61). This mild, earthy seasoning adds a vibrant yellow-orange color to the chicken. The WSM and offset recipe makes enough for four chicken halves and the kettle recipe for two chicken halves.

WSM AND OFFSET

MAKES 4 CUPS

2½ cups canola oil

1 cup dry white wine

¼ cup chopped shallots

3 tablespoons sweet curry powder

2 tablespoons soy sauce

2 tablespoons honey

2 tablespoons achiote paste (optional)

KETTLE

MAKES 2 CUPS

1¼ cups canola oil

½ cup dry white wine

2 tablespoons chopped shallots

1½ tablespoons sweet curry powder

1 tablespoon soy sauce

1 tablespoon honey

1 tablespoon achiote paste (optional)

In a medium bowl, whisk all of the ingredients together until the mixture is blended. If adding achiote for color, blend the paste into the mixture until it is fully dissolved.

For the WSM or offset, divide the marinade between two one-gallon zip-top bags.

For the kettle, pour all the marinade into one zip-top bag.

Add two chicken halves to each bag and press the air out of the bags and seal. Place the bags in a large bowl or on a rimmed baking sheet to catch drips. Allow the chicken to marinate for 4 to 6 hours in the refrigerator, turning the bags once or twice to redistribute the marinade.

FRENCH MARINADE

Smoked chicken probably isn't the first thing that comes to mind when you think of French cuisine, but the classic flavors translate well in barbecue. The French also have a history with this style of cooking—thanks to Catherine de Médicis's culinary influence—called de barbe et queue ("beard to tail"). Sound familiar? The WSM and offset recipe makes enough for four chicken halves and the kettle recipe for two chicken halves.

WSM AND OFFSET

MAKES ABOUT 3¼ CUPS

1¼ cups olive oil

¾ cup champagne vinegar

¼ cup chopped shallot

¼ cup Italian flat-leaf parsley, stemmed and chopped

15 whole peppercorns or 2 teaspoons freshly ground black pepper

1 shallot, chopped

1 teaspoon dried thyme

1 teaspoon kosher salt

2 bay leaves, crumbled

2 garlic cloves, peeled and chopped

KETTLE

MAKES A GENEROUS 2 CUPS

½ cup plus 2 tablespoons olive oil

¼ cup plus 2 tablespoons champagne vinegar

2 tablespoons chopped shallot

2 tablespoons Italian flat-leaf parsley, stemmed and chopped

7 whole peppercorns or 1 teaspoon freshly ground black pepper

½ shallot, chopped

½ teaspoon dried thyme

1 teaspoon kosher salt

1 bay leaf, crumbled

1 garlic clove, peeled and chopped

In a medium bowl, whisk all of the ingredients together until the mixture is blended.

For the WSM or offset, divide the marinade between two one-gallon zip-top bags.

For the kettle, pour all the marinade into one zip-top bag.

Add two chicken halves to each bag and press the air out of the bags and seal. Place the bags in a large bowl or on a rimmed baking sheet to catch drips. Allow the chicken to marinate for 4 to 6 hours in the refrigerator, turning the bags once or twice to redistribute the marinade.

BUILD-YOUR-OWN MARINADE TEMPLATE

WHAT IS A MARINADE? NOTHING MORE than a seasoned, acidic liquid that lends flavor to and tenderizes the meat. This simple liquid is, at its most basic, a mixture of two parts oil to one part acid. Got that? 2:1. Oil is a straightforward ingredient. It's oil. I recommend using canola because it has a neutral flavor and it's inexpensive. Cheap olive oil works fine, too. Acid, on the other hand, comes in many forms. Vinegar. Lemon juice. Mustard. There are many possibilities in the realm of acidic flavoring. Extra dashes of herbs or spices are also added to a marinade to infuse the meat with deeper and more complex flavors.

So the real question is, how do you make marinade? Now that you've made a few of the marinade recipes (because you're still practicing Lesson #1—let's not forget why you're here), it's time to gently shove you out of the nest. Stick to an approximate 2:1 oil to acid ratio, and the rest is up to you. Use this template as a guide.

OIL: 2½ CUPS

Oil is a fat, which helps to transfer the flavors of the marinade seasoning to the meat. To make four cups of marinade, you need to use about two and a half cups of oil. Canola and inexpensive olive oil are the ones I use most, but you can experiment with other light, neutral oils like grapeseed, safflower, and sunflower oil if you have those lying around the kitchen. I don't recommend using heavy, flavorful oils like corn or peanut oil in a marinade. The large amount required to make four cups of marinade will completely overwhelm the other flavors. Highly flavorful oils are best used as a seasoning. Sesame oil, for example, is very potent, but used sparingly—one or two tablespoons in one and a half cups canola oil—it imparts flavor without drowning out others. Remember to subtract the amount of seasoning oil you use from the amount of neutral oil in the marinade.

ACID: 1¼ CUPS

When balanced with oil, the acid in a marinade causes the tissue in meat to break down, which lets in more moisture and gives the meat a juicy, tender texture. Too much acid in a marinade, however, can toughen the proteins in meat. You can use a single acid, or mix them up—mustard and wine, for example—to get even more variety. Keep in mind that yogurt, papaya, pineapple, ginger, and kiwifruit contain protease enzymes that can turn your meat mushy if you marinate in these liquids too long. Use smaller amounts— one-quarter to one-half cup—mixed with other acids and cut your marinating time by half.

★ SUGGESTED OILS AND ACIDS ★

BASE		SEASONING	
OILS	**ACIDS**	**CITRUS JUICE**	**FRUIT OR**
Canola	**Vinegar**	Lemon juice	**VEGETABLE**
Grapeseed	Apple cider	Orange juice	**JUICE**
Olive	Champagne	Lime juice	Unsweetened
Safflower	Tarragon	Sour orange juice	cranberry juice
Sunflower	**Non-Vinegar**	Grapefruit juice	Pineapple juice
	Buttermilk	Yuzu juice	Mango juice
FLAVORED OILS	Yogurt		Tomato juice
Herb-infused	**Wine**	**OTHER**	
Pepper-infused	Red wine	Soy sauce	
Toasted sesame	Rice wine	Hot pepper sauce	
	White wine		

SEASONING:
1 TABLESPOON KOSHER SALT, PLUS ¼ TO ½ CUP HERBS OR SPICES

Oil and acid will contribute some flavor to a marinade, but they're mostly conduits for transferring the flavor of the seasonings to the meat. Not to be hyperbolic, but the sky's the limit with the type of herb, spice, aromatic, vegetable, or mineral you use in a marinade. This is where you get to start figuring out these things for yourself. If you like oregano, use oregano. Basil? Tamarind? Herbes de Provence? Whatever.

The quantity of any seasoning absolutely depends on the strength of the seasoning and the types and amounts of any other seasonings in the marinade.

TIME: 4 TO 6 HOURS

For an acidic marinade, 4 to 6 hours might seem like a long time. It's true that too much acid can make for chewy meat, and certain types of acids—those that break down protein with enzymes—can lead to mush. This longer suggested marinating time is based on using a well-balanced marinade that isn't too acidic. You're also using skin-on chicken halves, which are bigger and require more marinating time than the smaller cuts of chicken used in other recipes.

★ MARINATING TIPS ★

- Emulsify the marinade in a blender if it does not contain whole aromatics, herbs, or spices.
- Always marinate in a non-reactive container, such as the one-gallon zip-top bags I suggest, or a glass or ceramic dish. The acid in a marinade will react with aluminum and can cause off flavors in the marinated meat.
- Cover and refrigerate meat while it marinates. Flip the meat once or twice during the marinating time so that all sides are exposed to the marinade.
- If you plan to baste with your marinade or use it as a condiment, set aside $\frac{1}{4}$ to $\frac{1}{2}$ cup of the marinade before you pour it over the raw meat to prevent cross-contamination.

DEAR STUDENT,

YOU'VE LEARNED A FEW THINGS, GRASSHOPPER. AT THIS POINT, YOU SHOULD understand the fundamentals of building a clean-burning fire in your cooker and maintaining it for at least two to three hours. Hopefully you learned something about the chemistry of a marinade and how to make your own from scratch, too. You've laid a foundation of low and slow skills on which you will build with each lesson in the program.

Notice that I am not giving you a roster of sauces and condiments for your smoked chicken. You've learned enough already, and making barbecue sauce is a task you'll take on in Lesson #2 (page 104)—when you fully understand when and how to use one. In the meantime, I figure you probably have a favorite go-to sauce. If you need to douse your beautifully smoked chicken in something, use that one. Or try the Alabama White Sauce (page 105)—it's like an un-barbecue sauce.

Right now, I want you to practice more cooks and let what you've learned so far sink in slowly. Do it enough times so that it becomes second nature to you.

Congratulations,

Gary Wiviott

LOW & SLOW QUIZ: LESSON 1

There is no grade curve for this quiz. If you get more than two answers wrong, re-read chapters 1 through 3 and complete the first cook at least two more times before proceeding to Lesson #2.

1. Every time you open the cooker for no good reason, the stabilized temperature drops and the cook time is extended by . . .
a) 5 to 10 minutes
b) 15 to 20 minutes
c) 30 minutes
d) 1 hour

2. Why is it important to use three sheets of loosely rolled newspaper to light the chimney starter?

_____

_____

3. Charcoal briquettes burn faster and cleaner than any other type of charcoal. True or False?

4. Most barbecue "experts" recommend soaking wood in water to extend its burn time, but adding wet wood to a fire also . . .
a) causes the wood to smolder and produce tar
b) decreases the temperature in the cooker
c) smothers the fire
d) all of the above

5. What should you do if thick, dark smoke is billowing out of the cooker after you close it?

_____

_____

6. Where are the "hot zones" on a cooker?
a) in the middle of the cooking grate
b) around the edges of the cooking grate
c) the region on the grate closest to the lit charcoal or hot airflow
d) at the top of the cooker, where hot air rises

7. If smoked chicken has a pinkish tinge under the skin, it's probably undercooked. True or False?

8. The basic oil to acid ratio in a marinade is . . .
a) 2:1
b) 3:1
c) 1:1
d) depends on the type of meat

Answers: 1) b. 2) Packed paper smolders. The loose rings allow sufficient airflow to fully light the paper and ignite the charcoal. 3) False! Briquettes contain many chemicals. Natural lump charcoal burns cleaner and faster. 4) d. 5) Open the cooker until the clouds of dark smoke die down. When lit and unlit charcoal mix, it takes at least 5 to 10 minutes for the charcoal to catch and stop billowing smoke. 6) c. 7) False. Properly cooked, low and slow meat often has a smoke ring (page 54). 8) a.

★

4.

LESSON Nº2

BRINED CHICKEN

DEAR STUDENT,

SO YOU'VE LEARNED THE MOST IMPORTANT LESSON: HOW TO MAKE A CLEAN, non-smoldering fire in your cooker. It's a vital step, but please don't skip ahead to another, tastier-sounding dinner because you think you've mastered all the necessary skills. You have not. If you completed Lesson #1 and continued practicing the cook with different marinades, I don't doubt that you're tiring of chicken. The solution to your poultry ennui is in chapter 10: Smokin' Left-overs—a collection of my favorite recipes using smoked meat.

You still have much to learn. In this dinner, you will cook brined, air-dried chicken in almost exactly the same way as you cooked the chicken in Lesson #1, but with a critical new step: you will partially close a vent (or two, depending on the cooker) midway through the cook and use an oven thermometer. This new step demonstrates how the vents affect the grate temperature and cooking time. One small tweak to the vents lowers the temperature in the cooker and lengthens the cooking time. This isn't important when you're smoking chicken (the bird doesn't care if you're cooking at 350°F or 275°F—it'll taste good either way), but temperature and time will be factors later on with more heat-sensitive cuts of meat.

Instead of using a marinade for this cook, you will brine the chicken halves. Brines affect the flavor and texture of the meat as marinades do, but there's one key difference: brines are strong saltwater solutions, while marinades contain strong concentrations of acid. Brines typically contain little, if any, acid, and the saltwater solution actually penetrates and plumps the meat.

For Lesson #2, I'm giving you a basic brine recipe for the first time you attempt the cook. Please don't go messing with the brine right away. The point of making it my way the first time is to build your confidence in the basics and to slowly add to your understanding of low and slow cookery. Later in the chapter, you'll learn how to make your own brine, just as you learned the fundamentals of making a marinade after Lesson #1. Once you know the basics, you can fool around with brine to your heart's content. You'll also get one more low and slow building block—recipes for classic and not-so-traditional sauces and dips for chicken and other barbecue.

Be patient. The ribs you've been twitching to make are just around the corner.

Sincerely,

Gary Wiviott

BRINED CHICKEN

There's a lot of chemistry hoodoo that explains what brines do and how they do it, but now is not the time to discuss osmosis. All you need to know is that soaking the chicken halves in a strong saltwater solution keeps the meat moist and juicy. This basic brine can be used on most poultry and some lean cuts of pork.

WSM AND OFFSET

SERVES 4 TO 6

$2/3$ cup Morton kosher salt, plus more to taste

$1/2$ cup brown sugar

1 cup warm water

2 whole fryers (3- to 4-pound chickens),
  split in half, legs disjointed (page 50)

Olive oil for brushing

Freshly ground black pepper, to taste

KETTLE

SERVES 2 TO 4

$1/3$ cup Morton kosher salt, plus more to taste

$1/4$ cup brown sugar

$1/2$ cup warm water

1 whole fryer (3- to 4-pound chicken),
  split in half, legs disjointed (page 50)

Olive oil for brushing

Freshly ground black pepper, to taste

THE NIGHT BEFORE DINNER (6 TO 12 HOURS BRINING TIME)

In a large bowl or measuring cup, whisk the salt, sugar, and warm water together until the salt and sugar are dissolved. For the WSM or offset, divide four chicken halves between two one-gallon zip-top bags. Divide the brine between the bags. For the kettle, place two chicken halves in one one-gallon zip-top bag and pour all the brine into the bag.

Set the bag(s) in the sink and fill with cold water to within 1 inch of the zipper (8 to 10 cups depending on the water displacement of the chicken). Press the air out of the bags and seal. Place the bags in a large bowl or on a rimmed baking sheet to catch drips. Allow the chicken to brine for 6 to 12 hours in the refrigerator, turning the bags once or twice to redistribute the brine.

5 HOURS BEFORE DINNER

Remove the chicken from the bags and rinse the chicken under cold running water. Pat the chicken dry with paper towels. Lay the chicken halves on a cooling rack set on a rimmed baking sheet. Place the baking sheet, uncovered, in the refrigerator. Low-and-slow cooking typically makes chicken skin rubbery.

Air-drying the chicken for several hours in the refrigerator increases the odds of crisping the skin.

2 HOURS BEFORE DINNER

Set up and start a KISS method fire according to the instructions for your WSM (page 32), offset (page 34), or kettle (page36). If Lesson #1 was too smoky for your taste, remove one wood chunk from each level of charcoal.

While you're waiting for the charcoal in the chimney to engage, remove the chicken from the refrigerator. Brush the chicken halves with olive oil and season lightly with salt and pepper.

When the lit charcoal and wood are ready for cooking, arrange the chicken on the grate according to the illustrated instructions for your cooker.

WSM

PLACE THE CHICKEN HALVES in a circle, breast-side in on the top grate, as close to the center as possible without crowding. Use your tongs to nudge the thigh/leg portion higher on the breast. Place the oven thermometer in the center of the grate, between the chicken halves.

Set the lid on the cooker, with the top vent positioned on the opposite side of the cooker from the center ring door. The top and bottom vents should be open.

45 MINUTES INTO THE COOK

Close the two bottom vents closest to the side door by one-third.

Lift the lid—just this once—and check the

temperature on the oven thermometer, for informational purposes only. (See Addendum to the no-peeking policy, page 84.)

1¹/₂ HOURS INTO THE COOK

Remove the cooker lid and puncture the thickest part of the chicken breast with the tip of a sharp knife. If the juice running out of the chicken is clear, it's done.

If the juice is pinkish or cloudy, the chicken isn't done yet. Did you use bigger chickens? Is it really cold outside? These are things that can lengthen the cooking time.

If the chicken is not done, squirt the skin with cooking spray or olive oil so it doesn't stick to the grate; then flip the chicken over so it is skin-side down.

If the water pan is low, refill it so that the water level is about 1 inch from the rim.

Check the chicken every 10 minutes; it's ready when the juices run clear. Or, if you insist on using a digital meat thermometer, the meat is done when the breast reads 155°F and the thigh reads 165°F.

Again, for informational purposes, check the temperature on the oven thermometer when the chicken is done.

OFFSET SMOKER

TUCK EACH WING under the breast and place the chicken halves on the grate with the wing/leg facing the firebox. Set the first chicken half about a third of the way away from the firebox. Repeat with the remaining chicken halves, working away from the firebox. Use your tongs to nudge the thigh/leg portion higher on the breast. Place the oven thermometer on the grate between the chickens. Close the lid of the cooker. Both vents should be open.

30 MINUTES
INTO THE COOK

Close the vent on the firebox by one-third.

Lift the lid on the cooker and check the level in the water pan. If it is less than three-quarters full, add water. While you're in there, check the temperature on the oven thermometer, for informational purposes. (See Addendum to the no-peeking policy, page 84.)

1 HOUR INTO THE COOK

Fill the chimney starter halfway with charcoal and light it. When the charcoal is fully engaged, open the lid of the firebox and pour in the fresh charcoal. Add a split of wood to the charcoal.

Keep the firebox open until the charcoal and wood stop billowing smoke (about 10 minutes); then close it. While you're waiting for the charcoal to engage, open the cooker and check the water pan. If it is less than three-quarters full, refill it. Rotate the meat so that the chicken halves closest to the firebox are moved farthest away.

1½ HOURS INTO THE COOK

Remove the lid and puncture the thickest part of the chicken breast with the tip of a sharp knife. If the juice running out of the chicken is clear, it's done.

If the juice is pinkish or cloudy, the chicken isn't done yet. Did you use bigger chickens? Is it really cold outside? These are things that can lengthen the cook time.

If the chicken isn't done, squirt the skin with cooking spray or olive oil so it doesn't stick to the grate; then flip the chicken over so it is skin-side down.

Check the level in the water pan. If it is less than three-quarters full, refill it. Check the chicken every 10 minutes; it's ready when the juices run clear. Or, if you insist on using a digital meat thermometer, the meat is done when the breast reads 155°F and the thigh reads 165°F.

Again, for informational purposes only, check the temperature on the oven thermometer when the chicken is done.

PLACE THE CHICKEN HALVES on the grate, with the breast-side close to the edge of the grate without touching the side of the cooker. The breast should not face the water pan and bank of charcoal. Use your tongs to nudge the thigh/leg portion higher on the breast. Place the oven thermometer on the grate between the chickens.

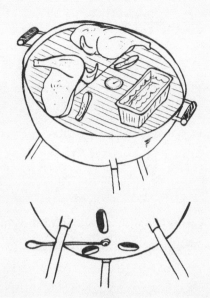

Set the lid on the cooker with the top vent positioned directly above the chicken. Open the top and bottom vents.

20 MINUTES INTO THE COOK

Close the bottom vent by one-third.

Pour the chimney starter one-third full with charcoal and light it (see Starting Your Chimney, page 28). After 5 minutes, when the charcoal in the chimney is fully lit, remove the cooker lid, slide the water pan aside, and open the top grate. Pour the fresh lit charcoal on the pile. Place 1 wood chunk on the fire and use your tongs to clean up and bank the pile.

Check the level in the water pan. If it is less than three-quarters full, add water.

When the fresh charcoal and wood chunk are engaged and no longer billowing smoke (about 10 minutes), put the lid on the cooker.

1 HOUR INTO THE COOK

Remove the cooker lid. For informational purposes, check the temperature on the oven thermometer. (See Addendum To The No-Peeking Policy, page 84.) Puncture the thickest part of the chicken breast with the tip of a sharp knife. If the juice running out of the chicken is clear, it's done.

If the juice is pinkish or cloudy, the chicken isn't done yet. Did you use bigger chickens? Is it really cold outside? These are things that can lengthen the cook time. If the chicken isn't done, squirt the skin with cooking spray or olive oil so it doesn't stick to the grate; then flip the chicken over so it is skin-side down. Check the chicken every 10 minutes; it's ready when the juices run clear. Or, if you insist on using a digital meat thermometer, the meat is done when the breast reads 155°F and the thigh reads 165°F. Again, for informational purposes, check the temperature on the oven thermometer when the chicken is done.

ADDENDUM TO THE NO-PEEKING POLICY

OKAY, YOU CAUGHT ME. I'VE TOLD YOU many times how unnecessary it is to obsess about exact temperatures and vent positions, and now I am telling you to close the vents—by one-third, no less—and to check the temperature on an oven thermometer.

What gives? This vent/temperature business has absolutely nothing to do with the chicken and everything to do with building your knowledge of and confidence in your cooker. You're checking to see how much the temperature changes when you slightly close the vents and comparing that temperature with the temperature readings through the end of the cook. There shouldn't be too much fluctuation in the temperature from beginning to end, and this thermometer check is a good, visual reminder of how steady your cooker temperature is if you build a clean-burning fire and resist the temptation to open the lid seventeen times. Not that it matters (chicken isn't particularly sensitive to heat fluctuations), but the temperature should be in the neighborhood of 250°F to 275°F. If it is higher than 300°F, check the water pan. A low water level can cause the temperature in the cooker to spike. For other troubleshooting tips, see Stop, or I'll Kick Your Ash (page 42).

CHARCOAL TEST

I'VE SAID MORE THAN ONCE THAT YOU'RE using far more charcoal than you actually need for these first two cooks. Before you start crying about the wasted $1.50 in charcoal, here's some extra credit work for you. After you take the chicken off the cooker, leave the oven thermometer on the grate and make a mental note of the temperature. When you finish eating dinner, check the temperature again. And if you really want to be a barbecue wanker, wait half an hour or so and check the temperature again, and again, until you get bored with it. The point? To show you that long after the dishes are done, your cooker is still cookin'. You will see exactly how long the cooker you're using—whether it's a WSM, kettle, or offset—maintains the proper low and slow temperature range. Kettle users will find that the temperature won't hold steady for as long because they're using less charcoal and a smaller cooker. This lesson will come in handy when you start to panic about whether you have enough charcoal to smoke a few racks of ribs for four hours.

CRISPY SMOKED CHICKEN

BECAUSE THE IDEAL BARBECUE temperature is lower than those for other styles of cooking, the big trade-off with properly smoked chicken is that the skin typically does not crisp. And, as we all know, crispy skin is one of the three great wonders of poultry. (The other two wonders? Crispy skin and crispy skin.) Air-drying the chicken after brining or marinating helps, but it's no guarantee. Instead, there are other, relatively simple post-cook solutions to the problem of rubbery skin.

If you have a blowtorch handy, blast the flame about five inches from the chicken skin until the skin turns brown and crisp. Or set the fully cooked chickens, skin-side up, under a broiler for three to four minutes. If you're using a kettle, flip the chicken skin-side down over the pile of hot charcoal and cook until the skin crisps, three to five minutes. If you're using a WSM, remove the center ring and set the grate over the charcoal bowl. Flip the chicken skin-side down. Use caution and don't walk away: the chicken will be very close to the coals, and the skin will crisp instantly— in less than one minute.

SWIM CAP CHICKEN

The brainchild of the Right Reverend Rock McNealy from the great state of Colorado, this technique also achieves the crispy-skinned chicken that's so elusive in low and slow barbecue. The chicken halves are smoked skin-side down for the first part of the cook. The skin acts as a "swim cap" for the pooling juices, which help crisp the skin when the chicken is flipped. Follow all of the directions for Lesson #2, with these adjustments.

WSM AND OFFSET
2 HOURS BEFORE DINNER
Place the chicken halves skin-side down on the grate, as instructed for the WSM (page 32) and the offset (page 34).
1 HOUR INTO THE COOK
Open the lid. Using tongs, flip the chicken skin-side up. Squirt the skin with cooking spray or brush with olive oil.

KETTLE
2 HOURS BEFORE DINNER
Place the chicken halves skin-side down on the grate, with the breast-side close to the edge of the grate without touching the side.
30 MINUTES INTO THE COOK
Open the lid. Using tongs, flip the chicken skin-side up. Squirt the skin with cooking spray or brush with olive oil.

CONTINUING EDUCATION

BRINE 101

THINK OF BRINING AS A WAY TO INCREASE your margin for error in low and slow. If something goes slightly wrong in a cook—a vent is blocked or the water pan runs too low—chicken that has been brined is less likely to suffer the consequences. The chicken will not dry out because brined meat is plumped full of water through a process called osmosis. Here's how it works: All meat contains saltwater, but not as much as the brine you soak it in. Osmosis happens when the meat "corrects" this imbalance. Meat will absorb a saltwater solution until the concentration of salt and water in the brine is the same as the concentration in the meat. When meat absorbs the brine, the salt in the brine unwinds the strands of protein in the meat. This reaction traps water from the brine inside the meat. This is how brines turn a lean piece of chicken juicy and tender and keep meat from drying out if the temperature spikes or drops in your cooker.

When you add herbs, spices, or even sugar to brine, the seasonings are pulled into the cell structure of the meat and trapped inside along with the saltwater. Unlike marinades, which mostly coat the outer surface of the meat with flavor, brines actually help the flavor penetrate the meat.

If you've brined meat before, you may notice that the salt-to-water ratio for the Basic Brine is not as strong as some other recipes. This recipe calls for one-third cup of salt to about ten cups (or slightly more than one half gallon) of water, give or take a few ounces depending on the weight of the chicken when you fill the bags. Chicken halves require more solution to soak in and a longer time to soak than smaller chicken pieces like legs or thighs.

This modified brine is also another example of how this program is built to compensate for any mistakes you might make along the way: the weaker brine is more forgiving and allows for a longer brining time. If your cooking schedule is thrown off by weather or any of life's other little curve balls, a window of six to twelve hours of brining time allows for plenty of leeway without risking overbrining the chicken. It's just my way of making sure your first few low and slow dinners are a success. This is also why I'm so adamant about not straying from the instructions.

Once you complete the first Lesson #2 cook with the basic brine, experiment with these recipes to see how brining can create subtle changes in the flavor of the chicken.

BUTTERMILK BRINE

This is one of my all-time favorite brines. The buttermilk lends a subtle undercurrent of tanginess to the chicken, and makes the meat extremely tender and juicy. Although I doubt there will be any, the leftovers of this brined chicken are superb in many of the chicken recipes in chapter 9. The WSM and offset recipe makes enough brine for four chicken halves and the kettle recipe for two chicken halves.

WSM AND OFFSET

$\frac{1}{2}$ gallon buttermilk

1 cup warm water

$\frac{2}{3}$ cup Morton kosher salt

$\frac{1}{2}$ cup brown sugar

$\frac{1}{4}$ cup Old Bay Seasoning (optional)

KETTLE

4 cups buttermilk

$\frac{1}{2}$ cup warm water

$\frac{1}{3}$ cup Morton kosher salt

$\frac{1}{4}$ cup brown sugar

2 tablespoons Old Bay Seasoning (optional)

In a large bowl, whisk all of the ingredients together until the salt and sugar are dissolved.

For the WSM or offset, divide four chicken halves between two one-gallon zip-top bags. Divide the brine between the bags.

For the kettle, place two chicken halves in one one-gallon zip-top bag and pour all the brine into the bag.

Set the bags in the sink and fill with cold water to within 1 inch of the zipper (8 to 10 cups of water, depending on the water displacement from the weight of the chicken). Press the air out of the bags and seal. Place the bags in a large bowl or on a rimmed baking sheet to catch drips. Allow the chicken to brine for 6 to 12 hours in the refrigerator, turning the bag once or twice to redistribute the brine.

BOURBON AND HONEY BRINE

Bourbon and barbecue go together like prom night and prophylactics. The natural affinity between the smoky flavor of the meat and the sweet smokiness of the liquor comes through in a subtle way in this brine. The WSM and offset recipe makes enough brine for four chicken halves and the kettle recipe for two chicken halves.

WSM AND OFFSET

1 cup warm water

1/2 cup bourbon whiskey

2/3 cup Morton kosher salt

1/2 cup honey

1 tablespoon grated lemon rind

1 teaspoon freshly ground black pepper

KETTLE

1/2 cup warm water

1/2 cup bourbon whiskey

1/3 cup Morton kosher salt

1/4 cup honey

1/2 tablespoon grated lemon rind

1/2 teaspoon freshly ground black pepper

In a large bowl, whisk all of the ingredients together until the salt and honey are dissolved.

For the WSM or offset, divide four chicken halves between two one-gallon zip-top bags. Divide the brine between the bags.

For the kettle, place two chicken halves in one one-gallon zip-top bag and pour all of the brine into the bag.

Set the bags in the sink and fill with cold water to within 1 inch of the zipper (8 to 10 cups of water, depending on the water displacement of the chicken). Press the air out of the bags and seal. Place the bags in a large bowl or on a rimmed baking sheet to catch drips. Allow the chicken to brine for 6 to 12 hours in the refrigerator, turning the bag once or twice to redistribute the brine.

SOY-GINGER BRINE

Classic Asian flavors like soy and ginger pair well with smoky barbecue. Chicken brined in tamari, a type of Japanese soy sauce, tastes great in recipes that feature complementary Asian herbs and spices, like the Asian Chicken Wraps (page 236). The WSM and offset recipe makes enough brine for four chicken halves and the kettle recipe for two chicken halves.

WSM AND OFFSET

1/2 cup soy sauce or tamari

1 cup warm water

1/2 cup Morton kosher salt

2/3 cup dark brown sugar

1 tablespoon freshly ground black pepper

1 (4-inch) piece fresh ginger, peeled and chopped

1 tablespoon Sriracha or chili garlic sauce (optional)

KETTLE

1/4 cup soy sauce or tamari

1/2 cup warm water

1/4 cup Morton kosher salt

1/3 cup dark brown sugar

1/2 tablespoon freshly ground black pepper

1 (2-inch) piece fresh ginger, peeled and chopped

1/2 tablespoon Sriracha or chili garlic sauce (optional – see Ingredient Finder, page 164)

In a large bowl, whisk all of the ingredients together until the salt and brown sugar are dissolved.

For the WSM or offset, divide four chicken halves between two one-gallon zip-top bags. Divide the brine between the bags.

For the kettle, place two chicken halves in one one-gallon zip-top bag and pour all of the brine into the bag.

Set the bags in the sink and fill with cold water to within 1 inch of the zipper (8 to 10 cups of water, depending on the water displacement of the chicken). Press the air out of the bags and seal. Place the bags in a large bowl or on a rimmed baking sheet to catch drips. Allow the chicken to brine for 6 to 12 hours in the refrigerator, turning the bag once or twice to redistribute the brine.

ORANGE-ROSEMARY BRINE

Rosemary can be overpowering in a recipe, so I don't recommend chopping the herb, which gives off too much flavor. Gently rub the leaves between your hands and let them fall into the brine. This bruises the herb and releases the oils. The WSM and offset recipe makes enough brine for four chicken halves and the kettle recipe for two chicken halves.

WSM AND OFFSET

1 cup warm water

2 oranges, juiced (about 1 cup juice)

$^2/_3$ cup Morton kosher salt

$^1/_2$ cup honey

2 tablespoons fresh rosemary, crumbled to bruise

1 tablespoon grated orange rind

1 teaspoon freshly ground white pepper

$^1/_2$ teaspoon ground cumin (optional)

1 serrano pepper, split in half (optional)

KETTLE

$^1/_2$ cup warm water

1 orange, juiced (about $^1/_2$ cup juice)

$^1/_3$ cup Morton kosher salt

$^1/_4$ cup honey

1 tablespoon fresh rosemary, crumbled to bruise

$^1/_2$ tablespoon grated orange rind

$^1/_2$ teaspoon freshly ground white pepper

$^1/_4$ teaspoon ground cumin (optional)

$^1/_2$ serrano pepper (optional)

In a large bowl, whisk all of the ingredients together until the salt and honey are dissolved.

For the WSM or offset, divide four chicken halves between two one-gallon zip-top bags. Divide the brine between the bags.

For the kettle, place two chicken halves in one one-gallon zip-top bag and pour all of the brine into the bag.

Set the bags in the sink and fill with cold water to within 1 inch of the zipper (8 to 10 cups of water, depending on the water displacement of the chicken). Press the air out of the bags and seal. Place the bags in a large bowl or on a rimmed baking sheet to catch drips. Allow the chicken to brine for 6 to 12 hours in the refrigerator, turning the bag once or twice to redistribute the brine.

TEQUILA LIME BRINE

This brine is a perfect example of how a good splash of liquor can add even more depth of flavor to smoked chicken. I don't have the science degree to prove it, but I've brined enough meat to know that alcohol also seems to make lean meat like chicken even juicier by aiding the salt in loosening up the proteins. Serve this chicken with a good margarita for Cinco de Mayo, and see if you agree. The WSM and offset recipe makes enough brine for four chicken halves and the kettle recipe for two chicken halves.

WSM AND OFFSET

1/2 cup tequila

2 limes, juiced (about 1/4 cup juice)

1 cup warm water

2/3 cup Morton kosher salt

1/2 cup honey

2 teaspoons grated lime rind

1/2 teaspoon freshly ground white pepper

1/2 teaspoon ground coriander

2 jalapeños, cut in half (optional)

KETTLE

1/4 cup tequila

1 lime, juiced (about 2 tablespoons juice)

1/2 cup warm water

1/3 cup Morton kosher salt

1/4 cup honey

1 teaspoon grated lime rind

1/4 teaspoon freshly ground white pepper

1/4 teaspoon ground coriander

1 jalapeño, cut in half (optional)

In a large bowl, whisk the tequila, lime juice, water, salt, honey, lime rind, pepper, and corriander together until the salt and honey are dissolved. Add the jalapeños, if using.

For the WSM or offset, divide four chicken halves between two one-gallon zip-top bags. Divide the brine between the bags.

For the kettle, place two chicken halves in one one-gallon zip-top bag and pour all of the brine into the bag.

Set the bag in the sink and fill with cold water, within 1 inch of the zipper (8 to 10 cups of water, depending on the water displacement from the weight of the chicken). Press the air out of the bags and seal. Place the bags in a large bowl or on a rimmed baking sheet to catch drips. Allow the chicken to brine for 6 to 12 hours in the refrigerator, turning the bag once or twice to redistribute the brine.

LEMONGRASS BRINE

Lemongrass is one of my favorite Southeast Asian herbs. It doesn't have the acidic twang of pure lemon, and combined with basil in a brine, the resulting smoked chicken has a distinct and unusual flavor. If you can't find purple Thai basil or palm sugar (also called jaggery), use regular sweet basil and brown sugar as substitutes. Serve the chicken with Thai-Style Sweet and Sour Cucumber Salad (page 205). The WSM and offset recipe makes enough brine for four chicken halves and the kettle recipe for two chicken halves.

WSM AND OFFSET

1 cup warm water

²/₃ cup Morton kosher salt

¹/₂ cup palm sugar or brown sugar

4 stalks lemongrass, trimmed and bruised

¹/₂ cup purple Thai basil leaves or sweet basil leaves, loosely packed (optional)

KETTLE

¹/₂ cup warm water

¹/₃ cup Morton kosher salt

¹/₄ cup palm sugar or brown sugar

2 stalks lemongrass, trimmed and bruised

¹/₄ cup purple Thai basil leaves or sweet basil leaves, loosely packed (optional)

In a large bowl, whisk all of the ingredients together until the salt and brown sugar are dissolved.

For the WSM or offset, divide four chicken halves between two one-gallon zip-top bags. Divide the brine between the bags.

For the kettle, place two chicken halves in one one-gallon zip-top bag and pour all of the brine into the bag.

Set the bag in the sink and fill with cold water, within 1 inch of the zipper (8 to 10 cups of water, depending on the water displacement). Press the air out of the bags and seal. Place the bags in a large bowl or on a rimmed baking sheet to catch drips. Allow the chicken to brine for 6 to 12 hours in the refrigerator, turning the bag once or twice to redistribute the brine.

TRIMMING AND BRUISING LEMONGRASS

Peel two or three of the dry, fibrous layers of the lemongrass stalks to the soft, pale yellow portion. Trim about one inch off the top and bottom of the stalk. To bruise the lemongrass and release its aromatic oils, whack the length of the stalk with the back of a heavy knife several times.

BUILD-YOUR-OWN BRINE TEMPLATE

BY NOW IT SHOULD BE CLEAR that brines (and marinades) are mind-numbingly easy to make, and there's simply no excuse for not making them from scratch. I could cram thousands more recipes onto these pages, but you're not here to be force-fed someone else's idea of tasty. You're here to learn how to cook reflexively, without having to reach for a recipe every time. When you're ready, make your own brine using this template, and follow the instructions for Lesson #2.

SALT:
⅓ CUP PER GALLON BAG

Although basic brines call for ½ cup of salt per gallon of water, when you add the chicken halves to a gallon zip-top bag, the amount of water drops to about 10 cups (or about 6 cups shy of a gallon). So, I recommend reducing the amount of salt to ⅓ cup per zip-top bag. Always use kosher salt. (See Kosher Salt 101 on page 17.) The iodine in regular table salt gives off a noticeable medicinal flavor in the large quantities you use in brines. Remember to reduce the amount of salt if you add a salty flavoring or seasoning, such as soy sauce, so that the total amount of salt is still around ⅓ cup per bag.

SUGAR:
¼ CUP PER GALLON BAG

Not all brine recipes call for sugar, but I like to add about ¼ cup of sugar or another sweetener to each bag of brine. Sugar doesn't make the chicken juicier; it minimizes the risk of the brined meat tasting too salty, and it can give chicken a nice, caramelized color. You can use brown or white sugar, honey, molasses, maple syrup, fruit, or fruit juice—anything sweet. This is where you get to start tinkering with the brine based on what you like or whatever ingredients you happen to have in your cupboard. One warning: adding too much sugar to the brine will give the meat a distinctly sweet, ham-like flavor.

SEASONING:
¼ TO ⅓ CUP PER GALLON BAG

Saltwater carries seasonings into the cell structure of the meat, so the addition of herbs, spices, and aromatics to the brine can contribute a subtle flavor to smoked meat. As with marinades, the amount of a seasoning you throw in each bag depends heavily upon how potent it is. With strong ingredients like hot sauce or rosemary, one or two tablespoons is plenty for this quantity of brine. If you want a note of heat, three toasted, crushed whole chiles or chopped fresh jalapeños get your point across. You can throw in onion halves, smashed ginger, cloves of garlic, or a few splashes of soy sauce. Go easy adding any acid, like citrus or vinegar. Too much acid can turn your brine into a salty marinade. Brining for six to twelve hours with too much acid will also turn your meat into mush and start cooking it. A teaspoon or two of citrus zest per bag is plenty.

The seasonings you choose can also complement any rub, paste, or sauce you plan to use. The Soy-Ginger Brine (page 89), for example, works well with the Five-Spice Rub (page 97). You can also flavor brines to match the seasonings in a dish you plan to make with the chicken; for instance, try adding one teaspoon of puréed chipotle in adobo per bag to the brine for chicken that will go into Tortilla Soup (page 239) or Chicken Enchiladas (page 234).

BOOZE:
2 TO 4 TABLESPOONS PER GALLON BAG

Alcohol loosens things up. Even chickens. Adding one or two ounces of liquor to a brine seems to aid the salt in breaking down the chicken's proteins and making it juicer.

LIQUID:

Always dissolve the salt and sugar (and optional seasoning or alcohol) in a half cup of warm water. Then place two chicken halves in each bag, pour the brine over the chicken, and fill the bag with cold water to within one inch of the top. Press as much air out of the bag as possible before sealing.

TIME:
6 TO 12 HOURS

The salt-to-water ratio in other brine recipes tends to be stronger and the brine time is shorter, but this also makes it easier to over-brine chicken. I recommend a weaker solution and a longer soak—a minimum of six hours for chicken halves—because it gives you a bigger window of time to start the cook without risking over-brining.

★ QUICK BRINES ★

LET'S SAY BAD WEATHER IS COMING and you've got to get those birds smoked quickly. You don't have six to twelve hours to brine. You have three to five hours, tops. For a quick brine, double the amount of salt and sugar so that each bag contains $^2/_3$ cup salt and $^1/_2$ cup sugar.

Generally, I don't recommend quick brining because it's not as easy to control. Chicken can soak in the basic brine from Lesson #2 for as long as twenty-four hours without hurting the meat. But when you substantially increase the salt, you don't have that leeway with time. If you need to postpone the cook for some reason and the chicken ends up soaking in the brine for more than five or six hours, you'll wind up with salty smoked chicken. But stuff happens. If you're in a hurry and have no other choice, quick brining can cut the brining time in half.

★ BRINING TIPS ★

- **DON'T USE "ENHANCED" OR KOSHER CHICKEN.** Brining this meat will make it too salty because it is injected with saltwater to improve texture and flavor or coated with salt to meet kosher guidelines.
- Always use kosher salt.
- Trim jagged bones to prevent sharp edges from puncturing the zip-top bag.
- Start with a cold brine. Add cold water to the dissolved brine solution, toss in a few ice cubes, or refrigerate the brine solution until it is cool before adding the meat.
- Completely submerge the meat in the brining liquid.
- Unless you use a quick brine solution, plan for at least $1^1/_2$ to 2 hours of brining time per pound of chicken.
- Never—ever—reuse brine.

RUBS, PASTES, AND COMPOUND BUTTERS

BRINES AND MARINADES ARE GREAT for infusing chicken with subtle flavor and making meat tender and juicy. But if you want your chicken to have the more assertive, concentrated flavor of a seasoning like lemon or spicy-hot chiles, the herbs and spices need to stick to the meat. This is where rubs, pastes, and compound butters come in. A coating or under-the-skin smear of a punchy seasoning mix will turn simple, well-cooked barbecued chicken into the legendary chicken your friends and family will worship. Rubs are dry herb, spice and salt mixes that can be sprinkled on meat. Pastes are thick, "wet" rubs—seasoning blends mixed with a liquid like oil, beer or mustard—that stick to meat. Compound butter is butter flavored with herbs and spices, and can be spread under chicken skin.

Rubs, pastes, and compound butters won't affect the texture or juiciness of the meat in a noticeable way, which is why I recommend (insist, really) that you brine the chicken to ensure that it will stay moist during the cook. But once you've dabbled with the brine recipes and started making your own, you should start thinking about how to build brines and rubs that go together. As when you pair wine and food, you can make brines that will contrast or complement the flavor of a rub. A soak in the Soy-Ginger Brine (page 89) followed by a coating of the Smoking Szechuan Pepper Rub (page 161) or the Five-Spice Rub (page 97) is an excellent pairing.

I don't mean to suggest that matching brines and rubs or pastes is an essential low and slow technique. You could use the basic brine every time and cover the chicken in whatever seasoning you're in the mood for. But once you develop some level of proficiency with your cooker, you might start to get bored with the process. Digging into the endless possibilities of pairing brines and rubs will keep you motivated and advance your low and slow education, as well as your general culinary skills.

RUBS

THE BEST-TASTING RUBS ARE MADE WITH the freshest ingredients you can get your hands on. Instead of using the pre-ground, flavorless seasonings you find in the spice aisle, always opt for freshly ground spices, real citrus zest, and dried whole peppers that have been toasted and ground in a spice mill or coffee grinder. Remember: commercial blends might be more convenient, but there is no comparison to the flavor of homemade.

★
BASIC BIRD RUB

This simple, savory rub gets added heat from the blend of toasted Mexican peppers. It's the perfect base rub to experiment with. Once you make it a few times, play with adding other seasonings like celery seed, garlic powder, or onion powder to change the flavor profile.

MAKES ABOUT ¼ CUP

1 tablespoon ground cumin

1 tablespoon curry powder

½ tablespoon Toasted Mexican Pepper Blend (page 18)

2 teaspoons ground allspice

2 teaspoons freshly ground black pepper

1 teaspoon Morton kosher salt

Combine all of the ingredients in a small bowl and stir until blended.

Sprinkle each brined, air-dried chicken half with 1 tablespoon of the rub. Follow the instructions for Lesson #2 on your cooker.

This recipe makes enough rub for 4 chicken halves. If you're cooking 2 chicken halves on a kettle, store the leftover rub in an airtight container for up to one month.

★
FIVE-SPICE RUB

Five-spice powder is a mix of equal parts cinnamon, cloves, fennel seed, star anise, and sometimes ginger or crushed Szechuan peppercorns. If you can't find whole peppercorns, substitute pre-ground Szechuan pepper. You can buy commercial five-spice powder in Asian markets and most supermarkets, but you're going to all of the trouble of making this delicious chicken, and you should want a better, homemade blend for it.

MAKES ABOUT ⅓ CUP

1 tablespoon ground cinnamon

1 tablespoon freshly ground cloves

1 tablespoon freshly ground fennel seed

1 tablespoon freshly ground star anise

1 tablespoon freshly ground Szechuan peppercorns

1 tablespoon Morton kosher salt

Combine all of the ingredients in a medium bowl and stir until blended.

Sprinkle each brined, air-dried chicken half with ½ tablespoon of the rub. Follow the instructions for Lesson #2 on your cooker.

Store the leftover rub in an airtight container for up to one month.

JERK WET RUB

This is not one of those girly "jerk" recipes you'll find in your mother-in-law's cooking magazines. It is unapologetically hot. Wear a pair of rubber gloves to stem and seed the peppers and to rub the paste on the chicken.

MAKES ABOUT 1 CUP

1 lime, juiced (about 2 tablespoons juice)

4 green onions, coarsely chopped

3 garlic cloves, peeled and coarsely chopped

2 jalapeño chiles, stemmed and seeded

2 habañero peppers, stemmed and seeded (optional)

1 teaspoon fresh thyme leaves

4 bay leaves, crumbled

4$\frac{1}{2}$ tablespoons freshly ground allspice

$\frac{1}{2}$ teaspoon freshly ground nutmeg

$\frac{1}{2}$ teaspoon cinnamon

1$\frac{1}{2}$ teaspoons Morton kosher salt

1 teaspoon freshly ground black pepper

2 tablespoons peanut oil

Combine all of the ingredients except the peanut oil in a food processor. Pulse to combine the ingredients, using a spatula to scrape down the sides of the bowl, until the mixture is blended. Add the oil and purée until the mixture forms a smooth paste.

Wearing a pair of disposable rubber gloves, smear each brined, air-dried chicken half with $\frac{1}{4}$ cup of the paste. Follow the instructions for Lesson #2 on your cooker.

Store the leftover rub in an airtight container for up to one week.

TIP: Allspice is expensive if you buy small jars of the whole berries from a regular grocery store. Buy it in bulk at Italian, Mexican, or other ethnic markets—it's used in many rub recipes, and it's a great all-purpose spice to have on hand.

LEMON PEPPER RUB

Coating brined chicken in freshly grated lemon zest is like dropping a V-8 into your 1976 AMC Pacer—it turbocharges the modest and humble.

MAKES ABOUT $\frac{1}{4}$ CUP

3 tablespoons freshly grated lemon rind

1 tablespoon Morton kosher salt

1 tablespoon freshly ground black pepper

1 teaspoon garlic powder

1 teaspoon onion powder

Combine all of the ingredients in a small bowl. Using the back of a spoon, smash the seasonings together to blend and release the aromatic oils in the lemon zest.

Smear each brined, air-dried chicken half with 1 tablespoon of the rub. Follow the instructions for Lesson #2 on your cooker.

Refrigerate any leftover rub in an airtight container for up to one week.

HERB PASTES
AND COMPOUND BUTTERS

IF YOU WANT TO TAKE A CHICKEN RUB TO THE NEXT LEVEL, smear a layer under the skin. Heat tends to mellow most seasonings, particularly in a long low and slow cook. Slipping the seasoning under the skin helps it penetrate the meat, and the blend retains a lot of its flavor because it stays moist.

You can work any of the dry rubs under the skin, but I recommend adding a liquid to the mixture to make a paste or wet rub, which is easier to spread and sticks to the chicken better. Add two tablespoons of canola oil, beer, or citrus juice, or blend it into half a stick of softened butter to make compound butter.

Applying a rub, paste, or butter under the skin may seem tricky at first. Take your time and gently loosen the skin over the breast and thigh by slipping your fingers between the skin and the meat. Spoon a dollop of the paste onto your fingers and massage it under the loosened skin. To prevent cross-contamination of the leftover wet rub or compound butter, do not dip into the seasoning with your hands (which will be covered in raw chicken juice). Use a spoon or spatula to scoop up and flick the mixture onto your fingers.

JALAPEÑO-ORANGE COMPOUND BUTTER

The tangy heat of jalapeño and the sweet orange notes are perfectly balanced with the subtle oniony scent of chive in this compound butter. To crisp the chicken skin, brush two tablespoons of the melted butter on the chicken at the end of the cook, then follow the directions for crisping chicken on your cooker (page 51).

WSM AND OFFSET

MAKES ABOUT ¾ CUP

2 tablespoons orange juice

¼ pound (1 stick) unsalted butter, at room temperature

1 jalapeño, stemmed, seeded, and minced

2 tablespoons grated orange rind

2 tablespoons finely diced chives

¼ teaspoon kosher salt

¼ teaspoon freshly ground white pepper

KETTLE

MAKES ABOUT ½ CUP

1 tablespoon orange juice

4 tablespoons (½ stick) unsalted butter, at room temperature

½ jalapeño, stemmed, seeded, and minced

1 tablespoon grated orange rind

1 tablespoon finely diced chives

Dash of kosher salt

Dash of freshly ground white pepper

Combine the orange juice with the softened butter in a medium bowl. Add the remaining ingredients and stir until blended.

To apply, slide your fingers between the skin and the chicken, and gently lift up the skin over the breast. Massage 2 tablespoons of compound butter directly onto the meat.

GARLIC AND ROSEMARY HERB PASTE

This one is for the garlic lovers. After an hour or so on a smoker, the slow-roasted garlic mellows and turns sweet, melding with the flavor of the rosemary.

WSM AND OFFSET

MAKES ABOUT ½ CUP

1 garlic head, cloves peeled and minced

1 lemon, juiced (about ¼ cup juice)

2 tablespoons olive oil

1 tablespoon grated lemon rind

½ teaspoon chopped fresh rosemary

2 teaspoons salt

Freshly ground black pepper, to taste

KETTLE

MAKES ABOUT ¼ CUP

½ garlic head, cloves peeled and minced

½ lemon, juiced (about 2 tablespoons juice)

1 tablespoon olive oil

½ tablespoon grated lemon rind

1 teaspoon chopped fresh rosemary

1 teaspoon salt

Freshly ground black pepper, to taste

Combine all of the ingredients in a small bowl and stir until the mixture is blended.

To apply, slide your fingers between the skin and the chicken, and gently lift up the skin over the breast. Massage an equal amount of the paste, about 2 tablespoons, under the skin of each chicken half.

★ THAI HERB PASTE ★

Like the Thai Marinade in Lesson #1, this herb paste is based on the classic Thai barbecued chicken, gai yang issan. *Pair it with the Thai Sweet and Spicy Garlic Sauce (page 107) or the Thai Chili Sauce (page 107).*

WSM AND OFFSET

MAKES ABOUT 1 CUP

5 to 7 garlic cloves

1 (2-inch) piece fresh ginger, peeled and coarsely chopped

1 cup fresh cilantro, stemmed and loosely packed

1 tablespoon freshly ground black pepper

1 tablespoon ground coriander

2 limes, juiced (about $1/4$ cup juice)

1 tablespoon canola oil

KETTLE

MAKES ABOUT $1/2$ CUP

3 to 5 garlic cloves

1 (1-inch) piece fresh ginger, peeled and coarsely chopped

$1/2$ cup fresh cilantro, stemmed and loosely packed

$1/2$ tablespoon freshly ground black pepper

$1/2$ tablespoon ground coriander

1 lime, juiced (about 2 tablespoons juice)

$1/2$ tablespoon canola oil

In a food processor, pulse the garlic, ginger, and cilantro to chop. Scrape the sides of the bowl and pulse a few more times, until the ingredients are blended in a rough and crumbly mixture. Pour the mixture into a large bowl and add the pepper, coriander, lime juice, and oil. Use a pestle or the back of a large spoon or spatula to smash and blend the mixture until it comes together in a chunky paste. To apply, slide your fingers between the skin and the chicken, and gently lift up the skin over the breast. Massage an equal amount of the paste, about 2 tablespoons, under the skin of each chicken half. Rub another 2 tablespoons of the paste on top of each chicken half.

SALTIMBOCCA HERB PASTE

Although barbecue purists might think it's too much of a stretch from traditional recipes, this twist on the classic Italian dish, which translates as "jump mouth," is a showstopper on smoked chicken.

WSM AND OFFSET

MAKES ABOUT $\frac{1}{2}$ CUP

4 tablespoons butter, cut into $\frac{1}{2}$-inch pieces

6 to 8 fresh sage leaves

5 ounces prosciutto (or cured country ham), cut into 1-inch pieces

1 tablespoon olive oil

Freshly ground black pepper, to taste

Dried crushed red pepper, to taste

KETTLE

MAKES ABOUT $\frac{1}{4}$ CUP

2 tablespoons butter, cut into $\frac{1}{2}$-inch pieces

3 to 4 fresh sage leaves

2.5 ounces prosciutto (or cured country ham), cut into 1-inch pieces

$\frac{1}{2}$ tablespoon olive oil

Freshly ground black pepper, to taste

Dried crushed red pepper, to taste

In a food processor, pulse the butter for 15 seconds. Add all of the remaining ingredients and pulse the mixture until the ingredients are blended.

To apply, slide your fingers between the skin and the chicken, and gently lift up the skin over the breast. Massage an equal amount of the paste, about 2 tablespoons under the skin of each chicken half.

SAUCES AND DIPS

GOOD BARBECUE REQUIRES LITTLE—if anything—in the way of sauce. Too often, people paint or pour on sweet sauces that are too heavy, masking the authentic, smoky flavor of good barbecued chicken. The few sauces I do use regularly are either built to complement the flavors of a marinade or rub or served very sparingly—more as an extra hint of flavor than an actual condiment.

★
SOUTH CAROLINA MUSTARD BARBECUE SAUCE

I've taken one of the classic South Carolina-style mustard sauces and added a blend of my favorite dried, ground Mexican chili peppers. I recommend toasting and grinding whole, dried peppers instead of using the store-bought powder, or you can substitute two tablespoons of the Toasted Mexican Pepper Blend (page 18). It is a delicious condiment on pulled pork sandwiches or dip for smoked chicken. It can also be used to baste smoked chicken in the last twenty minutes of a cook.

MAKES ABOUT 3 CUPS

$2/3$ cup yellow prepared mustard

$1/4$ cup white sugar

$1/4$ cup light brown sugar

1 cup cider vinegar

1 tablespoon ancho powder

1 tablespoon chipotle powder

1 tablespoon guajillo powder (optional)

1 teaspoon black pepper

1 teaspoon white pepper

1 teaspoon crushed red pepper

$1/4$ teaspoon cayenne pepper

1 tablespoon Louisiana-style or Mexican-style hot sauce, such as Texas Pete, Louisiana, or Búfalo

$1/2$ teaspoon soy sauce

2 tablespoon butter

Combine all of the ingredients except the soy sauce and butter in a medium saucepan. Simmer the mixture over a medium-high heat until the sugar dissolves, about 10 minutes. Remove the sauce from heat. Stir in the soy sauce and butter.

Store in an airtight container in the refrigerator for up to two weeks.

★
ALABAMA WHITE SAUCE

This barbecue sauce, often linked to Big Bob Gibson's Barbecue in Decatur, is a favorite in northern Alabama. Although barbecue is typically associated with tomato-based sauces, mayonnaise gives this sauce a rich, tangy flavor. The sauce should be used as a condiment because heat will cause the mayo to break down and separate if it is added while the meat is still on the cooker.

MAKES $1\frac{1}{4}$ CUPS

1 cup mayonnaise

3 tablespoons cider vinegar

1 tablespoon freshly squeezed lemon juice (about $1/2$ lemon)

2 teaspoons freshly ground black pepper

1 teaspoon kosher salt

1 teaspoon horseradish

1 teaspoon cayenne pepper

Combine all of the ingredients in a blender and blend until the mixture is smooth.

★ CLASSIC BARBECUE SAUCE

If you have a sweet tooth when it comes to barbecue sauces, this classic hits all the right notes. It doesn't have the cloying sugary rush of most bottled sauces, because it's balanced with the moderate heat of the Toasted Mexican Pepper Blend and tarted up with lemon juice.

MAKES ABOUT 3 CUPS

2 tablespoons unsalted butter

1/3 cup finely chopped onion

2 cups ketchup

1/4 cup brown sugar

1/4 cup molasses

2 tablespoons yellow prepared mustard

1 lemon, juiced (about 4 tablespoons juice)

1 tablespoon Worcestershire sauce

1/2 teaspoon garlic powder

1 tablespoon Toasted Mexican Pepper Blend (page 18) or 1/4 teaspoon cayenne pepper

1/2 teaspoon kosher salt

1/2 teaspoon freshly ground black pepper

Melt the butter in a saucepan over medium-high heat. Sauté the onion in the butter until the onion is softened and barely caramelized, about 5 minutes. Add the remaining ingredients and stir. Simmer the sauce for 20 minutes over medium-low heat.

Store, refrigerated, up to two weeks.

★ CHIMICHURRI

This classic sauce from Argentina is fresh and herbal— a perfect match for barbecued chicken or a steak just off the grill. Traditional recipes use only parsley, but adding an equal amount of cilantro smooths out the rough edges. This sauce is also excellent as a dip for breads or spread onto bruschetta and topped with roasted red peppers.

MAKES ABOUT 2 1/2 CUPS

1 cup fresh Italian flat-leaf parsley, stemmed and tightly packed

1 cup fresh cilantro, stemmed and tightly packed

1/2 cup olive oil

1/4 cup red wine vinegar

2 garlic cloves, peeled

1 teaspoon dried oregano

1 teaspoon freshly ground black pepper

1 teaspoon kosher salt

3/4 teaspoon dried crushed red pepper flakes

Combine all ingredients in a food processor. Blend until smooth.

Store, refrigerated, up to two weeks.

★ THAI SWEET AND SPICY GARLIC SAUCE

Smoked chickens bathed in the Thai Marinade (page 67) or slathered in Thai Herb Paste (page 102) are dynamite paired with this traditional dipping sauce. Authentic recipes use dried Thai chiles. If you can find them in a local gourmet or Asian market, use ten stemmed, toasted, and crumbled dried Thai chiles in place of the dried crushed red pepper flakes.

MAKES ABOUT 1 CUP

$^1/_2$ cup sugar

$^1/_2$ cup white vinegar

$^1/_2$ cup water

6 garlic cloves, peeled and grated

1 teaspoon kosher salt

1 tablespoon dried crushed red pepper flakes

Combine the sugar, vinegar, water, garlic, and salt in a nonreactive saucepan over medium-high heat. Bring the mixture to a boil, whisking continuously. Reduce heat to low and simmer the sauce until it has thickened to the consistency of runny syrup, 20 to 25 minutes. Remove from heat. Stir in the dried crushed red pepper flakes or toasted crumbled chiles. Let the sauce stand at room temperature for 1 hour before serving to allow the flavors to meld.

Store, refrigerated, for up to two days.

★ THAI CHILE DIPPING SAUCE

Straight out of the bottle, nam pla, or fish sauce, is not for the faint of heart. But a splash of the popular Southeast Asian seasoning adds depth and character to sauces and curries.

Another knockout dip for chicken with Thai Marinade (page 67), Lemongrass Brine (page 92), or Thai Herb Paste (page 102), this traditional sauce is the perfect example of how to balance very different flavors—from the sour tang of lime and the heat of chiles to the distinctly salty nam pla.

MAKES ABOUT $^1/_2$ CUP

$2^1/_2$ teaspoons uncooked rice, toasted until light brown (see Toasting Herbs and Spices, page 18)

$^1/_4$ cup *nam pla* (Thai fish sauce)

2 limes, juiced (about $^1/_2$ cup juice)

2 tablespoons dried crushed red pepper flakes

2 green onions, chopped

Grind the toasted rice to a fine powder in a spice grinder. Pour the rice into a medium bowl. Add the fish sauce, lime juice, dried crushed red pepper flakes, and green onions to the bowl and stir. Let the sauce stand at room temperature for 1 hour to allow the flavors to meld.

Store, refrigerated, for up to two days.

★ PEANUT DIPPING SAUCE

This sweet and savory sauce is a traditional side with chicken satay. It can be served with basic brined chicken, chicken with Thai Marinade (page 67), or chicken with Thai Herb Paste (page 102).

MAKES ABOUT 1½ CUPS

¾ cup crunchy peanut butter

½ onion, finely chopped (about ½ cup)

½ cup coconut milk

1 tablespoon *nam pla* (Thai fish sauce)

1 tablespoon soy sauce

2 teaspoons brown sugar or palm sugar

1 teaspoon cayenne pepper

1 stalk lemongrass, finely chopped or 1 lime, juiced (about 2 tablespoons juice)

Combine all of the ingredients in a medium saucepan. Whisk the mixture together and bring it to a simmer over low heat, stirring constantly, until it starts to thicken, about 8 to 10 minutes.

If the mixture becomes too thick to use as a dipping sauce, thin it with additional coconut milk. Remove the sauce from the heat and allow it to cool to room temperature before serving.

Store, refrigerated, for up to two days.

★ BUFFALO SAUCE

Why screw around with wings when you can have a whole Buffalo-sauced chicken? This sauce can be brushed onto the skin of the chicken halves at the end of the cook or served as a dip on the side.

MAKES ABOUT ¾ CUP

¼ pound (1 stick) unsalted butter

¼ cup Louisiana-style or Mexican-style hot sauce, such as Texas Pete, Louisiana, or Búfalo

1 garlic clove, peeled and minced

Pinch of kosher salt

Combine all of the ingredients in a medium non-reactive saucepan. Simmer over low heat for 5 minutes. Allow the sauce to cool to room temperature before serving.

Store, refrigerated, for up to one week.

LOW & SLOW QUIZ: LESSON 2

If you've successfully completed Lessons #1 and #2 at least two times apiece, you should know your cooker like an old friend. Answering these rudimentary questions should be second nature. If you strike out more than two times, repeat Lesson #2.

1. Because lump charcoal is a natural product, it's okay to re-use any leftovers from the previous cook. True or False?

2. Once the cook is under way, you should close the top vent . . .
a) when the cooker stops billowing dark smoke
b) about 30 minutes into the cook
c) for the final 30 minutes of the cook
d) when pigs fly

3. What benefit do you get from layering the wood chunks or splits in the charcoal?

_____

_____

4. What is the ideal temperature range in a low and slow cook?
a) 150°F to 200°F
b) 225°F to 250°F
c) 250°F to 275°F
d) Thermometers are for engineers. There is no "ideal" temperature in low and slow.

5. Only refill the water pan when it is less than half full. True or False?

6. Kosher salt is ideal for using in brines because . . .
a) it is flakier and dissolves quickly in the solution
b) it doesn't contain iodine and tastes better
c) you only use half the amount, compared to table salt
d) it does a better job of tenderizing meat than table salt

7. What does air-drying the chicken before cooking do?

_____

_____

8. Partially closing the bottom vent(s) on the cooker helps to stabilize the temperature by regulating the airflow over the lit charcoal. True or False?

Answers: 1. False. Charcoal absorbs moisture and odors that will give your barbecue off flavors. Always start with a fresh batch of charcoal. 2) d. Never, ever close the top vent on a cooker—it chokes off the oxygen, which smothers the fire. 3) The wood ignites and smoke penetrates the meat at different stages as the charcoal ignites. 4) c. The temperature will spike and drop throughout the cook as you open and restock the cooker, but the happy place in barbecue is in the 250°F to 275°F range. 5) False. The water pan should always be ½ to ¾ full. Check and refill as often as you open the cooker (which shouldn't be very often). 6) a. 7) Increases the likelihood that the chicken skin will brown and crisp. 8) True

5.

LESSON №3

BABY BACK RIBS

DEAR STUDENT,

CONGRATULATIONS! YOU HAVE REACHED THE HALFWAY POINT IN YOUR PATH TO low and slow greatness. If you're reading this note, you hereby swear a solemn oath that you have followed the instructions faithfully and completed at least two successful smoked chicken dinners. You are now trustworthy and skilled enough to attempt a more expensive and unforgiving meat: baby back ribs (a.k.a. pork loin ribs or back ribs).

After years of counseling students of this program, I already know that as soon as you skim over the instructions for the dinner, a voice in your head will start telling you that you might as well stuff the cooker with twice the number of racks of baby backs called for in the recipe. The voice will be very persuasive in rationalizing why it's okay to stray from the directions. It will say things like, "Well, as long as I'm going to the trouble . . ." and "Then, I can invite a few people over . . ." and "I've already smoked chicken ten times—it's not like I don't know what I'm doing . . ." Trust me: you still don't know enough to start wandering off and doing your own thing.

Of course you want to load up the smoker and invite over every neighbor and living relative you have to show off your new low and slow skills. Not only do I forbid you to do this, I guarantee that if you cook twice as many racks as instructed despite my warnings, the ribs will be so tough that your Aunt Hildred will break her eating teeth on the first bite she takes. You will sear the hair and skin on your forearms trying to rotate the meat around the grates. You will be exhausted and cranky by the end of the cook, and everyone you invite over will think you're an idiot.

I am trying to keep you from taking what could be an embarrassing learning experience public by limiting the number of racks you cook and restricting the number of people who will eat this dinner. I also want you to cook each rack for a different amount of time so that you can taste what a little extra time does to the texture of the meat. Each rack will help you figure out how you like your ribs cooked—from chewy and toothsome to fall-off-the-bone tender. Later in the course of your low and slow study, I will teach you how to stuff that cooker so full you'll be able to feed three generations of your family. But for now, keep it to three racks (one rack if you're using a kettle) and immediate family or a select group of very patient and forgiving friends.

Also in this chapter, you'll start making heavier barbecue rubs—from a simple salt-and-pepper blend to a screaming-hot Szechuan pepper concoction. Bigger, tougher, fattier cuts of meat, like ribs and pork shoulder, need the stronger seasoning because herbs and spices mellow over a long cook. In the first baby back rib cook, you must use my basic Rudimentary Rub (page 115), for the same reason you used the bottled mojo criollo and the basic brine in the first cooks for Lessons #1 and #2: because I said so. And because cutting your teeth on the most basic recipe is the quickest, most efficient way for you to learn the fundamentals of cooking ribs with the least chance of failure.

I'm not asking you. I'm telling you: follow the directions.

Sincerely,

Gary Wiviott

★ BABY BACK RIBS ★

Don't buy girly Niman Ranch, Whole Foods, or other gourmet-brand ribs. Not only are these ribs considerably more expensive, the upscale stuff is usually slightly smaller and leaner, which could skew the cooking time. And if things go wrong, it'll hurt less to wreck $20 in ribs versus $40. Grocery store ribs are often pumped full of saltwater (so 20 percent of what you're paying for is water) and other additives to "enhance" the flavor (and the price). Always read the label. If anything other than pork is listed in the ingredients (look for words like "enhanced," "injected," or "added water," or salt or phosphate), don't put it in your cart. I recommend inexpensive Costco or Sam's Club ribs because they tend to be meatier, and are not enhanced.

WSM AND OFFSET

SERVES 3 TO 6

3 (2- to 3-pound) racks baby back ribs

1½ cups white vinegar

¾ cup prepared yellow mustard

Rudimentary Rub (page 115)

Tart Wash (page 115; optional)

KETTLE

SERVES 1 TO 2

1 (2- to 3-pound) rack baby back ribs

½ cup white vinegar

¼ cup prepared yellow mustard

Rudimentary Rub (page 115)

Tart Wash (page 115; optional)

4 TO 5 HOURS BEFORE DINNER

Set up and start a KISS Method fire according to the instructions for your WSM (page 32), offset (page 34), or kettle (page 36).

While you're waiting for the charcoal in the chimney to engage, rinse the rib racks in the sink under cold water. Douse each rack with about ½ cup of vinegar, and lightly rub the vinegar into both sides. Rinse the racks again under cold water. Set the ribs on a rimmed baking sheet and slather both sides with a light coating of yellow mustard, about ¼ cup per rack. (The mustard helps the rub adhere to the meat.) Sprinkle about 2 tablespoons of rub over each rack, or more to taste.

(Continued on page 116)

> **TIP:** Ribs often have a slightly "off" smell and sticky feel when they are taken out of a vacuum-sealed package. Rinsing with vinegar removes the odor and tackiness, and vinegar is also a natural antibacterial agent.

★ RUDIMENTARY RUB

A basic rub doesn't get any simpler than this. A light dusting over the ribs, about two tablespoons per rack, will produce an excellent, chewy bark with just a touch of spice. You probably have most of the ingredients already, but I don't recommend using the musty, flavorless grocery store paprika in your spice cabinet. It's worth the extra dollar to buy fresh paprika at a specialty food store or online spice shop like Penzeys, The Spice House, or Kalustyan's.

MAKES ABOUT $^{1}/_{2}$ CUP

3 tablespoons paprika

2 tablespoons freshly ground black pepper

$1^{1}/_{2}$ tablespoons Morton kosher salt

2 teaspoons garlic powder

2 teaspoons onion powder

$^{1}/_{2}$ teaspoon cayenne pepper

Combine all of the ingredients in a small bowl and whisk until the mixture is thoroughly blended.

After slathering a thin, $^{1}/_{4}$-cup coating of yellow mustard on the ribs, sprinkle each rack with about 2 tablespoons of rub.

Store remaining rub in an airtight container for up to six months.

TIP: Double or triple this rub recipe and save the leftovers for Lesson #4 and Lesson #5. The rubs in these cooks are almost identical to this blend and can be twea-ked with the addition of one or two ingredients.

★ TART WASH

Although I caution against opening and closing the cooker too much, I often spritz ribs with this seasoned liquid when I have the cooker open to check the charcoal or water pan levels. But don't call it a mop. People think of mops as a panacea—a cure-all for keeping barbecue moist and tender. But it belies reason to think that any liquid could penetrate to the interior of a hot rack of ribs or a thick pork shoulder. It's more accurate to call it a wash. This wash adds a top note of flavor to the meat, the sprinkle of rub in the wash reinforces the rub on the meat, and the small shot of cranberry-colored liquid makes the ribs pretty.

MAKES 1 CUP

$^{2}/_{3}$ cup cranberry juice

$^{1}/_{3}$ cup olive oil

2 teaspoons Rudimentary Rub

Pour the cranberry juice, olive oil, and rub into a plastic condiment squirt bottle. Shake vigorously until the rub is dissolved and the mixture is blended (like a vinaigrette), about 1 minute.

Store in the refrigerator for up to two weeks. The olive oil in the wash will thicken when it is cold. Allow the wash to come to room temperature before using, and shake it vigorously to reblend.

WHEN THE LIT CHARCOAL and wood are in place and ready for cooking, put the smallest rack of the three in the middle of the top grate, meat-side down, bone-side up. Place the remaining two racks on the outside of the grate with the larger chine bone facing out. (Always face the thickest, fattiest, or largest bone side of the meat—which is most resistant to temperature fluctuations—toward the outer edge of the WSM.) If the racks are too long for the grate, scrunch them, like an accordion, to fit. Place the oven thermometer on the grate. Set the lid on the cooker with the top vent facing the back side of the cooker, at about 1 o'clock from the door at 6 o'clock on the center ring.

Set the oven thermometer on the grate.

Check the vents. The top vent and the bottom three vents should be completely open.

30 MINUTES INTO THE COOK

Close the two bottom vents on the front side of the cooker by one-third.

1 HOUR INTO THE COOK

Remove the lid and check the oven thermometer. Flip the ribs so that the racks are meat-side up, bone-side down. Check the level in the water pan and refill it if it is less than three-quarters full. For detailed instructions, see Refilling the WSM water pan (page 38).

2½ HOURS INTO THE COOK

Remove the lid and check the oven thermometer. Use the tongs to pick up one end of the smallest rack, holding the rack about four ribs in. If the rack bends and flexes a bit and looks as if it's about to crack or break, it's done. Remove this rack, but leave the other two racks on.

Vigorously shake the bottle of Tart Wash and spritz about 2 tablespoons over the racks left on the grate.

Check and refill the water pan. Close the lid.

If the smallest rack isn't ready? Chances are, the ribs will not be done at this point, but you should start checking the smallest rack for doneness at the 2½-hour mark. This part of the cook is highly subjective and it takes practice, because you're really trying to figure out how you like your ribs. Meaty and chewy? Fall-off-

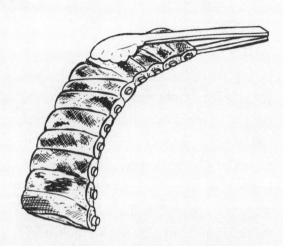

the-bone tender? When in doubt, cut a rib off the rack and sample it for taste and texture. If it's to your liking, it's ready. If you think it's too chewy, leave the ribs on the cooker and check them every 15 to 20 minutes until the ribs suit your style. It can take anywhere from 2½ to 3½ hours to cook a rack of baby back ribs, but barbecue will always fool you if you're cooking by the clock. No two racks ever cook alike.

ABOUT 20 MINUTES LATER

If the smallest rack of ribs wasn't done on the first check, open the lid and check the rack again. Remove this rack if it's done, and leave the other two racks on the grate. If the smallest rack isn't done, keep checking it every 10 or 15 minutes until it is. Spritz the racks with Tart Wash.

ABOUT 20 MINUTES AFTER YOU REMOVE THE FIRST RACK

Take the second rack of ribs off of the cooker. Spritz the last rack of ribs on the smoker with Tart Wash.

ABOUT 20 MINUTES AFTER YOU REMOVE THE SECOND RACK

Remove the last rack of ribs. Check the oven thermometer and close the lid.

THE SIREN SONG OF THE WATER PAN

NO MATTER HOW TEMPTING the water pan in the WSM might look after a cook—brimming with gravy made from rendered fat drippings—it is not usable. Anything you make with this meat juice soup will taste like liquefied ashtray.

WHEN THE LIT CHARCOAL and wood are in place and ready for cooking, open the lid and place the largest rack vertically on the cooking grate, about one-third of the way away from the firebox, bone-side up with the chine bone facing the firebox. (Always face the thickest, fattiest, or largest bone side of the meat—which is most resistant to temperature fluctuations—toward the firebox on the offset.) Repeat with the remaining two racks, working away from the first rack and the firebox. If the racks are too long for the grate, scrunch them, like an accordion, to fit.

Set the oven thermometer in the middle of the cooking grate. Close the cooker.

Check the vents. The top and side vents should be fully open.

30 MINUTES INTO THE COOK

Close the side firebox vent by one-third.

1 HOUR INTO THE COOK

Fill the chimney starter with charcoal and light it. While the charcoal is engaging, open the cooker and check the oven thermometer. Check the water pan. If it is less than three-quarters full, add more water. Use the tongs to flip the racks, meat-side up, and rotate the ribs so that the rack that was closest to the firebox moves to the spot farthest away. Close the cooker. When the charcoal is fully engaged,

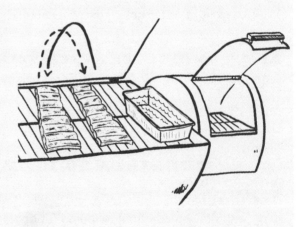

open the lid of the firebox and pour in the freshly lit charcoal. Add a split of wood to the charcoal. Keep the firebox open until the charcoal and wood stop billowing smoke (about 10 minutes); then close it.

2 HOURS INTO THE COOK

Fill the chimney starter with charcoal and light it. While the charcoal is engaging, open the cooker and check the oven thermometer. Check and refill the water pan if it is less than three-quarters full. Use the tongs to rotate the ribs again. Vigorously shake the bottle of Tart Wash and spritz about 2 tablespoons over each rack of ribs.

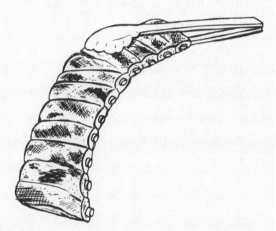

Close the cooker.

When the charcoal is fully engaged, open the firebox and pour in the freshly lit charcoal. Keep the firebox open until the charcoal stops billowing smoke (about 10 minutes); then close it.

2$^{1}/_{2}$ HOURS INTO THE COOK

Open the lid and check the oven thermometer. Pick up one end of the smallest rack with the tongs, holding the rack about four ribs in. If the rack bends and flexes a bit and looks as if it's about to crack or break, it's done. Take this rack out of the cooker, but leave the other two racks on. Spritz the ribs on the grate with Tart Wash. Check and refill the water pan, as needed.

Chances are, the ribs will not be ready at this point, but you should start checking the racks for doneness at the 2$^{1}/_{2}$-hour mark on an offset. This part of the cook is highly subjective and it takes practice, because you're really trying to figure out how you like your ribs. Meaty and chewy? Fall-off-the-bone tender? When in doubt, cut a rib off of the rack and sample it for taste and texture. If it's to your liking, it's ready. If you think it's too chewy, check the ribs every 15 or 20 minutes until the ribs suit your style. It can take anywhere from 2$^{1}/_{2}$ to 3$^{1}/_{2}$ hours to cook a rack of baby back ribs on an offset, but barbecue will always fool you if you're cooking by the clock. No two racks ever cook alike.

(continued on next page)

ABOUT 20 MINUTES LATER

If the smallest rack of ribs wasn't done on the first check, open the lid and check the rack again. Remove this rack if it's done, and rotate the two racks on the grate. If the smallest rack is not done, keep checking it every 10 or 15 minutes until it is ready to take off. Spritz the remaining racks with Tart Wash. Restock the water pan and charcoal as needed.

ABOUT 20 MINUTES AFTER YOU REMOVE THE FIRST RACK

Take the second rack of ribs off the cooker.

Spritz the last rack of ribs on the cooker with Tart Wash.

ABOUT 20 MINUTES AFTER YOU REMOVE THE SECOND RACK

Open the lid and remove the last rack of ribs.

Check the oven thermometer. Close the lid and open all vents on the cooker.

KETTLE

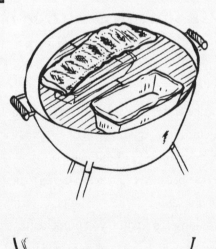

WHEN THE LIT CHARCOAL and wood are in place and ready for cooking, place the rack of ribs on the grate across from the water pan, bone-side up with the larger chine bone facing the fire. (Always face the thickest, fattiest, or largest bone side of the meat—which is most resistant to temperature fluctuations—toward the center of the grate and pile of live charcoal on the kettle.) If the rack is too long for the grate, scrunch it, like an accordion, to fit.

Place the oven thermometer next to the rack on the cooking grate. Set the lid on the cooker with the top vent positioned over the ribs.

Check the vents. The top and bottom vents should be completely open.

20 MINUTES INTO THE COOK

Close the bottom vent by one-third.

30 MINUTES INTO THE COOK

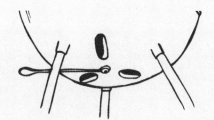

Remove the lid and check the oven thermometer. Slide the water pan to the side and flip open the grate over the charcoal. Add one wood chunk to the pile of lit charcoal. Close the grate and slide the water pan back over the charcoal.

Flip the rack over, meat-side up, but keep the chine bone facing the fire.

Check the water pan. If it is less than three-quarters full, add more water.

When the wood chunk stops billowing smoke (about 5 minutes), put the lid back on the cooker.

1 HOUR INTO THE COOK

Fill the chimney starter one-third full with charcoal. Open the lid and check the oven thermometer. Move the water pan, flip the top grate open, and pour in the unlit charcoal. Use the tongs to maintain the banked pile. Add one wood chunk to the charcoal. Close the grate.

Check the water pan and refill if it is less than three-quarters full.

Vigorously shake the bottle of Tart Wash. Spritz about 2 tablespoons over the rack of ribs.

When the charcoal and fresh wood chunk stop billowing smoke (about 5 minutes), put the lid back on the cooker.

1¹⁄₂ HOURS INTO THE COOK

Remove the lid and check the oven thermometer. Pick up one end of the rack with the tongs, holding the rack about four ribs in. If the rack bends and flexes a bit and looks as if it's about to crack or break, it's done. If the rack is not pliable, return the rack to the grate and close the cooker.

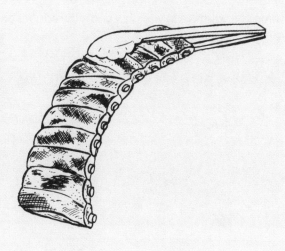

The rack may not be ready at this point, but you should start checking baby backs for

(continued on next page)

doneness at the 1½-hour mark on a kettle. This part of the cook is highly subjective and it takes practice, because you're really trying to figure out how you like your ribs. Meaty and chewy? Fall-off-the-bone tender? When in doubt, cut a rib off the rack and sample it for taste and texture. If it's to your liking, it's ready. If you think it's too chewy, check the ribs every 10 minutes until the ribs suit your style. It can take up to 2 hours to cook a rack of baby back ribs on a kettle, but barbecue will always fool you if you're cooking by the clock. No two racks ever cook alike.

If the ribs are not done, spritz the rack with Tart Wash and continue cooking. Keep an eye on the water pan and charcoal level and replenish as needed.

When the ribs are done, check the oven thermometer, close the lid, and open all the vents.

★ TASTER'S CHOICE ★

IN YOUR FIRST RIB COOK, it's all about the learning curve and teaching yourself what style of ribs you prefer. The point of leaving two of the racks on longer—even for as little as twenty minutes—is to show how a little more time on the cooker affects the meat. Did you notice a difference in the texture or flavor between the three racks of ribs? The first ribs were probably chewier. The second rack should have been less chewy, and the third rack approaching fall-off-the-bone. Which ribs did you like the best? This experiment should trigger one of many epiphanies you will have in your low and slow education. You have just learned to make barbecue the way you like it. Savor it.

CONTINUING EDUCATION

BABY BACKS ARE THE SHOW PONIES OF RIBS: compact, meaty, and picturesque on a plate. They're the most popular cut of ribs because they're naturally more tender than spare ribs, which makes them easier to cook and less vulnerable if there is a mishap in the cooker. They're also small—dainty, even. It's the slab I'd serve the Queen if she came over for dinner.

Baby back racks (also called slabs) are cut from the blade and center section of the loin, and in some grocery stores and meat markets, you might see them packaged or sold as pork loin ribs or back ribs. Baby backs weigh one and three-quarter pounds per rack. I don't waste too much thought on rib semantics. What you do want to know is what to look for when you're buying them.

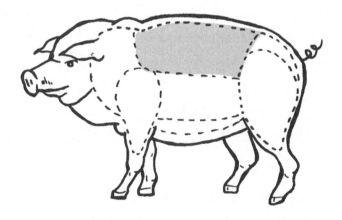

BUYING GUIDE

SIZE MATTERS. A typical rack has twelve to thirteen ribs. Go for the biggest, meatiest baby backs you can find that weigh about two to three pounds per rack.

AVOID SHINERS. A rib is a pork chop without the loin. When butchers cut baby backs, they sometimes cut too close to the bone to make a meatier boneless pork loin chop. If you can see the rib bone "shining" through the meat, it's been overtrimmed.

FAT IS YOUR FRIEND. Baby backs are leaner than spare ribs, but fat is what keeps the ribs tender and tasty. Buy racks with good marbling—the white, streaky fat that runs through the meat—but avoid racks with large, solid patches of surface fat.

APPLY COMMON SENSE LIBERALLY. Don't buy racks that have dark spots or dry edges. Vacuum-sealed ribs may have an off smell right out of the package, but the smell should dissipate. If the funky odor lingers, don't cook or eat the ribs.

DON'T BUY ENHANCED MEAT. The ribs will have a salty, chemical flavor. Racks are sometimes treated with saltwater, flavoring, and other preservatives so that amateur cooks can steam, bake, and otherwise abuse the meat and still make an edible rib. You know better.

One slab serves two to three people. It depends on the appetites, and whether ribs are the centerpiece dish or one of many barbecued meats you're serving.

RUB 101

THERE ARE PROBABLY ABOUT TEN original rub recipes in the world. The nine billion other rubs floating around are just slightly modified or bastardized versions of the original ten. People naturally want to futz with recipes. They feel a deep need to tweak a perfectly good rub by adding mint, eye of newt, and other secret ingredients because they think these Franken-rubs will make their barbecue taste better.

Good barbecue has nothing to do with magic rubs or sauce. Remember? It's about a clean, controlled fire. When it comes to good, savory rubs, I like what Leonardo da Vinci had to say on the subject: Simplicity is the ultimate sophistication. (Yes, he was talking about barbecue.)

MEMBRANE: ON <u>OR</u> OFF?

THE THIN, PAPERY MEMBRANE OVER the bone side of a rack of ribs can be removed—or not. Some people think the membrane prevents the flavor of a rub from sinking into the meat, so they take it off. Other people like the crisp, papery snap of biting into it, or they think it holds moisture in and keeps the ribs from drying out, so they leave it on. It's purely a matter of personal preference. If you want the best of both worlds, score the membrane with a fish scaler or paring knife. I don't think the membrane affects the taste or texture of the ribs enough to make a difference. If anything, removing the membrane is a bit like using good china. If you have company and want to impress, taking the membrane off makes for a better presentation. Here's how to remove it:

1. Slide a non-serrated butter knife under the membrane of the last rib at the narrow end of the rack. Be careful not to slice through the membrane.

3. Use a paper towel to grip the edge of the membrane and gently peel it away from the bones. If the membrane tears, use the knife to lift and loosen the edge and continue peeling.

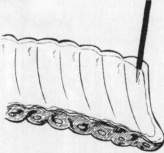

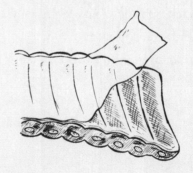

2. Gently pivot the knife back and forth under the membrane to loosen it enough to lift an edge with your fingers.

★ BLACK AND WHITE RUB

This basic blend, dubbed "dalmatian rub" by Indiana pitmaster Bruce Cook, is simplicity defined. It really lets the full flavor of the meat shine through, and it shows how wood smoke penetrates the meat and infuses it with flavor. If nothing else, this rub will teach you, once and for all, that there is no magic bullet in barbecue. It really is this easy.

MAKES ½ CUP

¼ cup Morton kosher salt
¼ cup freshly ground black pepper

Mix the ingredients in a small bowl, using a whisk to thoroughly blend.

To apply, sprinkle about 2 tablespoons over each rack of ribs, or more to taste.

Store leftovers in an airtight container for up to six months.

★ ALL-PURPOSE RUB

This is my all-occasion go-to rub for ribs. The smoky heat of the pepper blend is the perfect counterbalance to rich, fatty ribs. Thyme adds a zesty, herbal quality that never fails to leave people guessing the flavor. The rub can be used on chicken and beef, too.

MAKES ABOUT ½ CUP

⅓ cup Toasted Mexican Pepper Blend (page 18)
2 tablespoons Morton kosher salt
1 tablespoon freshly ground black pepper
½ tablespoon dried thyme
½ tablespoon dry mustard

Mix the ingredients in a small bowl, using a whisk to thoroughly blend.

To apply, sprinkle about 2 tablespoons over each rack of ribs, or more to taste.

Store leftovers in an airtight container for up to two months.

★ MUSTARD RUB

Pork and mustard have a natural affinity. In Lessons #3 and #4, the two rib cooks, the layer of cheap prepared yellow mustard is more functional than flavorful: it helps the rub adhere to the ribs, but its effect on flavor is nil by the end of the long cook. A rub heavy with freshly ground mustard seed is a different story. In this rub, the pungent, tangy spice gives the ribs' crusty outer layer a notable, zesty flavor.

MAKES ABOUT ½ CUP

2 tablespoons coarsely ground mustard seed
2 tablespoons freshly ground black pepper
2 tablespoons garlic powder
2 tablespoons Morton kosher salt

Mix the ingredients in a small bowl, using a whisk to thoroughly blend.

To apply, sprinkle about 2 tablespoons over each rack of ribs, or more to taste.

Store leftovers in an airtight container for up to two months.

★ KITCHEN SINK DRY RUB

There are a handful of herbs and spices that always seem to find their way into a rub, and this recipe uses a little bit of all of them. Feel free to tinker with the quantities. You can cut down on the pepper blend if you don't want the heat or reduce the amount of kosher salt and increase the celery salt to alter the flavor. This is a good base recipe to fiddle with to create your own signature rub. As I mentioned in the recipe for Rudimentary Rub (page 115), don't use the tasteless paprika you find in grocery stores. Splurge on fresh paprika from a gourmet store or specialty spice shop, like Penzey's, The Spice House, or Kalustyan's.

MAKES ABOUT ¾ CUP

3 tablespoons paprika
2 tablespoons Toasted Mexican Pepper Blend (page 18)
1 tablespoon celery salt
2 tablespoons Morton kosher salt
3 tablespoons freshly ground black pepper
2 teaspoons garlic powder
1 tablespoon dry mustard
2 teaspoons grated lemon rind

Mix the ingredients in a medium bowl, using a whisk to thoroughly blend.

To apply, sprinkle about 2 tablespoons over each rack of ribs, or more to taste.

Store leftovers in an airtight container for up to two months.

★
FENNEL
CORIANDER RUB

Fennel isn't the first flavor that comes to mind when you think of barbecue, but a thick crust on baby back or spare ribs makes an outstanding, crunchy bark. Then again, I can't think of anything this spice blend doesn't taste good on—fish, beef, chicken, veal, you name it. Do not substitute fresh orange zest for the dried in this recipe. It is too moist, and can burn or turn bitter on meat over the long haul of a low and slow cook.

MAKES ABOUT ¾ CUP

½ cup fennel seeds

1½ tablespoons whole coriander

1 tablespoon white peppercorns

1½ tablespoons Morton kosher salt

2 teaspoons granulated or dried orange peel

Preheat a heavy skillet over medium heat. Pour the fennel, coriander, and peppercorns in the skillet and swirl the seeds around in the pan to toast. Be careful: the seeds will burn quickly. When the seeds turn light brown and fragrant, after 4 to 5 minutes, remove from the heat. Add the salt and swirl to blend. Allow the mixture to cool completely.

When the spices have cooled, pour the mixture and the orange peel into a spice grinder or blender. Grind to a fine powder, shaking the grinder occasionally to redistribute the seeds.

To apply, sprinkle about 2 tablespoons over each rack of ribs.

Store leftovers in an airtight container for up to two months.

INGREDIENT FINDER: DRIED CITRUS PEEL

Granulated or dried orange peel isn't as common as, say, rosemary, but many grocery stores carry it, as do specialty stores and online spice shops like Penzeys, The Spice House, or Kalustyan's.

Or, you can make it. Use a vegetable peeler to remove strips of the very top orange layer of skin from the fruit. Trim away any white pith on the back of the peel. Lay the strips skin-side down on a plate and let them dry out at room temperature for three to four days, until the peel is shriveled and totally dry. If you're in a hurry, you can dry the orange peel in the oven: Preheat the oven to 200°F. Lay the fresh orange peel on a baking sheet and set it in the oven. Lower the oven temperature to 125°F or its lowest setting. Dry in the oven until there is no moisture left in the peel, about four hours.

moked Chicken halves (page 50)

Smoked Shrimp (page 224)

Spare Ribs (page 146) and Jalapeño Cheddar Skillet Corn Bread (page 213)

Pulled pork sandwich topped with Pickled Red Onions (page 205) and Lexington Red Slaw (page 202)

TOP: *Pulled Pork (page 175);* **BOTTOM:** *Smoked Tomato Bruschetta (page 219)*

Buttermilk-Brined Hot Wings (page 223)

TOP: *Trixie-Pea's Mac and Cheese* (page 209); **BOTTOM:** *Dragon Turds* (page 216)

Louisa Chu's White Peach, Blueberry and Lavender Cobbler (page 230)

★
TANDOORI RUB

Tandoor clay ovens and barbecue both put smoking-hot live coals to good use. It's only natural that the traditional flavors of this style of Indian cookery would translate well to low and slow. I usually avoid using sugar in a rub, but the small amount in this blend really balances the distinct flavors of this classic Indian seasoning.

MAKES ABOUT ½ CUP

3 tablespoons paprika

2 tablespoon Morton kosher salt

1 tablespoon ground coriander

1 tablespoon ground cumin

½ tablespoon freshly ground black pepper

1 tablespoon sugar

1 tablespoon ground ginger

1 teaspoon ground cinnamon

1 teaspoon turmeric

½ teaspoon cayenne pepper

Mix the ingredients in a small bowl, using a whisk to thoroughly blend.

To apply, sprinkle about 2 tablespoons over each rack of ribs, or more to taste.

Store leftovers in an airtight container for up to two months.

BUILD-YOUR-OWN RUB TEMPLATE

IF YOU'RE LOOKING FOR A DEFINITIVE, no-thinking-required guide to making rubs from scratch, you won't find it here. These are very simplified guidelines for building a rub, like the marinade and brine templates in Lessons #1 and #2. The suggested ratios and measurements are provided so that you can make a rub base and experiment with flavors and seasonings to create your own, unique rub. Don't worry about creating a masterpiece on your first attempt. Your technique and palate for rubs will develop over time, as you discover the flavors you like best on barbecue and learn how the sweet kiss of low and slow smoke affects the flavors of different herbs and spices over long cooks.

KOSHER SALT:
2 TABLESPOONS (2 PARTS)

Salt is the foundation of any rub. It not only enhances the flavor of the meat, it also carries the flavor of the other seasonings in the mix. Salt also draws a small amount of the moisture inside the meat to the surface. Under low and slow conditions, this light sheen of moisture helps caramelize the proteins on the outside of the meat to make the crunchy, browned bark. You don't have to be Harold McGee to know there's more flavor in the browned, caramelized bits.

PAPRIKA: 1 TABLESPOON (1 PART)

You'll find paprika in just about every traditional barbecue rub. It's in there to give a nice color to the surface of the meat, but it also has a good neutral flavor that adds depth to a rub without overpowering the other seasonings in the blend. You can use hot or sweet paprika, but I recommend using sweet until you figure out your baseline for heat. If you're blending in other hot spices like cayenne pepper or ancho chile powder, hot paprika might overwhelm the rub. Splurge on fresh paprika from a gourmet store or specialty spice shop, like Penzey's, The Spice House, or Kalustyan's. It makes all the difference in the world.

PEPPER: 1 TABLESPOON (1 PART)

Barbecue is nothing without the distinct flavor of black pepper. You can use other types of dried ground chiles as part of the overall pepper content, but at least half of the mix should be freshly ground or cracked black pepper. For example, you could use ½ tablespoon of the Toasted Mexican Pepper Blend (page 18) or ½ tablespoon of straight ancho chile powder with ½ tablespoon of black pepper in your rub.

HERBS AND SPICES:
1 TABLESPOON (1 PART)

A teaspoon of this, plus a teaspoon or two of that—what goes into your rub is purely a matter of personal taste. My rubs skew spicy-hot, and I use herbs to balance the heat. When you start selecting seasonings for a rub, think about the flavors that go well with the meat, whether it's pork, beef, chicken, fish, or lamb. Consider the side dishes the meat will be served with, and choose the rub seasonings to complement or contrast the sides. Example: Throw a teaspoon of celery seed in the rub if your cole slaw uses it too. You can also pair flavors by the category of cuisine—amping up the oregano if the sides have a Greek or Mediterranean influence or adding ground ginger and garlic powder if the meal has an Asian tone.

Until you're absolutely confident in the art of making your own rub, use dried herbs or spices. Ingredients like fresh thyme or minced onion can make a rub sticky or could burn or turn bitter during a long low and slow cook. Always toast and grind whole dried seeds and spice "berries" (like fennel or allspice). If a seasoning is larger than the other elements in the rub, like a whole bay leaf, give it a spin in a spice grinder so it disperses evenly in the rub.

Popular rub seasonings include garlic powder, onion powder, dry mustard, bay leaf, thyme, sage, cumin, allspice, clove, oregano, fennel seeds, coriander, curry powder, nutmeg, cinnamon, basil, rosemary, turmeric, and ginger.

★ RULES OF THE RUB ★

- Always taste the rub before you apply it to meat. If it's too heavy on spice or salt, bulk up the most neutral seasoning in the blend (probably the paprika), to balance the flavor.

- Apply rubs up to one hour before the meat goes on the cooker. Rubs stick to the surface of meat; they don't sink in. Therefore, there is no need to "marinate" a piece of meat in rub overnight. Too much salt in a rub can pull moisture out of thinner cuts of meat and cause them to dry out during the cook. It's important to make sure the rub adheres to the meat, either by using a mustard coating or by moistening the rub with oil or another liquid to make a wet rub.

- Don't put sugar in your rub. You read that right. I don't like sweet barbecue as a general principle, but sugar particularly has no place in a beginner's rub because too many things can go wrong with it. Sugar becomes tacky at 300°F and acts like flypaper—making soot and ash from the charcoal stick to the meat. And sugar starts to burn at 340°F. Although the ideal low and slow temperature is well below 300°F, it's not uncommon for the temperature in a cooker to spike, particularly when you're still honing your technique. If you like a sweeter barbecue, save the sugar for the sauce or glaze you paint on the meat at the end of the cook.

BABY BACK RIB MARINADES

POTENT RUBS ARE THE CLASSIC WAY TO ACHIEVE FLAVORFUL CRUSTS on ribs in American low and slow, but I also love the unique flavor of Asian barbecue, which comes from marinating the ribs. When ribs soak for several hours in a marinade, the acid and salt in the marinade break down the surface of the meat and the marinade works its way into the interior of the meat—unlike rubs, which rest on the surface of the meat. This is why, when you marinate ribs, it's important to remove the thin membrane (page 125) that covers the bones. Ribs with the membrane on will not absorb as much flavor.

KOREAN BARBECUE MARINADE

Traditionally, Korean barbecue—one of my favorite styles outside of American low and slow—is grilled directly over live charcoal. I've adapted this classic bulgogi *(boneless slices of beef) and* galbi *(short ribs) marinade for the longer, low-heat baby back cook. This variation gets natural sweetness from Asian pear juice, as too much sugar can caramelize and burn during the longer cook. If you can't find the large round Asian pear to purée for juice, regular pears are a fine substitute.*

WSM AND OFFSET

MAKES ABOUT 2 CUPS

2 Asian pears, peeled, cored, and grated

1 cup soy sauce

$1/2$ cup brown sugar

$1/3$ cup sake or dry sherry

$1/4$ cup Asian sesame oil

12 garlic cloves (6 cloves minced,
    6 cloves thinly sliced)

8 green onions, chopped, reserve 2 tablespoons

4 tablespoons toasted sesame seeds,
    reserve 2 tablespoons

1 (1-inch) piece fresh ginger, peeled and grated

1 teaspoon freshly ground black pepper

$1/2$ teaspoon cayenne pepper (optional)

KETTLE

MAKES ABOUT 1 CUP

1 Asian pear, peeled, cored, and grated

$1/2$ cup soy sauce

$1/4$ cup brown sugar

$2^1/2$ tablespoons sake or dry sherry

2 tablespoons Asian sesame oil

6 garlic cloves (3 cloves minced,
    3 cloves thinly sliced)

4 green onions, chopped, reserve 1 tablespoon

2 tablespoons toasted sesame seeds,
    reserve 1 tablespoon

1 ($1/2$-inch) piece fresh ginger, peeled and grated

$1/2$ teaspoon freshly ground black pepper

$1/4$ teaspoon cayenne pepper (optional)

Combine all of the ingredients (except the reserved green onion and sesame seeds) in a large bowl and whisk to blend. Pour the marinade in a shallow glass baking dish big enough to accommodate the racks of ribs. Lay the racks, meat-side down, in the marinade. Cover the dish with plastic wrap and allow the racks to marinate 6 to 8 hours in the refrigerator, flipping the racks three or four times to marinate both sides.

Cook ribs as instructed for your cooker in Lesson #3. Garnish ribs with reserved sesame seeds and scallions.

CHAR SIU-STYLE MARINADE

This marinade is based on the popular Cantonese dish—sweet and salty roasted pork that turns a brilliant, shiny red when meat meets fire. This marinade gives baby back ribs the same shiny red glaze. Although I caution beginners against the potential for burning sugary rubs, this marinade is an excellent litmus test of your new skills.

WSM AND OFFSET

MAKES ABOUT 3 CUPS

15 garlic cloves, minced

1 (5-inch) piece fresh ginger, peeled and minced

1/2 cup Shaoxing wine or dry sherry

1/2 cup hoisin sauce

1/2 cup sugar

1/3 cup *nam pla* (Thai fish sauce)

1/3 cup soy sauce

1/3 cup Asian sesame oil

2 teaspoons five-spice powder

4 star anise seeds, crushed

KETTLE

MAKES ABOUT 1 1/2 CUPS

7 garlic cloves, minced

1 (2-inch) piece fresh ginger, peeled and minced

1/4 cup Shaoxing wine or dry sherry

1/4 cup hoisin sauce

1/4 cup sugar

1/3 cup nam pla (Thai fish sauce)

2 1/2 tablespoons soy sauce

2 1/2 tablespoons Asian sesame oil

1 teaspoon five spice powder

2 star anise seeds, crushed

Combine all of the ingredients in a large bowl. Whisk or blend until the sugar is dissolved. Pour the marinade in a shallow glass baking dish big enough to accommodate the racks of ribs. Lay the racks, meat-side down, in the marinade. Cover the dish with plastic wrap and allow the racks to marinate 6 to 8 hours in the refrigerator, flipping the racks three or four times to marinate both sides. Follow the instructions for Lesson #3

INGREDIENT FINDER: SHAOXING WINE

The "drunken" in popular dishes like "drunken shrimp," Shaoxing (a.k.a. "Shao hsing") is one of the most famous Chinese fermented rice wines. Buy the good stuff—in an Asian market, either the most expensive "cooking" Shaoxing on the shelf or the type sold for drinking. Or substitute dry sherry.

THE SAUCE PHILOSOPHY:
IT'S A CONDIMENT, NOT A SIDE DISH

I THINK OF BARBECUE SAUCE AS THE POOR MAN'S (or in this case, cook's) cover-up. If you have to rely on secret award-winning sauces to make your ribs taste good, it's probably because your ribs need a strong sauce to make up for your lack of barbecue savvy. Or, giving you the benefit of the doubt, the ribs taste just fine on their own, and you simply don't know any better than to overuse the sauce. It never ceases to amaze me when I see people who have devoted hours upon hours to buying, prepping, and cooking a rack of ribs drown all of their efforts in a sugar, mustard, ketchup, or vinegar sauce that completely overwhelms the delicious, smoky flavor of the meat. This is why I'm a fan of the Tart Wash (page 115). The simple cranberry and olive oil blend adds a hint of moisture and color and the faintest of flavors without detracting from the overall flavor of the smoked meat.

If you're going to get serious about barbecue, you need to start thinking of sauce as a simple condiment. It should be an ethereally light coating that gives your barbecue an easy twang and a whack of color. It should be served in a small, squeezeable condiment bottle—not ladled out of a bubbling cauldron or spackled onto every rack that leaves your cooker. If sauce is dripping down your wrists while you munch on a rib, you have to ask yourself: what am I trying to hide? As you learn more about low and slow and begin to refine your techniques and recipes, you'll make better and better barbecue and use less and less sauce.

It's not that I don't like a good sauce. I do. I'm only trying to teach you what it takes most barbecue fanatics years to figure out: until you get a handle on the clean-burning fire and the perfectly cooked meat, sauce is secondary. Then again, while you're learning the techniques of low and slow, a killer sauce can be the barbecue equivalent of a wing man: a reliable tool that can keep your dinner from crashing and burning. These are a few of my favorites.

TANGY SEVEN-PEPPER SAUCE

Some people have a "house wine"; this is my "house bar-becue sauce." It's my answer to all of the cloying, sweet, thick glop served on most competition barbecue. It has a good kick and is the perfect accent for meat coated in my signature blend, Gary Wiviott's Rub (page 160). You can use Tabasco or any other vinegar-based Louisiana-style hot sauce, but I am adamant about using Búfalo Chipotle Mexican Hot Sauce. It's very common in Mexican and Latino markets and can be ordered online from MexGrocer.com.

MAKES 6 CUPS

4 cups ketchup

²/₃ cup cider vinegar

¹/₂ cup sugar

¹/₂ cup brown sugar

¹/₄ pound (1 stick) unsalted butter

2 to 3 lemons, juiced (about ¹/₂ cup juice)

4 limes, juiced (about ¹/₂ cup juice)

2 teaspoons freshly ground black pepper

2 tablespoons dried crushed red pepper flakes

2 tablespoons Búfalo Chipotle Mexican Hot Sauce

2 tablespoons Louisiana-style hot sauce

2 tablespoons Toasted Mexican Pepper
  Blend (page 18)

Combine all of the ingredients in a medium nonre-active saucepan. Gently simmer the sauce over medium heat for 20 minutes, stirring occasionally.

Store the sauce in an airtight container in the refrigerator for up to one week.

INGREDIENT FINDER: CHIPOTLE HOT SAUCE

Okay, okay. You can't find Búfalo Chipotle Mexican Hot Sauce, and you don't feel like ordering it online. Fine. Go to your regular grocery store and buy a can of chipotles in adobo. Pour the whole can in your blender and purée it. Use one tablespoon of the purée in place of the Búfalo sauce. Save the rest of the purée to use in mayo, sour cream, or any sauce, soup, or stew that needs a smoky, spicy kick.

★ DANNY'S GLAZE

This is a highly regarded recipe from respected barbecue veteran Danny Gaulden. Although undeniably sweet and slightly tart, the main idea is to use it to pretty-up ribs that aren't necessarily so—for example, on ribs that have overlapped on the cooker and need some cover-up to hide gray patches. This sweet glaze gives the rack the kind of burnished red gloss that many people have come to expect from ribs.

MAKES ABOUT 1 CUP

1 cup brown sugar
¼ cup prepared yellow mustard
¼ cup cider vinegar

Combine the sugar, mustard, and cider vinegar in a medium nonreactive saucepan and stir until the sauce is mixed. Cook the sauce over medium heat until it comes to a low simmer, about 10 minutes, stirring frequently. Do not let the sauce come to a full boil. When the sauce has thickened slightly, remove it from the heat.

To apply, paint the sauce on the ribs immediately after removing the racks from the cooker. The heat from the ribs continues to cook and thicken the sauce, turning it into a light glaze.

Store the leftovers in an airtight container in the refrigerator for up to one week.

★ GUAVA GLAZE AND SAUCE

You don't see a lot of guava in barbecue country, but this tropical sauce fits the island style of charcoal cookery. It puts a typical native ingredient—in this case, guava—to good use, just like a barbecue guy would use a native ingredient like beer.

MAKES ABOUT 3 CUPS

1½ cups chopped onion
4 to 5 garlic cloves, peeled and chopped (about 2 tablespoons)
2 (11.5-ounce) cans guava nectar
⅔ cup guava jelly or red currant jelly
¼ cup dry sherry
¼ cup light molasses
3 tablespoons red wine vinegar
2 tablespoons tomato paste
1 tablespoon cumin seeds, toasted and ground
2 teaspoons dry mustard

Purée the onion and the garlic in a food processor. Combine the purée with all the other ingredients in a large saucepan. Whisk the mixture over medium heat until the jelly dissolves and the sauce comes to a slow boil, about 5 minutes. As soon as the sauce begins to bubble, decrease the heat to low and simmer. Stir frequently to keep the sauce from burning, and simmer until the sauce is reduced to about 3 cups, 35 to 45 minutes.

Store in an airtight container and keep refrigerated for up to one week.

BARBECUE CLASSICS: KANSAS CITY-STYLE SAUCES

SAUCE IS KING IN KANSAS CITY BARBECUE, and no rack of ribs is considered complete without a pool of it on the plate. There are two distinct styles: the gritty, peppery sauce from legendary Arthur Bryant's Barbecue, and a sweeter, molasses-based sauce made famous by Gates and Sons Bar-B-Q. Both restaurants can trace their roots back to Tennessee native Henry Perry, who transported Memphis-style barbecue to K.C. and started selling it from a street stand in 1908. Arthur Bryant's brother, Charlie (who bought Perry's business when he died in 1940), and Gates and Sons pitmaster, Arthur Pinkard, both worked for Perry.

NOT ARTHUR BRYANT'S BARBECUE SAUCE

Generations of backyard cooks have tried to replicate the signature grit and spice of Arthur Bryant's sauce to no avail. Do dried ground peppers make it gritty? Is pickle juice the secret ingredient? There's no short supply of theories. This version is a fair likeness. I recommend using half-sharp paprika (page 160) because it lends a perfect balance of sweetness and fiery heat to a recipe. This paprika is made from a pepper that has more punch than the red bell peppers used to make sweet paprika.

MAKES ABOUT 4 CUPS

2 cups water

1½ cups white vinegar

1 (8-ounce) can tomato paste

¼ cup lard

¼ cup molasses

2 tablespoons half-sharp paprika

1 tablespoon celery seed, ground

2 teaspoons kosher salt

2 teaspoons garlic powder

2 teaspoons onion powder

1 teaspoon ground cumin

½ teaspoon dry mustard

Combine all of the ingredients in a large saucepan. Bring the sauce to a boil over medium-high heat, stirring frequently. Reduce heat and simmer for 45 minutes, stirring occasionally.

INGREDIENT FINDER: LARD

Yes, *lard*. I can't imagine a student devoted to learning the art of barbecue would be squeamish about using a little pork fat. That's not broccoli juice dripping off those ribs. Lard is stocked in the oil and shortening aisle, and in Mexican markets, it's labeled "manteca" or "manteca de cerdo." You can also use bacon grease if it's been properly stored and refrigerated. If you really want to get gourmet, buy fresh rendered lard from a farmers' market pork vendor or order it from a specialty butcher or meat market and render it yourself. "Leaf lard" is the finest, purest white fat from the kidneys of the pig. It's what pastry chefs use in pie crusts. In the lard quality (and price) hierarchy, "fatback" is the next best, then "caul fat." To render the fat, cube it and place it, skin-side down, in a large, heavy pot. Render in a 200°F oven until most of the fat is liquefied, up to six or seven hours. Tasty bonus: the leftover pieces of crispy, crackling skin.

NOT GATES AND SONS BAR-B-Q SAUCE

In one corner: thin, gritty, and vinegary Arthur Bryant's. In the other corner: this thick and sugary concoction. When the two heavyweights duke it out in a down and dirty fight, there's no question where my money is. Sweet and sticky sauce can cover a multitude of sins, and this is the thick, sugary sauce to trot out if you tank the ribs. It is most definitely not to my taste, but this sauce has big fans, including my brother-in-law, John P., who also puts sugar by the tablespoon on Frosted Flakes.

MAKES ABOUT 4 CUPS

2 cups ketchup

³/₄ cup molasses

1 (8-ounce) can tomato sauce

¹/₃ cup chopped onion

3 tablespoons brown sugar

2 tablespoons Worcestershire sauce

1 lemon, juiced (about 4 tablespoons juice)

1 tablespoon minced garlic

1 tablespoon kosher salt

1 teaspoon freshly ground black pepper

1 teaspoon cayenne pepper

¹/₂ teaspoon celery salt

Combine all of the ingredients in a saucepan and, stirring, bring the mixture to a boil over medium-high heat. Reduce the heat to low and simmer the sauce, uncovered, for 1 hour, stirring frequently.

Store in an airtight container in the refrigerator for up to two weeks.

LOW & SLOW QUIZ: LESSON 3

You are almost there, grasshopper. Two more lessons and you're on the way to barbecue enlightenment. But before you attempt the next cook, you must pass this test. If you get one wrong, repeat Lesson #3.

1. If you buy "enhanced" ribs that have been injected with saltwater and other flavorings, you don't have to brine or baste the racks. True or False?

2. The primary reason for using the rub-spiked tart wash is . . .
a) to ensure the meat does not dry out
b) to reinforce the rub and add a splash of flavor
c) to seal in moisture in the first part of the cook
d) none of the above

3. Why should you coat ribs in a light layer of yellow mustard before the rub?

_____

_____

4. When shopping for ribs, buy racks with "shiners"—ribs covered with a thick, solid layer of surface fat. True or False?

5. If the oven thermometer on the grate reads 300°F, what should you do?
a) Nothing
b) Partially close the bottom vent(s) by one-third.
c) Check and refill the water pan or charcoal as needed.
d) a and c

6. Why is it important to face the thickest, fattiest or largest bone side of the meat toward the hot zone on the cooker?

_____

_____

7. To check a rack of baby back ribs for doneness...
a) cut off a rib and eat it. If you like it, it's done.
b) with a pair of tongs, hold the rack four ribs in. If it flexes and the meat cracks, it's done.
c) a and b
d) a only

8. Why should beginners avoid using sugar in rubs?

_____

_____

Answers: 1) False. You should never buy enhanced ribs. 2) b. 3) Mustard helps the rub stick to the meat. 4) False. Shiners are ribs that have been trimmed too close to the bone, so that the bone shows through the meat. Buy meaty ribs with good marbling, but no large patches of fat. 5) d. Temperature fluctuations happen when the water pan or charcoal is low or the cooker is restocked with fresh, lit charcoal. 6) Because these sections are more resistant to higher temperatures and temperature fluctuations in the cooker. 7) c. 8) Ash blowing around in the cooker will stick to the meat, and sugar will burn if the temperature in the cooker gets too high.

6.

LESSON №4

DEAR STUDENT,

RAISE YOUR RIGHT HAND, REACH IT OVER YOUR LEFT SHOULDER AND GIVE yourself a hearty pat on the back. You've made it to Lesson #4, which means you are clearly made of sturdier stuff than was apparent when you started this program. Because you did complete Lessons #1 through #3, correct? You wouldn't skip ahead to the second most difficult cook in the book because spare ribs are your favorite and you just couldn't resist, would you? You're far too smart to do something so dumb. Besides, the majority of this cook is very similar to Lessons #1 through #3. It requires the same charcoal and wood setup, and you'll use all of the techniques and sharpened barbecue instincts you picked up in the other cooks to make these spare ribs. Without that base of knowledge, well . . . I'd rather not even think about the culinary disaster that awaits you if you skip a Lesson and attempt this cook.

The biggest difference in this cook is that spare ribs are meatier and tougher than any meat you've smoked so far on your cooker. Spare ribs are not as naturally tender as baby back ribs and will require a longer cook—four hours, at a minimum, on the offset and WSM. In some cases, depending on your cooker and such factors as the temperature outside, the wind, and the musculature of the piggy, it could take as long as six hours to complete this cook.

Because this cook is longer than the previous cooks, you will also begin to use the full potential of the fire you build. In Lessons #1 through #3, I noted several times that you would be burning up far more charcoal than was necessary for cooks on the WSM and offset, purely as a way of learning how long your cooker can go before the charcoal needs restocking to maintain the proper temperature. In Lesson #4, you're actually using the right amount of charcoal for the amount of time you'll be cooking. When it's all over, you'll see that the smoker—particularly the WSM—is capable of cooking for extended periods of time without much futzing.

Sadly, this knowledge and futz-free methodology does not apply to kettle users, particularly in the longer cooks. Because the kettle grill is reconfigured for indirect heat and, thus, has less surface area for charcoals and cooking, the charcoal requires constant maintenance. The kettle also cooks hotter and faster. You learned in Lesson # 3 to check the charcoal and water pan every thirty minutes to one hour and restock as needed. This cook is no different—it's just a bigger piece of meat that requires more cooking time. As much as I love the kettle for grilling, the biggest downside to it is that these frequent checks are a must when the grill is set up for for low and slow. I'm willing to bet that if you complete this program, a WSM or offset will be on your very next birthday wish list.

As in the other Lessons, I'm also sharing a handful of my favorite barbecue rubs, sauces and marinades that are excellent on spare ribs, including the aptly-named and highly-acclaimed (by my friends, at least) Gary Wiviott's Rub (page 160)—a blend I've kept secret, until now. Well, okay, I left out a secret ingredient or two. Even a barbecue life coach can't reveal all of his tricks.

You'll also be thrilled to find out I'm finally giving you permission to explore the full meat-cooking potential of your equipment with instructions on how to stuff your smoker (page 000). After you successfully complete Lesson #4, I hereby grant you permission to invite a friend or two over to sample your tasty, perfectly-cooked ribs.

Good luck, and may the pork be with you.

Sincerely,

Gary Wiviott

★ SPARE RIBS ★

Racks of spare ribs are bigger, tougher and fattier than baby back ribs, and the cook will be longer than any of the previous lessons. Because of the increased size, you may have to scrunch or fold the ends of the racks to fit the grate. You will also restock the charcoal and water—at least once on the WSM, and about every hour on the offset and kettle. Otherwise, this cook is like the others. There should be no surprises if you've successfully completed the first three Lessons.

WSM AND OFFSET

SERVES 4 TO 6

2 (4- to 6-pound) racks untrimmed spare ribs

2 cups white vinegar

$\frac{1}{2}$ cup prepared yellow mustard

Junior Rub (next page)

Tart Wash (page 115)

KETTLE

SERVES 2 TO 3

1 (3- to 5-pound) rack untrimmed spare ribs

1 cup white vinegar

$\frac{1}{4}$ cup prepared yellow mustard

Junior Rub (next page)

Tart Wash (page 115)

6 TO 7 HOURS BEFORE DINNER

Set up and start a KISS Method fire according to the instructions for your WSM (page 32), offset (page 34), or kettle (page 36).

While you're waiting for the charcoal in the chimney to engage, rinse the rib racks in the sink under cold water. Splash each rack with about 1 cup of vinegar and lightly rub the vinegar into both sides. Rinse the racks again under cold water. Set the ribs on a rimmed baking sheet and slather both sides with a light coating of yellow mustard, about $\frac{1}{4}$ cup per rack. Sprinkle about 2 tablespoons of rub over each rack, or more to taste.

TRIMMED VS. UNTRIMMED SPARE RIBS

THE INSTRUCTIONS AND TIMING for the spare rib cook are based on untrimmed (tips-on) spare ribs. However, butchers in many stores trim spares "St. Louis–style," with the tips removed. The presentation is neater, and the store can sell the rib tips separately. If you can only find St. Louis spares, keep in mind that the cooking times may decrease slightly, but hardly enough to worry about. Just use your instincts.

⭐
JUNIOR RUB

This easy blend is nearly identical to the Rudimentary Rub (page 115), with one addition: chipotle powder. It infuses the rub with a distinct smokiness and a little bit of heat without being spicy-hot.

MAKES ABOUT ½ CUP

3 tablespoons paprika

2 tablespoons freshly ground black pepper

1½ tablespoons kosher salt

2 teaspoons garlic powder

2 teaspoons onion powder

1 teaspoon chipotle powder or Toasted Mexican Pepper Blend (page 18)

½ teaspoon cayenne pepper

Combine all of the ingredients in a small bowl and whisk until the mixture is thoroughly blended.

After slathering a thin coating of yellow mustard on the ribs, sprinkle each rack with slightly more than 3 tablespoons of rub.

Store in an airtight container for up to two months.

INGREDIENT FINDER: CHIPOTLE POWDER

Chipotles are smoked jalapeños, and the powder is made from toasted and finely ground dried chipotle peppers. This chile is to the new millennium what sun-dried tomatoes were to the nineties. When KFC is serving up chipotle fried chicken, you can pretty much assume it won't be tough to find the powder. You can also make the powder by toasting and grinding dried chipotles, which may be easier to find in some rural locales.

To make chipotle powder, stem and seed one dried chipotle. Tear the chipotle into small pieces. Toast the pieces in a hot skillet until fragrant, about five minutes. Allow the peppers to cool. Grind the toasted pepper in a coffee grinder or food processor until it is pulverized to a fine powder.

WHEN THE LIT CHARCOAL and wood are in place and ready for cooking, lay the racks on the top grate, meat-side down, bone-side up. Place the side of the rack with the angled "tip" section facing the outer edge of the WSM. If the racks are too long for the grate, scrunch them, like an accordion, to fit. Or roll the narrow end of the rack under. Set the lid on the cooker with the top vent facing the back side of the cooker, at about 1 o'clock from the door at 6 o'clock on the center ring.

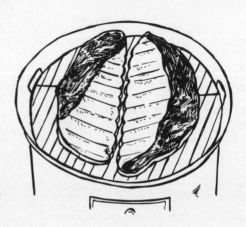

Set the oven thermometer on the grate.

Check the vents. The top vent and the bottom three vents should be completely open.

30 MINUTES INTO THE COOK

Close the two bottom vents on the front side of the cooker by one-third. Remember, the top vent should always remain completely open and sit at about 1 o'clock from the door at 6 o'clock on the center ring. This ensures even airflow throughout the cooker.

2¹/₂ HOURS INTO THE COOK

Remove the lid, check the oven thermometer, and flip the ribs so the racks are meat-side up, bone-side down.

Check the water pan. If it is less than three-quarters full, refill it to within 1 inch of the edge. For pointers, see Refilling the WSM water pan (page 38).

4 HOURS INTO THE COOK

Check the water pan and the oven thermometer. If the pan is less than three-quarters full, refill it.

Spritz each rack with about 2 tablespoons of Tart Wash.

Use the tongs to check the ribs for doneness, holding the ribs one-third of the way into the rack to see if the rack flexes and cracks, as instructed for Lesson #3.

The ribs will not be ready at this point, but doing the flex test here will illustrate the look and feel of the ribs at an early stage, for comparison with the later stages in the cook.

4½ HOURS INTO THE COOK

Check the oven thermometer. Check the ribs for doneness again. Chances are the ribs will not be ready at this point, either. This check provides another reference point to gauge the changing appearance and texture of the ribs.

Spritz the ribs with Tart Wash.

5 HOURS INTO THE COOK

Check the oven thermometer.

Check the ribs. The racks should be approaching the point where the meat around the ribs is starting to crack and break apart when you do the flex test with the tongs.

If one rack is done, leave the other rack on the cooker (for comparison), meat-side up, and spritz with Tart Wash again. Check the water pan. If it is less than three-quarters full, refill it.

If the rack isn't done, check the ribs every 30 minutes until one rack is done, and refill the water pan as needed. It can take up to 6 hours to cook a big, meaty rack of spare ribs. You cannot go by the clock on this cook. You must use your barbecue instincts.

Remove the second rack of ribs 30 minutes after you pull the first rack off of the cooker.

WHEN THE LIT CHARCOAL and wood are in place and ready for cooking, open the lid and place the first rack vertically on the cooking grate, about one-third of the way away from firebox, bone-side up. Face the angled "tip" side of the rack away from the firebox. Repeat with the remaining rack. If the racks are too long for the grate, scrunch them, like an accordion, to fit. Or roll the narrow end of the rack under.

Set the oven thermometer on the grate between the two racks and close the cooker.

Check the vents. The top vent and side firebox vent should be fully open.

30 MINUTES INTO THE COOK

Close the side firebox vent by one-third.

1 HOUR INTO THE COOK

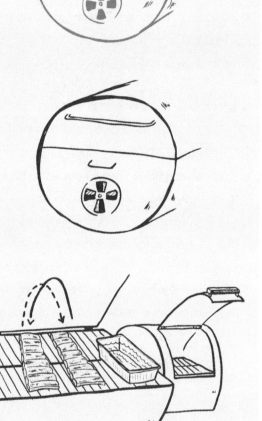

Fill the chimney starter with charcoal and light it. When the charcoal is fully engaged, open the lid of the firebox and pour in the fresh charcoal. Add a split of wood to the charcoal. Keep the firebox open until the charcoal and wood stop billowing smoke (about 10 minutes); then close it.

While you're waiting for the charcoal to engage, open the cooker and check the oven thermometer and the water pan. If it is less than three-quarters full, refill it. Use the tongs to flip the racks, meat-side up, and swap the placement of the ribs on the grate.

Close the cooker.

2 HOURS INTO THE COOK

Fill the chimney starter with charcoal and light it. While the charcoal is engaging, open the cooker and check the oven thermometer. Refill the water pan. Use the tongs to flip the racks, bone-side up, and swap the placement of the ribs on the grate. Close the cooker.

When the charcoal is fully engaged, open the firebox and pour in the fresh charcoal. Add a split of wood to the charcoal. Keep the firebox open until the charcoal and wood stop billowing smoke (about 10minutes), then close it.

2½ HOURS INTO THE COOK

Check the oven thermometer. Check and refill the water pan if it is less than three-quarters full. Use the tongs to flip the racks, meat-side up, and swap the placement of the ribs on the grate.

Spritz the ribs with about 2 tablespoons of Tart Wash.

Close the cooker.

3 HOURS INTO THE COOK

Fill the chimney starter with charcoal and light it. When the charcoal is fully engaged, open the lid of the firebox and pour in the fresh charcoal. Add a split of wood to the charcoal. Keep the firebox open until the charcoal and wood stop billowing smoke (about 10 minutes); then close it.

Open the cooker. Refill the water pan. Use the tongs to flip the racks, bone-side up, and swap the placement of the ribs on the grate.

4 HOURS INTO THE COOK

Check the water pan and charcoal level. Restock as needed.

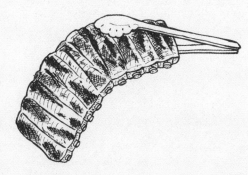

Spritz the racks with Tart Wash.

Use the tongs to check the ribs for doneness, holding the ribs one-third of the way into the rack to see if the rack flexes and cracks, as instructed for Lesson #3.

(continued on next page)

The ribs will not be ready at this point, but doing the flex test here will illustrate the look and feel of the ribs at an early stage, for comparison with the later stages in the cook.

Use the tongs to flip the racks, meat-side up, and swap the placement of the ribs on the grate.

4½ HOURS INTO THE COOK

Check the water pan and charcoal level. Restock as needed.

Check the ribs for doneness again. Chances are, the ribs will not be ready at this point, either. This check provides another reference point to gauge the changing appearance and texture of the ribs.

Spritz the ribs with Tart Wash. Use the tongs to swap the placement of the ribs on the grate. (The racks should stay meat-side up for the remainder of the cook.)

5 HOURS INTO THE COOK

Check the ribs. The racks should be approaching the point where the meat around the ribs is starting to crack and break apart when you do the flex test with the tongs.

If the ribs are not done, leave the racks on the cooker, meat-side up, and spritz with Tart Wash again. Use the tongs to swap the placement of the ribs on the grate.

Check the ribs every 20 to 30 minutes until one rack is done. Restock the charcoal and water pan as needed. If the ribs are done, remove one rack from the cooker. Spritz the other rack with Tart Wash and leave it on the cooker for an additional 30 to 45 minutes for comparison.

It can take anywhere from 4 to 6 hours to cook a big, meaty rack of spare ribs. You cannot go by the clock on this cook. You must use your barbecue instincts.

WHEN THE LIT CHARCOAL and wood are in place and ready for cooking, place the rack of spare ribs on the grate across from the water pan, bone-side up. Place the side of the rack with the angled "tip" section facing the water pan and charcoal. If the rack is too long for the grate, scrunch it, like an accordion, to fit. Or, roll the narrow end of the rack under.

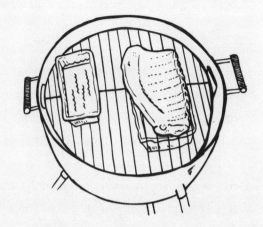

Set the oven thermometer next to the rack on the cooking grate. Close the cooker.

Check the vents. The top and bottom vents should be completely open.

20 MINUTES INTO THE COOK

Close the bottom vent by one-third.

30 MINUTES INTO THE COOK

Check the oven thermometer. Slide the water pan to the side and flip open the grate over the charcoal. Add one wood chunk to the pile of lit charcoal. Flip the rack over, meat-side up, but keep the angled "tip" side facing the fire.

Check the water pan. If it is less than three-quarters full, add more water.

When the wood chunk stops billowing smoke (about 5 minutes), put the lid back on the cooker.

1 HOUR INTO THE COOK

Fill the chimney starter one-third full with charcoal and light it. When the charcoal stops billowing smoke and is ready for the cooker, open the lid, move the water pan, and flip the top grate open with the tongs. Pour in the lit charcoal and use the tongs to maintain the banked pile. Add one wood chunk to the pile. Close the grate. Check and refill the water pan as necessary.

Flip the rack over, bone-side up, with the angled "tip" side facing the fire.

When the charcoal and fresh wood chunk stop billowing smoke (about 5 minutes), put the lid back on the cooker.

1¹/₂ HOURS INTO THE COOK

Check the oven thermometer. Check the water pan and charcoal levels. If the water pan is less than three-quarters full, refill it. If the charcoal is low but still burning red and hot, add five medium pieces of unlit charcoal to the pile. If most of the charcoal has burned through, you may need to restock the pile with a half-chimney of lit charcoal.

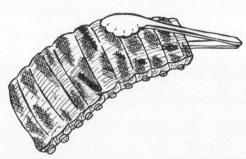

Flip the rack over, meat-side up. If the tip side, which has been facing the fire throughout the cook so far, is beginning to look dry or charred, rotate the rack so the tip faces out, away from the fire. Spritz the ribs with about 2 tablespoons of Tart Wash.

When the fresh charcoal engages and stops billowing smoke (about 5 minutes), close the cooker.

2 HOURS INTO THE COOK

Check the oven thermometer.

Use the tongs to check the ribs for doneness, holding the ribs one-third of the way into the rack to see if the rack flexes and cracks, as instructed for Lesson #3.

A kettle grill cooks hotter and faster than traditional smokers, and the ribs may or may not be done. Checking for doneness at this point also illustrates the look and feel of the ribs at an early stage, for comparison with the later stages in the cook.

Refill the water pan. Spritz the ribs with Tart Wash.

2¹/₂ HOURS INTO THE COOK

Check the ribs. The rack may be approaching the point where the meat around the ribs is starting to crack and break apart when you do the flex test with the tongs. If the ribs aren't done, leave the rack on the cooker, meat-side up, and spritz with Tart Wash again. Check the water pan and charcoal and restock as needed.

Check the ribs every 15 to 20 minutes until the rack is done. Spritz the ribs with Tart Wash and restock the water pan and charcoal as needed.

It can take up to 3 or 4 hours to cook a big, meaty rack of spare ribs on a kettle. You cannot go by the clock on this cook. You must use your barbecue instincts.

READING CHARCOAL AND TEMPERATURE

LOW AND SLOW IS NOT AN EXACT SCIENCE. Using your senses is vital in charcoal cookery because every cook will be slightly different. I can't tell you exactly when your cooker will need restocking or whether you should add lit or unlit charcoal to the pile, because there are too many variables, from the brand and size of the lump charcoal you use to the direction the wind is blowing that day. For some, the thrill of barbecue is in sharpening those instincts so that you can gauge the condition of your fire just by glancing at a pile of lit charcoals or waving your hand over the top vent. If you stick with this program, you will get there.

To hone this skill, start making mental notes about the relationship between the pile of charcoals and the temperature on the oven thermometer whenever you open the cooker to check the water pan or charcoal level. As I've already preached, I'm not obsessive about temperature. The number on the thermometer can waver between 225°F and 275°F throughout a cook. But a combination of the temperature and the condition of the charcoal pile can tell you a lot.

LOW TEMP + LOW, BURNED-UP CHARCOAL: Add a fresh batch of lit charcoal.

LOW TEMP + LOW, RED-HOT CHARCOAL: Add a fresh batch of unlit charcoal.

LOW TEMP + HIGH, PARTIALLY BURNING CHARCOAL: The fire is choking. Check the vents for ash or stray charcoal blocking the openings.

HIGH TEMP + LOW, RED-HOT CHARCOAL: Too much air is circulating over the coals or the water pan is low. Refill the water pan and check the vents to make sure they are closed to the right degree for your cooker.

HIGH TEMP + HIGH, RED-HOT CHARCOAL: The water pan is low, the vents need to be closed by one third, or there's too much charcoal on the pile.

CONTINUING EDUCATION

SPARE RIBS ARE THE BRUISERS OF PORK RIBS—they're the rack you want on your side in a bar fight and the one you don't want to meet in a dark alley. The ribs come from the belly of the pig, a.k.a. bacon country, and are bigger, tougher, and fattier than a rack of baby backs. It's what you serve when the real eaters in your crowd are coming over for dinner.

The meat on a spare rib needs a longer smoke in order to turn the tough connective tissue and layers of internal fat into unctuous, pork perfection. Because the meat spends more time on the cooker and it's laced with fat, these ribs can (and should) be seasoned more aggressively, whether you use a dry or wet rub. Seasonings tend to mellow in low and slow cooks, and you want a flavor that can cut through the rich, fatty meat. Keep this in mind when you're choosing seasonings to make your own rub.

BUYING GUIDE

THINK OUTSIDE THE SUPERMARKET. Independent butchers, retail meat lockers, and food clubs like Sam's Club and Costco tend to have better butchers, better-quality meat, and a better price.

DON'T BUY WHAT YOU CAN'T SEE. With loose slabs of ribs or racks vacuum-sealed in clear plastic, you can inspect the condition and cut of the meat. Bulk boxes of ribs may include odds and ends of trimmings or poor cuts you don't want.

CHECK THE TRIM. Ideally, you want untrimmed spare ribs, but most supermarkets trim the tips and brisket bone and package the racks as St. Louis–style ribs.

AVOID SHINERS. If you can see rib bone "shining" through the meat, it's been over-trimmed and signals poor butchering.

INSPECT THE FAT AND MEAT. You want even white streaks of fat running through the meat. Avoid (or trim) racks with big patches of fat. Don't buy a rack with dark spots or dry edges.

SAY NO TO "ENHANCED" RIBS. These racks are treated with saltwater, flavoring, and other preservatives that can make the ribs too salty.

CHECK THE WEIGHT. "$3\frac{1}{2}$ down" refers to trimmed racks of spare ribs under $3\frac{1}{2}$ pounds—the ideal weight, according to some pitmasters. We're using untrimmed racks, which can weigh up to 6 pounds. Heavier racks can indicate an older animal and tougher meat. One slab serves 3 to 4 people.

RIB-TIONARY

SPARE RIBS: A whole section of ribs cut from the belly, with tips still attached.

RIB TIPS: Belly-side strip of cartilage and meat on spare ribs.

ST. LOUIS-STYLE: Spare ribs with rib tips trimmed off.

KANSAS CITY-STYLE: Spare ribs with rib tips and the "skirt" of flap meat trimmed from the bone side.

TRIM ST. LOUIS STYLE

YOUR FAVORITE CARNIVORES will delight at the sight of big, meaty slabs of untrimmed spare ribs piled high on a cutting board, but sometimes you've got to dish out a classier spread to help convert the shy and picky eaters. Here's how to put a party dress on your pig.

1. Remove the membrane (page 125).

2. Trim off the triangular "points" on both ends of the spare ribs, leaving ½ to 1 inch of meat from the first bone on either side.

3. Cut off the rib tips at the line of fat that runs horizontal to the bones. (Don't throw the rib tips away! Season the tips and throw them on the cooker at the same time as the ribs. Tips are the chef's snack, and the early tasting will let you know if you need to re-season the racks at the end of the cook.)

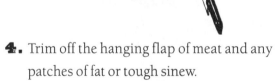

4. Trim off the hanging flap of meat and any patches of fat or tough sinew.

RIB SERVICE

ONCE THE SPARES ARE OFF THE COOKER, you can cut and serve the ribs several ways.

HOLLYWOOD CUT: Cut flush against the inner side of the first bone on both sides of the rack. Skip the second bone and cut flush against the outer side of the third bone. Repeat. You'll end up with several rib bones with meat on both sides, as well as a few ribs stripped of meat. The big, double-meaty, flashy ribs are to serve. The stripped bones and ends are chef's treats.

COMPANY CUT: Cut the racks so that there are three bones per serving; then slice between each rib bone, about three quarters of the way through. The ribs will stay attached, so eaters still get the satisfying, visceral tug of pulling the meat apart.

FINE CHINA CUT: Slice down the middle of the meat between each rib, all the way through. Each rib will be separate and easy to handle—a meaty, yet delicate serving (if such a thing exists in barbecue ribs) for your refined Aunt Hildred to nibble.

HUNGRY MAN CUT: Toss a full rack of ribs on the table before each hungry, snarling fellow. Move quickly, or risk losing a finger. Have a garden hose ready for cleanup.

CURSES! FOILED AGAIN.

THE QUESTION OF WHETHER OR NOT TO wrap ribs in aluminum foil pops up frequently on barbecue forums, so let me address it here and now: foiling is for weenies. Foiling is often associated with the 3-2-1 method: three hours bare on the cooker, two hours wrapped in foil on the cooker, one hour unwrapped. The foil traps in steam and juices, so the ribs are braised and steamed in their own liquid. This cuts the cooking time and the amount of charcoal you use. The foil also "protects" the meat from absorbing too much smoke, and it keeps the exterior of the ribs from getting too dark.

To this, I have four responses. First, you're making barbecue ribs, not braised ribs. By definition, that means cooking with a clean, controlled charcoal and wood fire, and if you follow the tenets of this program, you won't need "cheats" like foil to make tender, perfect ribs. Braised ribs also have a mealy, unappealing texture. Second, in case the title of the book didn't give it away, this is low and slow cookery. Making beautiful barbecue takes time. If you want a shortcut, throw the ribs in the microwave or boil them. Third, are you really worried about the extra $2.50 you might blow in charcoal doing the cook properly? And fourth, you don't have to worry about over-smoking if you use the KISS setup and follow the instructions for the cook—using the right number of wood chunks or splits (not chips) and maintaining a clean, controlled fire.

MORE RUBS AND SAUCES

MOST BARBECUE RUBS AND SAUCES can be used on any type of ribs (or chicken, for that matter), but I tend to turn up the heat or choose stronger flavors when I'm making blends specifically for spare ribs. Big, bold flavors are right at home on meaty spare ribs, and the longer cook and the all-around fatty goodness of the ribs have a mellowing effect on even the most aggressive seasonings on the meat.

GARY WIVIOTT'S RUB

This is my signature rub—the recipe I'm asked for most often and the one I'm most protective of. To be honest, my version never stops evolving. Sometimes I add pequín chile and habañero powder to amp up the heat. I'll add cumin, coriander, and turbinado sugar if I'm making beef ribs. Lemon zest in the mix works well on chicken, and ground sage goes in if I'm making pork. In other words, this is a highly futz-able rub. This recipe yields a big batch of rub, but I think you'll find many other uses for it, including Lesson #5. I throw it into everything, including dips, mayo, and salad dressing. Shameless self-promotion: The rub is also available online through The Spice House. I like to use a blend of my favorite dried, ground Mexican chili peppers. I recommend toasting and grinding whole, dried peppers instead of using the store-bought powder, or you can substitute two tablespoons of the Toasted Mexican Pepper Blend (page 18).

MAKES ABOUT 2½ CUPS

10 tablespoons hot Hungarian or "half sharp" paprika

6 tablespoons garlic powder

6 tablespoons kosher salt

5 tablespoons freshly ground black pepper

3 tablespoons cayenne pepper

3 tablespoons onion powder

2 tablespoons dried oregano

2 tablespoons dried thyme

2 tablespoons chipotle powder

2 tablespoons ancho powder

1 tablespoon guajillo powder

Mix the ingredients in a medium bowl, using a whisk to thoroughly blend.

To apply, sprinkle about 2 tablespoons over each rack of ribs, or more to taste.

Store leftovers in an airtight container for up to two months.

INGREDIENT FINDER: PAPRIKA

Surely, you know my position on grocery store paprika at this point: Buy the best, or don't even bother. For my rub, I strongly recommend going a step further, and seeking out hot or half-sharp Hungarian paprika, available at some gourmet and ethnic markets, as well as The Spice House or Penzey's. This type of paprika, ground from a hotter variety of pepper than sweet paprika, gives the rub extra bite.

★ GARRY HOWARD'S 180 RIB SAUCE

A force in barbecue, talented pitmaster Garry Howard runs The Smoke Ring, a hub of hundreds of barbecue Web sites. He's also a multiple grand champion on the barbecue competition circuit, although I try not to hold that against him. The "180" in the name refers to the perfect score in competition barbecue.

MAKES ABOUT 5 CUPS

1 large onion, chopped (about 1 1/2 cups)

4 garlic cloves, peeled and chopped

1 tablespoon canola oil

2 tablespoons chili powder

1 tablespoon freshly ground black pepper

2 teaspoons ground ginger

1 teaspoon allspice

1/2 teaspoon mace

1 tablespoon paprika

1 (28-ounce) can tomato purée

1 (14-ounce) can whole tomatoes

1 1/2 cups ketchup

1 cup cider vinegar

4 tablespoons Worcestershire sauce

3/4 cup prepared yellow mustard

1/3 cup honey

1/3 cup molasses

1 cup orange juice

1/2 cup turbinado sugar

1/2 cup dark brown sugar

Sauté the onion and garlic in the oil until golden brown and soft. Add all dry spices and stir for about 30 seconds. Add all the remaining ingredients. Simmer on very low heat for 4 hours. The long cooking time is needed to remove the acidity from the tomatoes.

Store in an airtight container in the refrigerator up to 2 weeks.

★ SMOKING SZECHUAN PEPPER RUB

Szechuan pepper is not an actual peppercorn. It is the dried outer pod of a small berry that grows on an ever-green tree in Asia. Although it's not spicy-hot like a habañero pepper, Szechuan pepper has a tongue-numbing effect that enhances the flavor of other herbs and spices it accompanies—in this case, cayenne pepper and black pepper.

MAKES ABOUT 1/2 CUP

3 tablespoons ground Szechuan pepper

2 tablespoons kosher salt

1 tablespoon cayenne pepper

1 tablespoon freshly ground black pepper

Mix the ingredients in a medium bowl, using a whisk to thoroughly blend.

To apply, sprinkle about 2 tablespoons over each rack of ribs, or more to taste.

Store leftovers in an airtight container for up to two months.

THAI CURRY SLATHER

I'd like to say I work hard to make this killer Thai green curry paste—that I use a mortar and pestle to grind exotic ingredients like coriander root, kaffir limes, galangal (an unusual, earthy herb common in Thai cuisine), and the fresh "bird's eye" green Thai chiles that give the paste its trademark color. The truth? The only energy you'll expend on this slather is twisting a can opener. I guarantee anyone who tastes your well-cooked spare ribs schmeared with this paste 1) will love it and 2) will never guess what the subtle, spicy flavor is. A 1 to 1 curry paste to mustard ratio creates a great flavor for the ribs, but if you like more kick, reduce the amount of mustard in the mix.

MAKES ABOUT 1 CUP

1 (4-ounce) can Thai green curry paste
$\frac{1}{4}$ to $\frac{1}{2}$ cup prepared yellow mustard

Stir the curry paste and mustard together in a medium bowl. Follow the instructions for Lesson #4, using the mustard-curry paste in lieu of the mustard and rub steps.

Use $\frac{1}{3}$ cup of slather per rack of ribs.

INGREDIENT FINDER: THAI CURRY PASTE

Any brand of Thai green curry paste will get the job done, but I typically use Maesri—and not just because I like the picture of the Thai Betty Crocker on the can. The lingering, spicy heat is nice, but not overpowering. Thai curry paste is becoming more common in large grocery stores, including Wegmans. Specialty gourmet stores like Whole Foods and Central Market carry at least one brand, and you can also buy cans online at—I kid you not—Amazon.com.

CHINESE SPARERIBS MARINADE

If you're on the fence about experimenting with ethnic flavors in barbecue, this marinade will be your gateway drug. One taste and you'll start stockpiling five-spice powder, hoisin sauce, ginger, and other classic Chinese ingredients. Remember to remove the thin membrane on the ribs (page 137) so that the meat drinks up as much marinade as possible.

WSM AND OFFSET

MAKES 2½ CUPS

1 cup hoisin sauce

¾ cup soy sauce

½ cup dry sherry

10 garlic cloves, peeled and finely chopped

⅓ cup sugar

1 (4-inch) piece fresh ginger, peeled and minced

1 teaspoon five-spice powder

KETTLE

MAKES 1¼ CUPS

½ cup hoisin sauce

⅓ cup soy sauce

¼ cup dry sherry

5 garlic cloves, peeled and finely chopped

2½ tablespoons sugar

1 (2-inch) piece fresh ginger, peeled and minced

½ teaspoon five-spice powder

Combine all of the ingredients in a large bowl or food processor. Whisk or blend until the sugar is dissolved.

Pour the marinade in a shallow glass baking dish big enough to accommodate the racks of ribs. Lay the racks, meat-side down, in the marinade. Cover the dish with plastic wrap and allow the racks to marinate 6 to 8 hours in the refrigerator, flipping the racks three or four times to marinate both sides. Follow the cook instructions for Lesson #4.

★
HOISIN
BARBECUE SAUCE

This is the sauce to whip up when you don't have time to soak the ribs in one of the Asian marinades, or if you want a sauce to go on ribs hit with the Smoking Szechuan Pepper Rub (page 161) or the Five-Spice Rub (page 97). You can slather it on in the final minutes of the cook, or serve it as a side sauce to drizzle on the ribs to taste. One warning: the sauce may taste salty and unbalanced on its own, but it improves greatly once painted on spare ribs. The sauce is excellent on duck, too.

MAKES ABOUT 1 CUP

1 teaspoon canola oil

1 teaspoon Asian sesame oil

2 tablespoons finely minced onion

2 garlic cloves, peeled and finely minced

$1/3$ cup hoisin sauce

2 tablespoons brown sugar

1 tablespoon soy sauce

$1/4$ cup dry sherry

1 tablespoon ketchup

1 tablespoon rice vinegar

1 teaspoon chile-garlic sauce

Heat the canola and sesame oil in a small saucepan and then cook the onion and garlic over medium-low heat until fragrant, about 2 minutes. Add the remaining ingredients and simmer, stirring frequently, until thickened, about 15 minutes. Serve warm. If you find the pieces of minced onion and garlic unappealing, smooth out the sauce with an immersion blender.

Store in an airtight container for up to two days.

INGREDIENT FINDER: CHILE-GARLIC SAUCE

If this chunky, chile-red sauce is unfamiliar to you, slow down the next time you're cruising the grocery aisle with soy sauce and chow mein noodles. Chile-garlic sauce is sold in plastic or glass jars, and the one with the green plastic screw-top—by the same manufacturer as the Sriracha with the rooster on the bottle—is fairly common. You can also substitute Sriracha, a Thai-style hot sauce made with chiles, vinegar, and garlic, or *sambal oelek,* a pure chile sauce.

★
BOURBON-CUE SAUCE

It is possible to make barbecue without having a slosh of bourbon, but four out of five pitmasters do not recommend it. For sipping, I like Old Rip Van Winkle, but don't use the good stuff in this sauce. Old Crow or Evan Williams will do just fine.

MAKES ABOUT 3 CUPS

2 cups ketchup

$1/3$ cup mild molasses

$1/3$ cup bourbon

$1/4$ cup prepared brown mustard

2 tablespoons Louisiana-style or Mexican-style hot sauce, such as Texas Pete, Louisiana, or Búfalo

2 tablespoons Worcestershire sauce

2 teaspoons paprika

1 teaspoon garlic powder

1 teaspoon onion powder

Combine all of the ingredients in a large saucepan. Bring the sauce to a boil over medium heat, stirring occasionally. Reduce the heat to low and simmer, stirring frequently, until the sauce thickens, about 15 minutes.

Store in an airtight container in the refrigerator for up to one week.

★
CITRUS GLAZE AND SAUCE

Oil and vinegar. Laurel and Hardy. Perfect examples of how opposites attract and cause good things to happen, much like rich, fatty spare ribs and this zesty, spicy sauce. Applied in the last few minutes of the cook, it works as a glaze and gives the ribs a glossy finish, striking the perfect balance between sweet and tart. I find pineapple juice sweet enough on its own, so I cut out the brown sugar if I use it in place of OJ.

MAKES ABOUT 2 CUPS

1 tablespoon canola oil

1 medium onion, minced (about 1 cup)

1 tablespoon Toasted Mexican Pepper Blend (page 18)

1 fresh jalapeño, stemmed, seeded, and minced

1 cup orange juice or pineapple juice

4 limes, juiced (about $1/2$ cup juice)

$1/2$ lemon, juiced (about 2 tablespoons juice)

2 tablespoons brown sugar

1 tablespoon chopped cilantro

1 teaspoon kosher salt

Heat the oil in a small saucepan and cook the onion, pepper blend, and jalapeño over medium-low heat until the onion and jalapeño are tender and fragrant, about 5 minutes. Add the remaining ingredients and bring the sauce to a boil, stirring. Reduce heat to low and simmer, uncovered, until thickened, about 10 minutes.

Store in an airtight container for up to two days.

★ COFFEE AND A SMOKE SAUCE

Good coffee, like fine wine, has complex undertones—nutty aromas, caramel flavors, spice, chocolate notes, and more, depending on the bean—and it's a natural match for smoky barbecue. In a tomato-based sauce, coffee adds a dark richness to the flavor. It's not quite bitter, but it has a slight edge.

MAKES ABOUT 4 CUPS

2 tablespoons unsalted butter

1 tablespoon canola oil

1 medium onion, finely chopped (about 1 cup)

3 garlic cloves, peeled

2 tablespoons toasted and freshly ground ancho powder (see Toasted Herbs and Spices, page 18)

1 tablespoon ground cumin

$\frac{1}{2}$ teaspoon ground coriander

$\frac{1}{2}$ teaspoon ground fennel seed

1 teaspoon paprika

$\frac{3}{4}$ cup ketchup

$\frac{1}{2}$ cup dark brown sugar

$1\frac{1}{2}$ cups brewed dark roast coffee

$\frac{1}{2}$ cup cider vinegar

2 tablespoons Worcestershire sauce

Kosher salt and freshly ground black pepper to taste

In a large saucepan, heat the butter and oil over medium heat. When foam subsides, add the onion and garlic and cook, stirring frequently, until soft and translucent, about 8 minutes. Add the ancho powder, cumin, coriander, fennel, and paprika and cook, stirring, until fragrant, about 1 minute. Add the ketchup and brown sugar and cook, stirring, until the sugar is dissolved, about 2 minutes. Stir in the coffee, vinegar, and Worcestershire sauce. Season with salt and pepper. Simmer over medium-low heat until the liquid is reduced by half, about 20 to 30 minutes. Use an immersion blender or transfer sauce to a blender and process until smooth.

Store in an airtight container in the refrigerator for up to one week.

NOSTALGIA IN A BOTTLE

Despite rather strong opinions about making sauces (and marinades and rubs) from scratch, I am not ashamed to say I like Original Open Pit Barbecue Sauce. It's the only bottled sauce that crosses the threshold of my home, partly because I genuinely like the tangy vinegar zip, but also for sentimental reasons. It's the sauce I grew up on. My father would boil some type of animal flesh, drown it in Open Pit, and then burn the living daylights out of it on the grill. It wasn't just caramelized. It was call-the-fire-department blackened. Years later, I learned that Michael Morowitz, a Chicago friend and food enthusiast's grandfather, was one of the three men who created the sauce for their food service company after World War II. Culinary kismet.

BARBECUE CLASSICS: MEMPHIS-STYLE RIBS

IN MEMPHIS, RIBS ARE SERVED UP DRY OR WET. That is, dripping-wet with sauce or dry-crusted with rub.

MEMPHIS DRY RIBS

At Charlie Vergos' Rendezvous restaurant, the so-called birthplace of the Memphis dry rib, layers and layers of dry rub go on the rib racks via a rub-heavy basting liquid similar to the Tart Wash. The wash of seasoned liquid throughout the cook builds a thick, rub-crusted bark.

DRY RIB RUB, MAKES ABOUT 1 CUP

$\frac{1}{2}$ cup Morton kosher salt

$\frac{1}{4}$ cup freshly ground black pepper

1 tablespoon garlic powder

1 tablespoon dried oregano

1 tablespoon celery seed

1 tablespoon paprika

1 tablespoon Toasted Mexican Pepper Blend (page 18)

DRY RIB WASH, MAKES 2 CUPS

1 cup water

1 cup white vinegar

3 tablespoons Dry Rib Rub or rub of choice

To prepare the rub, mix the ingredients in a medium bowl, using a whisk to thoroughly blend.

To prepare the wash, pour the water, vinegar, and rub into a plastic condiment squirt bottle. Vigorously shake the bottle until the salt in the rub dissolves and the seasoning and liquid are blended.

Smear both sides of the rack with $\frac{1}{4}$ cup prepared yellow mustard. Shake 2 tablespoons of Dry Rib Rub over the racks, front and back.

Follow the cook instructions for Lesson #4. Every 30 to 45 minutes during the cook—when you open the cooker to check the water pan or charcoal level or to flip the ribs—spritz the ribs with the Dry Rib Wash. When the ribs are done, remove them from the cooker and baste the meat with more Dry Rib Wash. Shake a final layer, about 1 tablespoon, of Dry Rib Rub over each rack.

MEMPHIS WET RIBS

Neely's Bar-B-Que in Memphis serves one of the most famous examples of the wet rib. The ribs are repeatedly mopped with a sweet tomato-based sauce in the final thirty minutes of the cook, then doused again when the racks are pulled off the cooker. Don't baste earlier in the cook with this sauce; the high dose of sugar in the sauce can burn easily. This is not my personal preference in rib styles, but it certainly is a crowd-pleaser. Add more hot sauce or a pinch of the Toasted Mexican Pepper Blend (page 18) if you want more heat.

MAKES ABOUT 4 CUPS

2 cups ketchup

1 cup water

$^2/_3$ cup cider vinegar

6 tablespoons light brown sugar

6 tablespoons sugar

1 lemon, juiced (about $^1/_4$ cup juice)

1 tablespoon Worcestershire sauce

1 tablespoon freshly ground black pepper

$^1/_2$ tablespoon onion powder

$^1/_2$ tablespoon garlic powder

$^1/_2$ tablespoon dry mustard

$1^1/_2$ teaspoons Louisiana-style Louisiana-style or Mexican-style hot sauce, such as Texas Pete, Louisiana, or Búfalo

Combine all of the ingredients in a large saucepan. Bring the sauce to a rolling boil, stirring frequently. When the sauce comes to a boil, reduce the heat to low. Simmer the sauce, uncovered, for 2 hours, stirring frequently.

Follow the cook instructions for Lesson #4. When checking the ribs for doneness and when checking the charcoal and water pan levels in the last 30 minutes of the cook, paint a thick layer of the sauce on the ribs. Paint on a second layer of sauce in the last 15 minutes, and a third as soon as you pull the ribs off the cooker.

STUFFING YOUR SMOKER

While you're learning the basics in this program and until you really understand how your cooker works, I strongly suggest moderation in the amount of meat you cook. It's partly because I don't want you to open the cooker eight hundred times to rotate the meat. And if the cook is a disaster, you're only losing a couple of chickens or racks of ribs. Also, for practical reasons, if you're using a kettle, there's just not enough space to cook more.

But as you get savvier about barbecue and the ways of your cooker, the fact is, you can stuff it full enough to feed your neighborhood (at least the people you like) by rolling, standing, or stacking the ribs. For all of these techniques, flipping and rotating the racks is of the utmost importance to ensure that all of the slabs are equally exposed to the smoke and heat inside the cooker.

ROLLING

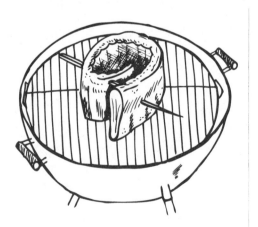

Roll the rack into a very loose "O" shape and use a wooden skewer to secure the roll. Depending on the size and type of ribs you're cooking, you can fit up to ten rolled racks on an offset, five racks per grate on a WSM, and two racks on a kettle. Remember to flip and rotate the rolled racks every twenty minutes on a kettle or every thirty to forty-five minutes on a WSM or offset.

STANDING

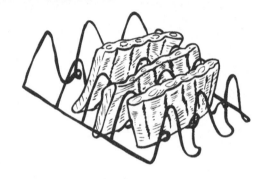

With a rib rack (or an inverted roasting rack), you can fit as many slabs on each cooking grate as the rack allows, usually three to five slabs per rib rack. Flip and rotate the racks every twenty minutes on a kettle or every thirty to forty-five minutes on a WSM or offset.

STACKING

Flipping and rotating is the key with this technique—every thirty to sixty minutes, depending on the cooker—to equalize the amount of time the racks are exposed to smoke and the cooker's "hot zone." This method adds time to the cook because you're opening the cooker more often and because each rack should go through the flip/rotate cycle twice.

WSM: Stack five racks per grate, with three racks on the bottom and two racks laid cross-hatch on top. The larger chine bone of each rack should be facing the edge of the grate, where heat flows up sides of the cooker. Flip, reposition, and rotate the racks between the top and bottom grate every hour. The two cooking grates are not interchangeable, and you will have to remove the ribs on the bottom grate before you switch them with racks from the top grate. Ribs on the bottom grate will cook more slowly. When the ribs on the top grate are done, move the ribs on the bottom grate up, and give them a final fifteen or twenty minutes to finish.

OFFSET: Lay as many racks as will fit on the grate vertically without touching to make a bottom layer. Face the larger chine bone of each rack toward the firebox, the hottest zone on the offset. Then crosshatch racks horizontally to make a top layer. Flip and rotate the racks every forty-five minutes, always keeping the side of the rack with the larger chine bone facing the firebox.

KETTLE: Overlap two or three racks on the grate across from the water pan, with the larger chine bone of each rack facing the water pan and bank of charcoal—the hottest zone on a kettle. Flip and rotate the racks every thirty minutes.

A CAUTION ON ROLLING, STANDING OR STACKING

The only issue with stuffing a smoker is that any part of the meat that overlaps and touches another part will not brown or crust or absorb as much smoke. The meat will have a grayish cast in those spots. This doesn't affect the flavor at all, but it's not as appealing to the eye.

Although I caution against drowning good barbecue in sauce, this is the perfect time to use something like Danny's Glaze (page 138) or a sauce to make ribs more visually appealing. A glaze, which contains more sugar than a sauce, should be applied as soon as the ribs come off the cooker. If you're using a sauce with less sugar, it's okay to paint the ribs at three intervals: thirty minutes before the rack is done, then fifteen minutes later, and then immediately after you take the ribs off the cooker. Whether you layer a sauce on or give the meat one shellacking with a glaze, this masks the grayish spots and give the ribs a photo-worthy gloss.

LOW & SLOW QUIZ: LESSON 4

Answer all of these questions correctly, and I give you my blessings to move forward and conquer Lesson #5: Pulled Pork. Flub just one question, and it's in your best interest to redo Lesson #4. But don't look at it as punishment or failure. Spare ribs are a delicious price to pay for the wisdom you need to cook a solid pork butt.

1. Approximately how often do you need to restock the charcoal in your cooker?

_____

_____

2. When restocking, it is acceptable to add fresh, unlit charcoal to the pile when at least half of the charcoal is lit and glowing bright. True or False?

3. The trick to stuffing your cooker with more meat (once you master each Lesson, of course) is flipping and rotating the racks every _____ in order to _____.

4. St. Louis-style ribs are . . .
   a) whole racks of spare ribs
   b) spare ribs with the tips removed
   c) spare ribs with tips, membrane and skirt removed
   d) none of the above

5. Wrapping the ribs in aluminum foil for half of the cook makes barbecue fall-off-the-bone-tender. True or False?

6. If the temperature on the oven thermometer in the cooker is low, and the pile of charcoal is high and only partially burning . . .
   a) the fire is choking from lack of oxygen
   b) check to see if charcoal or ash is blocking the bottom vent(s)
   c) add a fresh batch of lit charcoal
   d) be sure the top vent is fully open and the bottom vents are open to the right degree

7. Rubs made for spare ribs and other thick, fatty meats should be stronger and more aggressive because . . .

_____

_____

8. "3½ down" refers to . . .
   a) the temperature check taken at the midpoint of a spare rib cook
   b) a full rack of spare ribs that has been cut in half
   c) the weight, in pounds, of an untrimmed rack of spare ribs
   d) 3½ pounds or less, the ideal weight of a fully trimmed rack of spare ribs

Answers: 1) WSM, 4 to 5 hours; offset, about every hour; kettle, every 45 to 60 minutes. 2) True. If the charcoal is mostly burned through, restock with a full chimney starter (or half-full, if you're using a kettle) of lit charcoal. 3) 20 to 45 minutes, depending on the cooker; ensure that all sides of the meat are equally exposed to the smoke and heat inside the cooker. 4) c. 5) True, but don't call it barbecue. Foiling traps moisture and steams the ribs, which turns ribs into meat Jell-O. If you get the urge to foil ribs, reread chapters 1 through 6, very slowly and out loud. 6) Trick question! a, b, and d are correct. 7) The longer the cook, the more the flavor of a seasoning mellows. 8) d.

7.

LESSON Nº5

PULLED PORK

DEAR STUDENT,

YOU STAND AT THE THRESHOLD OF BARBECUE GREATNESS. WHEN YOU COMPLETE this cook, you will possess the skills and instincts required to truly master the art of barbecue. Your prowess and commitment to the program have impressed even me.

Now you will embark upon the most challenging lesson you have yet faced: an all-day, meaty pork shoulder cook. This is the true test of the skills you've learned up to this point. It will require time, patience, and barbecue intuition as you've never used it before. And it will be labor-intensive. The pork shoulder needs to be flipped and rotated throughout the cook, and there are several charcoal and water pan restocks, depending on the cooker you're using. As the most efficient cooker of the bunch, the WSM will require the least amount of futzing. The offset requires restocking about every hour. And if you're using a kettle, brace yourself to fiddle with it, in some way, about every forty-five minutes to an hour.

At first glance, you'll notice that the cook instructions are very specific and repetitive, with exact times for restocks and temperature checks. Despite the engineered, linear construction of the cook, this lesson is—more than anything—about learning to ignore rigid instructions and relying on your barbecue instincts. In the first few lessons, the inflexibility of my directions was intended to help you develop those senses and gradually become less dependent on recipes and exact temperatures and times. Now is the opportunity to test your barbecue instincts. While I was unbending and adamant about following directions before, you are now allowed to use your knowledge and get interactive.

With this cook, you should fully realize that barbecue is three things: delicious, highly variable, and delicious. Your ability to handle the challenges of the cook is directly related to how tasty the barbecue will be.

Be one with the pork.

Sincerely,

Gary Wiviott

★ PULLED PORK ★

Aside from the basic, essential details I insist on—the weight of the pork butt, the timing of the vent closures, and the broad six- to twelve-hour cooking span—you should be using your five senses to determine what needs to happen throughout the cook. If you're paying attention, the meat or the fire will tell you exactly what it needs and when it needs it. You may decide at one checkpoint or another that the charcoal doesn't need to be restocked or that adding a few pieces of unlit charcoal is sufficient to maintain the fire. You might sense that the cooker is too hot or that the water pan is running low before a prescribed check. You should have all of the wisdom and troubleshooting instincts you need to assess and deal with these issues without my telling you what to look for or what to do.

WSM AND OFFSET

SERVES 20 TO 25

2 (7- to 9-pound) pork butts
   (See Buying Guide, page 188)

2 cups white vinegar

1 cup yellow prepared mustard

Graduate Rub (page 176)

Tart Wash (page 115)

KETTLE

SERVES 8 TO 10

1 (4- to 6-pound) pork butt
   (See Buying Guide, page 188)

1 cup white vinegar

½ cup yellow prepared mustard

Graduate Rub (page 176)

Tart Wash (page 115)

9 TO 10 HOURS BEFORE DINNER

Start a KISS Method fire according to the instructions for your WSM (page 32), offset (page 34), or kettle (page 36).

While you're waiting for the charcoal in the chimney to engage, rinse the pork shoulder(s) with cold water. Pour about 1 cup of vinegar over each shoulder, and lightly rub the vinegar into all sides. Rinse the shoulder(s) again under cold water. Slather each shoulder with a light coating of mustard, about ½ cup per butt. Smear a heavy coat of rub, about ¼ to ½ cup, over all sides of each piece of meat.

GRADUATE RUB

Making this rub should be a walk in the park at this point. In fact, if you made a big batch of the Junior Rub (page 147) and you have about one cup left over, just add one teaspoon of dried oregano to the blend, and you're done. Or if you have one cup of Rudimentary Rub (page 115), add one teaspoon of chipotle powder and one teaspoon of oregano. And to prove I'm not a barbecue tyrant, I won't even insist that you use this rub for the final lesson. You can also substitute the multipurpose Gary Wiviott's Rub (page 160).

Because the flavor of a rub mellows over time, you need to use a quarter cup to a half cup of rub to thoroughly coat each shoulder. Using enough rub also ensures that, once the meat is cooked and pulled and you mix in Mr. Brown and Mrs. White (page 187), each bite will be a balanced, three-part harmony of crispy, spicy, bark, and tender, delicious pork.

WSM AND OFFSET

MAKES ABOUT 1 CUP

6 tablespoons paprika

4 tablespoons freshly ground black pepper

3 tablespoons Morton kosher salt

4 teaspoons garlic powder

4 teaspoons onion powder

2 teaspoons chipotle powder or Toasted Mexican Pepper Blend (page 18)

2 teaspoons dried oregano

1 teaspoon cayenne pepper

KETTLE

MAKES ABOUT ½ CUP

3 tablespoons paprika

2 tablespoons freshly ground black pepper

1½ tablespoons Morton kosher salt

2 teaspoons garlic powder

2 teaspoons onion powder

1 teaspoon chipotle powder or Toasted Mexican Pepper Blend (page 18)

1 teaspoon dried oregano

½ teaspoon cayenne pepper

Combine all of the ingredients in a small bowl and whisk until the mixture is thoroughly blended.

Store in an airtight container for up to two months.

FLIPPING AND ROTATING
★ HOT PORK SHOULDERS ★

IN THE PREVIOUS LESSONS, flipping and rotating the meat was essential to ensure that all sides of the meat were equally exposed to the hottest zone in the cooker. This lesson is no different, except for the fact that you're handling up to nine pounds of solid, hot, fatty meat. When the instructions say "flip," turn the meat vertically so the top side of the shoulder is flipped to the bottom side. To "rotate" the four-sided shoulder, spin the side facing the hot zone ninety degrees horizontally, so a new side faces the hottest area on the grate.

After years of juggling hot pork shoulders between grates, I can make this switch quickly and easily with a few paper towels in hand. Until you're more experienced, wear insulated gloves and use an extra-wide, heavy-duty grill spatula and a pair of tongs to flip and rotate the meat.

WHEN THE FIRE IS FULLY ENGAGED and the cooker is reassembled, place both pork butts fat-side up on the top grate, positioning them as close to the center of the grate as possible without touching.

Set the oven thermometer in the center of the grate, between the pork shoulders.

The vents should be open.

30 MINUTES INTO THE COOK

Partially close all three bottom vents by one-third. (As always, keep the top vent completely open.)

2 HOURS INTO THE COOK

Check the oven thermometer. Refill the water pan.

4 HOURS INTO THE COOK

Check the oven thermometer. Refill the water pan.

Flip the meat fat-side down and rotate the shoulder 90 degrees so that a new side is facing the outer edge of the grate. (See Flipping and Rotating Hot Pork Shoulders, page 177.)

5 HOURS INTO THE COOK

Light a chimney starter full of charcoal. Check the oven thermometer.

When the charcoal is fully engaged, after about 10 minutes, put on a pair of heavy-duty oven mitts or work gloves. Grip the side of the center ring and carefully remove it (with the lid on) and set it on even ground. Take extreme caution and move slowly to avoid sloshing the water pan over the charcoals or on your feet. (For detailed instructions, see Restocking the WSM charcoal chamber, page 39.)

Redistribute the hot coals in the ring with tongs. Pour in fresh, unlit charcoal until the ring is three-quarters full, or the charcoal level is about one full inch below the top edge of the ring. Lay two chunks of debarked wood on top of the unlit charcoal.

Pour the lit charcoal in the chimney starter over the charcoal and wood in the ring.

Check the area around the outside of the ring to make sure there are no stray pieces of charcoal blocking the vents. Use the tongs to pick up any strays and return them to the charcoal ring.

When the charcoal stops billowing white smoke, about 10 minutes, add two more chunks of wood to the pile. Carefully reassemble the cooker, returning the center ring (with lid) to the charcoal bowl. Refill the water pan (page 38). Spritz the meat with Tart Wash. Flip the meat fat-side up and rotate the shoulders 90 degrees so that a new side is facing the outer edge of the grate.

7½ HOURS INTO THE COOK

Check the oven thermometer. Refill the water pan. Open one bottom vent.

Poke the meat with your finger. At this point, the meat should be starting to "yield," which is a fancy way of saying that it's not as firm. Stick an instant-read thermometer into a meaty—not fatty—section of the shoulder to gauge how things are going. Remember: temperature is only one indication of doneness. The temperature will probably be in the range of 160°F to 170°F. The internal temperature of a pork shoulder plateaus during the cook (see page 185) and can hover at this temperature for hours. Be patient, and know that this check is more for educational purposes. Observe, don't act.

Spritz the meat with Tart Wash. Check the water pan and refill as needed.

8½ TO 9 HOURS INTO THE COOK

Poke the meat and check the temperature again to see if it is done. (See The Wabba Wabba, page 186.)

Pork shoulders in the 7- to 9-pound range can take anywhere from 8 to 12 hours to cook. If you are beginning to think the meat might be done, it's not done yet and could easily use another hour or more.

After this check-in, give the pork shoulder a look and a poke every 20 minutes to check for doneness. Spritz the meat with Tart Wash and refill the water pan as needed. When the smaller of the two pork butts is truly, indisputably done, take that shoulder off. Leave the other shoulder on the cooker for an additional 45 minutes to 1 hour to compare the different stages of doneness.

Let the meat rest for 15 to 20 minutes before handling. The meat "pulls" most easily when warm.

WHEN THE FIRE IS FULLY ENGAGED and the cooker is ready, open the lid and place both pork shoulders fat-side up on the grate, about one-third of the way down the grate from the opening to the firebox.

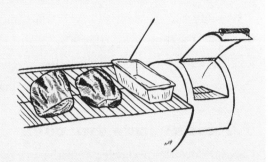

Set the oven thermometer in the middle of the grate, between the pork shoulders.

The vents should be open.

30 MINUTES INTO THE COOK

Close the firebox vent by one-half.
Open the firebox and add one split of wood to the pile of charcoal.

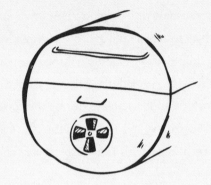

When the wood is fully engaged and stops billowing smoke, about 5 minutes, close the firebox.

1 HOUR INTO THE COOK

Open the cooker and check the oven thermometer and the water pan. If the water pan is less than three-quarters full, refill it.

Flip and rotate the meat so that it is fat-side down and the shoulder closest to the firebox shifts to the position away from the firebox. Close the cooker.

Open the firebox and check the charcoal pile. Are most of the coals burned down? If so, you may need to light a full chimney of charcoal to pour onto the pile. (For detailed instructions, see Restocking the offset firebox, page 40.) If the pile is high with lit, glowing-hot charcoal, you may need only to pour one chimney of unlit charcoal on the pile to maintain the fire. Use your barbecue judgment.

Add one split of wood to the charcoal. Close the firebox when the charcoal and wood stop billowing smoke, about 5 minutes.

EVERY HOUR IN THE COOK

Open the cooker and check the oven thermometer. Refill the water pan as needed.

Flip the meat, alternating fat-side up or down, and rotate the meat so that the shoulder closest to the firebox shifts away from the firebox. Close the cooker.

Restock the firebox with lit or unlit charcoal, as needed. Add one split of wood to the charcoal at every restock up to the 5-hour mark. Close the firebox when the charcoal and wood stop billowing smoke, about 5 minutes.

7 HOURS INTO THE COOK

Check the oven thermometer and refill the water pan.

Spritz the meat with Tart Wash.

Poke the meat with your finger. At this point, the meat should be starting to "yield," which is a fancy way of saying that it's not as firm. Stick an instant-read thermometer into a meaty—not fatty—section of the shoulder to gauge how things are going. Remember: temperature is only one indication of doneness. The temperature will probably be in the range of 160°F to 170°F. The internal temperature of a pork butt plateaus during the cook (see page 185), and can hover at this temperature for hours. Be patient, and know that this check is more for educational purposes. Observe, don't act.

Restock the firebox with lit or unlit charcoal, as needed. Close the firebox when the charcoal and wood stop billowing smoke, about 5 minutes.

8 HOURS INTO THE COOK

Restock the charcoal as needed and refill the water pan.

Poke the meat and check the temperature again to see if it is done. (See The Wabba Wabba, page 186.) Pork shoulders in the 7- to 9-pound range can take anywhere from 8 to 12 hours to cook. If you are just beginning to think the meat might be done, it's not done yet and could easily use another hour or more.

After this check-in, give the pork shoulder a look and a poke every 30 minutes to check for doneness and spritz the meat with Tart Wash. Keep an eye on the charcoal and water pan levels, and restock or refill as needed.

When the smaller of the two pork butts is truly, indisputably done, take that shoulder off. Leave the other one on the cooker for an additional 45 minutes to 1 hour to compare the different stages of doneness.

Let the meat rest for 15 to 20 minutes before handling. The meat "pulls" most easily when warm.

WHEN THE LIT CHARCOAL AND WOOD

are in place and ready for cooking, place the pork shoulder fat-side up on the grate across from the water pan. It should be close to the outer edge of the grate without touching the lid.

Set the oven thermometer next to the meat on the cooking grate. Close the cooker.

Check the vents. The top and bottom vents should be completely open.

20 MINUTES INTO THE COOK

Close the bottom vent by one-half.

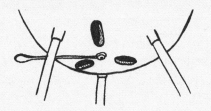

45 MINUTES INTO THE COOK

Open the cooker and check the oven thermometer.

Use the tongs to slide the water pan to the side and flip open the grate. Check the charcoal. Are most of the coals burned down? If so, light a half chimney of charcoal to pour onto the pile. (For detailed instructions, see Restocking the kettle two-zone fire, page 41.) If the pile is high with lit, glowing-hot charcoal, you may need only to pour a handful or one-half chimney of unlit charcoal on the pile to maintain the fire. Use your barbecue judgment.

Add two wood chunks, and use the tongs to maintain the banked pile of charcoal.

Close the grate and slide the water pan back into place with the tongs.

Check the water pan. If it is less than three-quarters full, refill it. (For detailed instructions, see Refilling the kettle water pan, page 41.)

Flip and rotate the meat so that it is fat-side down and the side of the shoulder facing the fire is shifted away.

After you restock, wait until the billowing smoke from the wood and charcoal dies down, about 5 minutes, before closing the cooker.

EVERY 45 MINUTES TO 1 HOUR IN THE COOK

Check the oven thermometer.

Assess the charcoal pile. Restock the charcoal as needed, add two wood chunks, and refill the water pan.

Flip the meat, alternating fat-side up or down, and rotate the meat so that the side facing the fire is shifted away from the fire. After you restock, wait until the billowing smoke from the wood and charcoal dies down, about 5 minutes, before closing the cooker.

5 HOURS INTO THE COOK

Check the oven thermometer.

Poke the meat with your finger. At this point, the meat should be starting to "yield," which is a fancy way of saying that it's not as firm. Stick an instant-read thermometer into a meaty—not fatty—section of the shoulder to gauge how things are going. Remember: temperature is only one indication of doneness. The temperature will probably be in the range of 160°F to 170°F. The internal temperature of a pork butt plateaus during the cook (see page 185), and can hover at this temperature for hours. Be patient, and know that this check is more for educational purposes. Observe, don't act.

Restock the charcoal as needed and refill the water pan.

Flip and rotate the meat. Spritz with tart wash.

After you restock, wait until the billowing smoke from the wood and charcoal dies down, about 5 minutes, before closing the cooker.

6 HOURS INTO THE COOK

Check the oven thermometer.

Restock the charcoal as needed and refill the water pan.

Flip and rotate the meat.

Spritz the meat with Tart Wash

Poke the meat and check the temperature again to see if it is done. (See The Wabba Wabba, page 186.)

Pork shoulders in the 4- to 6-pound range can take anywhere from 6 to 9 hours to cook. If you are just beginning to think the meat might be done, it's not done yet and could easily use another half hour or more.

After this check-in, give the pork shoulder a look and a poke every 20 minutes to check for doneness and spritz the meat with Tart Wash. Keep an eye on the charcoal and water pan levels, and restock or refill as needed.

Let the meat rest for 15 to 20 minutes before handling. The meat "pulls" most easily when warm.

DEAR STUDENT,

DID YOU NOTICE HOW THE DIRECTIONS INSTRUCT YOU TO CHECK THE TEMPERATURE on the oven thermometer, but neglect to explain what you're checking for? I don't want to worry you with an exact temperature or temperature range at these checkpoints. I'm afraid that if the temperature on your oven thermometer doesn't jive with that "ideal" temperature so many books and barbecue experts tout, it might incite some kind of panic or overreaction on your part, and you'll end up botching the cook or second-guessing what your instincts are telling you.

This is my last chance to drill it into your skull that the grate temperature is not the most important factor in barbecue. The most important element is a clean-burning fire. The grate temperature is simply a piece of information that tells you what's going on in your cooker—a way to gauge how your clean-burning fire is doing. There is no reason to panic if the grate temperature is slightly above or below the 250°F to 275°F low and slow range. The temperature will fluctuate throughout the cook. It dips when you open the lid. It spikes when you add fresh charcoal or wood. It drops when the coals are burning low. It increases when the water pan is low. But you know all of this intuitively now. If the temperature is too high or low (well above 300°F or below 225°F), trust your instincts and respond accordingly. (See Reading Charcoal and Temperature, page 155).

Cordially yours,

Gary Wiviott

P.S. Please don't confuse "grate temperature" and "internal temperature." The oven thermometer gives you the ambient temperature of your cooker. The instant-read thermometer gives you the internal temperature of the meat.

★ WHEN MEAT "PLATEAUS" ★

MEAT BEGINS TO SHRINK AND BREAK DOWN as soon as it hits the grate. When the meat's internal temperature hits the 160°F to 170°F range, the streaks of fat and connective tissue inside the meat begin to liquefy and run out, which has a cooling effect on the meat. At this point the meat enters a sort of limbo: the temperature can stall in this range for several hours while the connective tissue continues to break down.

When the cell structure in the meat has shrunk as much as possible and most of the fat has been rendered, the internal temperature of the meat will start to rise again. At some point in the last hours of the cook, when you check the internal temperature of the meat, you will notice the temperature slowly increasing. It will break away from the plateau and start creeping past 175°F. This is your cue to start checking the meat for doneness every twenty to thirty minutes. (See The Wabba Wabba, page 186.)

THE WABBA WABBA, OR WHAT BUTTS DO WHEN THEY'RE DONE

IN BARBECUE, IT'S CALLED THE "WABBA wabba"—the point when the tough connective tissue, fat, and meat in a pork shoulder finally surrenders. It wabbas. The pork slumps under its own weight, and the meat looks as if it is pulling itself apart, particularly in the area around the blade bone. There are various general indicators of doneness, but the shoulder is only truly done when you observe all three of these signs in the meat.

EASY PIERCING Insert a meat fork into the shoulder. Does the fork glide easily into the meat?

PULLING AWAY Check the blade bone. Is the meat pulling away from the bone? Is the bone loose when you wiggle it with a pair of tongs?

RIGHT TEMPERATURE Poke an instant-read thermometer into a meaty (not fatty) section of the shoulder. Is the temperature 197°F to 200°F?

If you can say "yes" unequivocally to all three questions, the pork is done.

POINTERS FOR SERVING PORK SHOULDER

CHOPPED BARBECUE HAS A SOFTER TEXture. It's the typical method of serving whole hog barbecue because chopping allows mixing in of pieces of skin and different parts of the pig. Since you're only cooking a shoulder, chopping is a matter of personal preference.

PULL THE MEAT WHEN IT IS STILL WARM. If the meat is allowed to cool completely, the fat in the meat hardens and you lose the fall-apart-tender pull-ability. Use two forks to pull the meat apart in threads.

SLICE IT when practicality and personal safety dictate pulling the meat off the cooker before the wabba wabba happens. Or when the meat just isn't giving it up after ten hours. If you've got hungry, angry guests who are going cannibal on you, slice the meat like you would any roast. You should also slice it if you're starting from a cold, cooked shoulder.

MIX MRS. WHITE (see opposite page)—the pockets of rendered fat—with the rest of the meat. You can also save a hunk of her to throw in any barbecue sauce.

CONTINUING EDUCATION

PORK SHOULDER IS ONE OF THE MEATIEST, TOUGHEST, AND FATTIEST cuts on a pig, which is what makes it ideal for low and slow cookery. Under the proper care, this burly piece of meat turns into fall-apart-tender pork, and can change even the most effete eater into a slobbering carnivore.

Pork shoulder goes by a few aliases, including Boston butt, pork butt, and pork shoulder roast. There are two sections to a pork shoulder: the top portion, called the "butt," and the "picnic ham" or "picnic roast" from the bottom, leg section of the shoulder. Skilled barbecue cooks might do a whole shoulder, but for this lesson, use the butt section only. The instructions are specific to the top portion of the shoulder, and the cook would go differently for the tougher and less forgiving picnic portion.

★ MEET MR. BROWN AND MRS. WHITE ★

PLEASE REFER TO THE CRUSTY, caramelized bark on a pork shoulder as Mr. Brown. The fatty bit that runs through the meat is Mrs. White. Both are so delicious, you have to be formal. No doubt many fistfights have started over these coveted pieces, and they deserve the utmost respect.

BUYING GUIDE

BEFRIEND A BUTCHER. Meat counter staff can help you pick the right piece of meat if you have good rapport.

AIM FOR UNIFORMITY. For the WSM or off-set cooks, the butts don't have to be exactly seven pounds, but try to get two shoulders of approximately the same weight.

FAT IS GOOD. Look for cuts with a good, solid surface fat cap and even marbling throughout.

SHAKE (YES, SHAKE) THE MEAT. Fat hardens when it's cold, so at refrigerator temperature, the shoulder should be firm. This indicates good marbling. It should not be floppy—a sign that it's too lean.

CHECK THE BLADE BONE. Ideally, it should be smack in the middle of the roast. A well-centered bone will help conduct heat more evenly through the meat.

RUBS AND WASHES

AFTER EIGHT TO TWELVE HOURS ON a cooker, the herbs and spices in a rub mellow and lose some bite. For a more assertive flavor, rubs built for a long low and slow cook should be considerably more aggressive than rubs you use for quick grilling. A wash or mop—like the Tart Wash (page 115)—spiked with your rub of choice is another way to layer flavors and reinforce the punch of the rub at the end of the cook.

A warning on "mops": most people use them incorrectly and with the wrong intentions. A mop should not be applied throughout the cook, and it does not make pork shoulder or other barbecued meat juicy. It is physiologically impossible for a thin coat of liquid—no matter how tasty it is—to penetrate an eight-pound hunk of meat. Opening the cooker 703 times to douse the meat is also a good way to guarantee a longer cook and, possibly, a plate full of mediocre barbecue.

To minimize temperature fluctuations in the cooker and maximize the flavor in the rub, the seasoned liquid should be used only in the last half hour of the cook and only when you are already opening the lid of the cooker to check for doneness or the level in the water pan.

★ ROSEMARY-SAGE RUB

The combination of rosemary and sage can be overpowering, but this strong blend turns sublime when rubbed on a pork butt and cooked low and slow for hours. It's very different from the paprika and pepper rubs common in barbecue—and that's the point. Backed by the Rosemary-Sage Wash, this is the rub you go to when you want to fancy-up pulled pork or other barbecued pork to serve to barbecue dilettantes.

MAKES ABOUT $^{3}/_{4}$ **CUP**

3 tablespoons crumbled dried rosemary

$1^{1}/_{2}$ tablespoons crumbled dried sage
    or $^{1}/_{2}$ tablespoon ground sage

3 tablespoons Morton kosher salt

3 tablespoons cracked black peppercorns

$1^{1}/_{2}$ teaspoons garlic powder

$1^{1}/_{2}$ teaspoons onion powder

Combine all of the ingredients in a small bowl and whisk until the mixture is thoroughly blended.

Sprinkle each pork shoulder with about $^{1}/_{4}$ cup of rub, reserving 2 tablespoons to use in the Rosemary-Sage Wash.

TIP: Cracking peppercorns is a good way to get a bold, aggressive pepper flavor in a rub. To crack, place the peppercorns in a zip-top bag and lightly crush with a rolling pin or the flat side of a cleaver. Peppercorns can also be cracked using a mortar and pestle.

★ ROSEMARY-SAGE WASH

Apple, rosemary, and sage are classic flavor matches for pork, and this wash brings them all together in perfect harmony. The contrast of the savory and herbal seasonings with the sweetness of the apple juice creates an incredible bark on a pork shoulder layered with the Rosemary-Sage Rub.

MAKES 1 CUP

$^{3}/_{4}$ cup apple juice

$^{1}/_{4}$ cup vegetable oil

2 tablespoons Rosemary-Sage Rub

Pour the juice, oil and rub into a plastic condiment squirt bottle. Shake vigorously until the rub is dissolved and the mixture is blended, like vinaigrette, about 1 minute.

Store in the refrigerator for up to two weeks. The oil in the wash will thicken when it is cold. Allow the wash to reach room temperature before using, and shake vigorously to re-blend.

To use, spritz a light coat of the wash—enough to moisten, but not soak—over pork shoulder or ribs when you check for doneness during the last 30 minutes of the cook.

★
SOUTHWEST RUB

Cumin is a familiar flavor in Southwest cuisine. Paired with the distinct, smoky and spicy Mexican pepper blend, this rub holds up very well over a long, slow pork shoulder cook.

MAKES ABOUT ³/₄ CUP

¹/₄ cup kosher salt

¹/₄ cup Toasted Mexican Pepper Blend (page 18)

2 tablespoons cracked black peppercorns
  (see tip, page 189)

1 tablespoon Mexican oregano

1 teaspoon cumin

¹/₂ teaspoon dry mustard

Combine all of the ingredients in a small bowl and whisk until the mixture is thoroughly blended.

Store in an airtight container for up to two months.

★
SOUTHWEST WASH

Cumin and I have something in common: an affinity for beer. The big, bold spice is a natural companion for the strong chile pepper blend, too. Blended with beer and oil, the rub makes a fine wash for ribs or pork shoulder.

MAKES 1¹/₄ CUPS

8 ounces (1 cup) beer

¹/₄ cup vegetable oil

2 tablespoons Southwest Rub

Pour the beer, oil, and rub into a plastic condiment squirt bottle. Shake vigorously until the rub is dissolved and the mixture is blended, like a vinaigrette, about 1 minute.

Store in the refrigerator for up to two weeks. The oil in the wash will thicken when it is cold. Allow the wash to reach room temperature before using, and shake vigorously to re-blend.

To use, spritz a light coat of the wash—enough to moisten, but not soak—over pork shoulder or ribs when you check for doneness during the last 30 minutes of the cook.

★
HERBES DE
PROVENCE RUB

French cuisine and wine are not the first things that come to mind with low and slow cookery, but the classic blend of herbes de Provence is a good match for pork. Lavender enhanced by a chorus of aromatic herbs creates a subtle flavor—at least by barbecue standards—but coriander gives it bite. The crisp, clean, fruit-forward French rosé in the wash is a natural pairing with rich, fatty pork, and it really picks up the flavor of the rub.

MAKES ABOUT ½ CUP

4 tablespoons Morton kosher salt

4 tablespoons herbes de Provence

1 tablespoon freshly ground white pepper

1 teaspoon ground coriander

Combine all of the ingredients in a small bowl and whisk until the mixture is thoroughly blended.

Store in an airtight container for up to two months.

★
HERBES DE
PROVENCE WASH

MAKES ABOUT 2 CUPS

12 ounces (1½ cups) French rosé wine

½ cup vegetable oil

2 tablespoons Herbes de Provence Rub

Pour the wine, oil, and rub into a plastic condiment squirt bottle. Shake vigorously until the rub is dissolved and the mixture is blended, like a vinaigrette, about 1 minute.

Store in the refrigerator for up to two weeks. The oil in the wash will thicken when it is cold. Allow the wash to reach room temperature before using, and shake vigorously to re-blend.

To use, spritz a light coat of the wash—enough to moisten, but not soak—over pork shoulder or ribs when you check for doneness during the last 30 minutes of the cook.

BUILD-YOUR-OWN-WASH TEMPLATE

I TYPICALLY USE THE TART WASH (page 115) for any meat graced with Gary Wiviott's Rub (page 160) because I think the sweet-tart flavor of the cranberry juice lends itself to that particular blend of herbs and spices. However, as with the marinade (page 72), brine (page 93), and rub (page 130) templates, you should experiment with different flavors and customize the wash based on what you like.

WASH LIQUID: ¾ CUP

Think of the liquid as a conduit for the rub—although you should consider the acidity, sugar content and flavor of the liquid when you choose it, it's really a way to get an additional coating of the rub on the meat. Beer, unsweetened fruit juice and broth impart a subtle flavor to the meat and can be paired to complement or contrast the flavors in a rub. Stay away from highly acidic citrus juices, like lemon or lime, and be wary of liquids loaded with sugar, including sodas and fruit juice. And think about flavors that make sense with the rub on the meat. For example, use orange juice if the meat is coated in the Fennel Coriander Rub (page 128).

OIL: ¼ CUP

You can use olive oil, but canola, vegetable, sunflower, and safflower oil are cheaper, readily available and are more neutral in flavor. Do not use corn, peanut, sesame or any other heavy, flavorful oils.

RUB: 2 TABLESPOONS

Use whatever rub you're coating on the meat.

★ BARBECUE CLASSICS: ★
THE CAROLINAS DIPS

A GREAT JOKE THAT exemplifies how ubiquitous barbecue is in North Carolina and South Carolina: How can you tell you're in the Carolinas? The car washes have signs that say "No Pig Cookers Allowed."

The regional barbecue of North Carolina and South Carolina is partly defined by the different types of sauces used. South Carolina tends toward mustard-based sauces, and North Carolina is known for its vinegar-based dips. The Carolinas and I agree on the role of sauce—it's strong, and it's thought of as a condiment or dip, like hot sauce or ketchup.

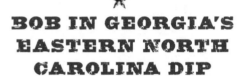

BOB IN GEORGIA'S EASTERN NORTH CAROLINA DIP

One of the more interesting barbecue men of my acquaintance, Bob in Georgia not only talks the talk, he walks the walk—raising his own pigs, sheep, goats, and other delicious animals. Bob and his wife, Ginger, are true keepers of the traditional barbecue flame, and his dip is barbecue simplicity at its finest. It's an eastern North Carolina classic: straight-up vinegar and pepper. Out of the bowl, this dip will seem harsh and overpowering. But sprinkled—lightly, like hot sauce—over pulled pork piled on a bun, it is perfectly balanced with the rich, fatty meat.

MAKES 2 CUPS

2 cups cider vinegar

2 tablespoons Morton kosher salt

1 tablespoon dried crushed red pepper flakes

Pinch of sugar

Freshly ground black pepper, to taste

Whisk together all of the ingredients in a medium bowl until the salt is dissolved.

WESTERN NORTH CAROLINA DIP

As you move west in North Carolina, dips get slightly sweeter with the addition of tomato—usually ketchup or tomato paste, or occasionally tomato juice. Barbecued pork shoulders are the meat of choice in the Carolinas, and this dip is a classic for drizzling on pulled pork sandwiches. It's thin and peppery, but a whack of brown sugar and ketchup take some of the edge off. If you're smart, you'll whip up this sauce after you take the pork off of the cooker. While the meat is getting cool enough to handle, tear off a hunk of Mrs. White (page 187) and whisk it into the sauce as it simmers.

Makes about 6 cups

4 cups water

1¼ cups white vinegar

1 cup ketchup

5 tablespoons brown sugar

1 tablespoon Morton kosher salt

2 tablespoons freshly ground black pepper

2 tablespoons dried crushed red pepper flakes

½ teaspoon cayenne pepper

½ cup Mrs. White (optional)

Whisk all of the ingredients together in a large non-reactive saucepan over medium heat, stirring occasionally. When the sauce comes to a low boil, lower the heat and simmer for 10 minutes. Serve at room temperature.

Store in an airtight container in the refrigerator for up one week.

CANDY WEAVER'S MUSTARD BARBECUE SAUCE

Highly respected on the competition circuit, Candy Weaver gives a lot of thought and consideration to the art of barbecue. Candy's addition of grated apple and Jack Daniel's to this South Carolina mustard sauce turns this sauce into a completely different animal. Right off the burner, it has a bite, but give it two or three days to mellow in the refrigerator. Her recipe calls for John Willingham's W'ham Seasoning, but you can substitute another rub.

Makes about 4 cups

1 cup cider vinegar

1 cup white vinegar

1 cup honey

½ cup prepared yellow mustard

¼ cup Worcestershire sauce

½ cup Jack Daniel's

1 apple, peeled, cored, and grated

3 tablespoons Willingham Original BBQ Rub (W'ham Seasoning)

1 tablespoon onion powder

1 tablespoon garlic powder

Simmer all of the ingredients over low heat until the apple falls apart, or until the sauce reaches the desired thickness and consistency.

Store in the refrigerator for several days to allow the flavors to meld before using.

TEXAS-STYLE BARBECUE SAUCE

This is my amped-up version of the barbecue sauce served at Cooper's, in Llano, Texas—where God goes when she's in the mood for brisket. You can't make this sauce before the pork is cooked because the key ingredient is a big rich hunk of the browned fatty bits (a.k.a. Mr. Brown and Mrs. White) from the cooked shoulder. Dropped into the sauce, the fat and spices from the rub dissolve into the other ingredients and make for one damn-fine condiment.

MAKES ABOUT 6$\frac{1}{2}$ CUPS

2 cups white vinegar

2 cups ketchup

2 cups water

1 tablespoon Louisiana-style or Mexican-style hot sauce, such as Texas Pete, Louisiana, or Búfalo

1 tablespoon Worcestershire sauce

2 teaspoons freshly ground black peppercorns

1 teaspoon garlic powder

1 teaspoon onion powder

$\frac{1}{2}$ teaspoon Morton kosher salt

Large (hand-size) chunk of fat cap/bark from cooked pork shoulder

Combine all of the ingredients in a large stockpot over medium heat and simmer, stirring occasionally, for 20 minutes. Serve warm.

Store in an airtight container in the refrigerator for up to one week.

HOW TO REHEAT PULLED PORK

Not that there will be any leftovers, but if you make a huge quantity of pulled pork and hold it for a day or two, the reheat requires a deft hand. The meat can dry out and overcook quickly, so it needs a preventative hit of moisture. I use a mix of apple juice and cider vinegar seasoned with salt and pepper, but you could use an equal amount of beer or soda, too. If you want to use beer or soda, use 1 cup of liquid, $\frac{3}{4}$ teaspoon salt, and $\frac{1}{2}$ teaspoon freshly ground black pepper.

1. Preheat the oven to 300°F.
2. Mix about $\frac{1}{4}$ cup of reheating liquid per pound of meat. (For 1 cup of liquid, stir together $\frac{3}{4}$ cup apple juice, $\frac{1}{4}$ cup cider vinegar, $\frac{3}{4}$ teaspoon kosher salt, and $\frac{1}{2}$ teaspoon freshly ground black pepper.)
3. Gently toss the pulled meat with the reheating liquid.
4. Cover the container tightly with foil.
5. Place the pan in the oven. Check the pork every 10 to 15 minutes, depending on the quantity of meat. It takes about 5 minutes to heat 1 pound of meat.

DEAR LOW & SLOW GRADUATE,

CONGRATULATIONS—YOU MADE IT THROUGH ALL FIVE COOKS WITH MEAN OLD Wiviott riding you like a rented mule. You think that was tough? Now comes the hard part, when neighbors, friends, and long-lost relatives start dropping by unannounced and clamoring for some of your exquisite barbecue. Pretty women will be nicer to you, free beers will appear in your hand at the local tavern, and, if your reputation spreads far enough, you may even get out of a few speeding tickets.

Despite the deliciousness that is good barbecue, this program has never been about the food. The perfect ribs or pulled pork sandwich are but a delectable side effect of the real challenge of developing your barbecue senses and learning to build a clean-burning fire. You probably made a few mistakes along the way—you strayed from the program or tried some neat shortcut you read about online. All is forgiven. (The great thing about barbecue is, even when you screw it up, you get to eat your mistakes.)

I should warn you about the one unfortunate side effect of learning such a delicious and highly coveted skill. People tend to get evangelical about barbecue once they learn the true and righteous way. It will become very difficult—even impossible—for you to keep your mouth shut when you bear witness to the unspeakable acts of cruelty inflicted on meat in the name of barbecue. You will get anxious watching a neighbor hose down briquettes with lighter fluid, or worse, fire up the propane for some "barbecue." You will cringe when so-called friends speak of boiling or baking as the secret to great ribs. The taste of liquid smoke will make you angry. Feelings may get hurt—probably not yours—and you'll spend a day or two in the doghouse paying for it.

I have learned, the hard way, the art of tempering barbecue-related conversations: the closer the relative or friend, the less inclined I am to set them straight. I advise you to do the same. But by all means, go forth and teach the good word of true barbecue, and give every one of those poor barbecue-challenged souls a copy of this book.

May the smoke be with you,

Gary Wiviott

8.

MASTER
THE ART OF
BARBECUE
ON A GAS OR
ELECTRIC GRILL

GOTCHA!

Shame on you for even thinking it.

You cannot make low and slow barbecue on a gas or electric grill.

9.

MEAT AND THREE

SIDES

AT DIVE BARBECUE JOINTS, HOMESPUN DINERS, AND COMFORT FOOD CAFES
across the South, the menu is "Meat and Three"—your choice of a meat and three vegetable side
dishes. Big scoops of crusty molten macaroni and cheese, potato salad made with bacon drippings, and molasses-sweetened baked beans all fall into the category of vegetable. It's a beautiful thing, this menu. It's also the inspiration for the handpicked group of sides, appetizers, and
desserts in this chapter. These are the standouts—the recipes I turn to time and again when I'm
planning to fire up the smoker.

Like everything else in this program, these recipes come with a caveat: Don't get so wrapped
up in side dishes that you lose sight of the meal's headliner. You're working too hard learning the
proper techniques of low and slow barbecue to let a pile of coleslaw overshadow your efforts. It's
like focusing on the color of a strikingly beautiful woman's toenail polish. There's nothing wrong
with serving a pile of perfectly cooked ribs or pulled pork with a smear of sauce and a few slices
of cheap white bread. Once your skills on the cooker become second nature, you'll have plenty
of free time to fool around with these side dishes.

COLD SIDES

 ## GARLIC SLAW

Danny Gaulden is a well-known barbecue man from Carlsbad, New Mexico, and this recipe is my spicy adaptation of his Garlic Slaw. The recipe was near perfect on its own, but I'm rarely content with strictly following recipes. If a little of something is good, a lot of something is better. So I added a hit of cayenne, threw in a few grated jalapeños, and nearly tripled the amount of garlic. Because the cabbage wilts and can turn the dressing thin and watery, don't dress the coleslaw more than three hours before serving. Use tongs to grab the coleslaw out of the mixing bowl and strain the excess dressing from it before putting it in a serving bowl.

SERVES 10 TO 12

2 cups mayonnaise

1/2 cup plus 2 tablespoons sugar

2 tablespoons prepared yellow mustard

1/3 cup cider vinegar

1 1/8 teaspoons kosher salt

1/4 teaspoon freshly ground white pepper

1/4 teaspoon freshly ground black pepper

1/4 teaspoon cayenne pepper

4 garlic cloves, peeled and grated

1/2 lemon, juiced (about 2 tablespoons juice)

1 small green cabbage, quartered, cored, and thinly sliced (about 6 cups)

1/2 small red cabbage, quartered, cored, and thinly sliced (about 3 cups)

2 medium carrots, peeled and grated (about 1/2 cups)

1/2 bunch green onions, thinly sliced

3 jalapeños, grated

1/2 red bell pepper, diced

Whisk the mayonnaise, sugar, mustard, vinegar, salt, pepper, cayenne, garlic, and lemon juice in a large bowl until combined. Toss with the cabbage, carrot, green onion, jalapeño, and bell pepper. Cover the slaw with plastic wrap and refrigerate until it's cold and the flavors blend—at least 1 hour, but no more than 3 hours to keep the slaw from wilting and getting runny.

★ GRANDMA SCHULER'S POTATO SALAD

From my lovely bride, Ellen's, mother, this straightforward potato salad is a delicious mainstay at family picnics. The Kraft mayo is more tradition than taste-maker. Feel free to substitute your favorite mayonnaise.

SERVES 6 TO 8

2 $\frac{1}{2}$ pounds small red-skinned potatoes, scrubbed, but not peeled

$\frac{1}{2}$ tablespoon salt

4 eggs, hard-cooked and coarsely chopped

$\frac{1}{2}$ medium onion, grated

1 $\frac{1}{2}$ cups Kraft Real Mayo

1 tablespoon sweet pickle relish

$\frac{1}{2}$ tablespoon crushed garlic

Kosher salt and freshly ground black pepper, to taste

Paprika, for garnish

Parsley, for garnish

Place potatoes, $\frac{1}{2}$ tablespoon salt, and water to cover in a large pot. Bring the water to a boil over high heat; then reduce heat and simmer until the potatoes are tender, about 20 minutes; a toothpick or fork should slide easily into the flesh. Drain and quarter the potatoes. Place the potato, egg, and grated onion in a large bowl. In a separate bowl, stir the mayonnaise, relish, garlic, and salt and pepper together. Pour the dressing over the potato mixture and gently fold to combine.

Cover and refrigerate the potato salad until cold, about 1 hour. After cooling, taste and reseason as needed. To serve, mound the potato salad in a bowl and garnish with a dusting of paprika and a topknot of parsley. Store in the refrigerator for up to two days.

★ LEXINGTON RED SLAW

A pulled pork sandwich is not a pulled pork sandwich in North Carolina without this tangy barbecue slaw thrown on. As in the barbecue sauce or "dip" native to western North Carolina, tomato (in this case, ketchup) makes an appearance. And because it contains no mayonnaise, this different breed of coleslaw is picnic-friendly.

SERVES 8 TO 10

$\frac{1}{3}$ cup vegetable oil

$\frac{1}{4}$ cup ketchup

3 tablespoons cider vinegar

1 tablespoon sugar

1 $\frac{1}{2}$ teaspoons celery seeds

1 medium green cabbage, quartered, cored, and thinly sliced (about 8 cups)

3 large carrots, peeled and grated (about 1 $\frac{1}{2}$ cups)

Kosher salt and freshly ground black pepper, to taste

Whisk the oil, ketchup, vinegar, sugar, and celery seeds in a large bowl. Toss with the cabbage and carrot. Season with salt and pepper. Cover and chill in the refrigerator at least 2 hours, but no more than 6 hours, before serving.

★ CREAMY MACARONI SALAD

On a blistering-hot day, a tangy cold macaroni salad is an excellent counterpoint to warm barbecue. If you make the salad and refrigerate it for a few hours before serving, the macaroni will absorb a lot of the liquid in the dressing. Stir in a few tablespoons of cold water to revive some moisture. Taste the salad and adjust the seasonings after it has been refrigerated.

SERVES 8 TO 10

1 pound elbow macaroni, cooked al dente in salted boiling water and drained

$1/2$ red onion, minced

1 celery rib, minced

3 tablespoons minced Italian flat-leaf parsley or 1 tablespoon dried parsley

$1/2$ lemon, juiced (about 2 tablespoons juice)

1 tablespoon brown prepared mustard

$1/4$ teaspoon garlic powder

$1/2$ teaspoon Louisiana-style hot sauce

$1^1/2$ cups mayonnaise

Kosher salt and freshly ground black pepper, to taste

Place the cooked pasta in a large mixing bowl. Stir in the onion, celery, parsley, lemon juice, mustard, garlic powder, and hot sauce. Fold in the mayonnaise. Add salt and pepper. Refrigerate, covered, for 1 hour before serving.

Store in an airtight container in the refrigerator for up to two days.

★ TEXAS CAVIAR

This simple dish belies its highbrow name, but the humble cowpea, or black-eyed pea, is a beloved legume in Texas—particularly when served with barbecue. (Athens in East Texas is the "black-eyed pea capital of the world," in case you have any doubts.) The peas are nearly pickled in the strong vinaigrette overnight. The caviar can be served as a side salad or as a scoopable salsa with tortilla chips.

SERVES 6 TO 8

$1/2$ cup olive oil

$1/4$ cup white vinegar

2 garlic cloves, finely minced

$1/4$ teaspoon dry mustard

1 teaspoon Morton kosher salt

1 teaspoon freshly ground black pepper

2 cups black-eyed peas, cooked, or 2 (15-ounce) cans black-eyed peas, drained and rinsed

1 jalapeño, minced

4 green onions, sliced

1 celery rib, finely diced

Whisk the oil, vinegar, garlic, mustard powder, salt, and pepper together in a bowl. Add black-eyed peas, jalapeño, onion, and celery and toss. Refrigerate overnight.

Store in an airtight container in the refrigerator for up to one week.

★
TUSCAN WHITE
BEAN SALAD

Simple and delicious, this is a long-time favorite dish from my friend Jan Bloom, a terrific cook and an even better tango dancer. I regularly make this to serve at my own backyard gatherings or to bring to parties. It's low maintenance, and with no spoilable ingredients, it holds up well over several hours.

SERVES 6 TO 8

1$\frac{1}{2}$ cups dried cannellini beans, cooked, or 2 (15-ounce) cans cannellini beans, drained and rinsed

1 cup Italian flat-leaf parsley, stemmed and chopped

2 medium tomatoes, chopped

5 tablespoons extra-virgin olive oil

1 lemon, juiced (about 3 tablespoons juice)

5 garlic cloves, minced

$\frac{1}{2}$ tablespoon kosher salt, or to taste

$\frac{1}{2}$ teaspoon freshly ground black pepper, or to taste

Combine the beans, parsley, and tomato in a bowl. In a separate bowl, whisk the oil, lemon juice, garlic, salt, and pepper to emulsify. Pour the dressing over the beans and gently toss to blend. Serve at room temperature. Store in the refrigerator for up to one week.

TIP: If you double the recipe, do not increase the amount of salt in the salad.

INGREDIENT FINDER:
CANNELLINI BEANS

Popular in Southern Italian cuisine, these nutty white beans are a common staple in Italian markets. Most supermarkets stock canned cannellini beans in the aisle with Italian or Mexican ingredients (labeled "alubias" in Spanish). If you can't find cannellinis, substitute with great Northern or white navy beans.

★
THAI-STYLE SWEET AND SOUR CUCUMBER SALAD

This traditional Thai salad is a classic accompaniment with grilled, skewered satay, but over years of searching for new, non-traditional sides, I've found this to be the perfect foil for American barbecue. Tart, hot, and just a little sweet, it works with any barbecue, but it is a terrific match with ribs bathed in the Char Siu-Style Marinade (page 135) or chicken made with the Thai Marinade (page 67), Thai Herb Paste (page 102), or Lemongrass Brine (page 92).

SERVES 6

2 large cucumbers, peeled, halved lengthwise, seeded, and thinly sliced

1 small red onion, thinly sliced

1 teaspoon dried crushed red pepper flakes

4 tablespoons sugar

$^1/_2$ cup water

5 tablespoons white vinegar

$^1/_2$ teaspoon kosher salt

Place the cucumber slices, onion, and pepper flakes in a heatproof mixing bowl. Combine the sugar and water in a saucepan over medium heat, and gently simmer until the sugar dissolves, about 5 minutes. Remove from the heat and stir in the vinegar and salt. Pour the liquid over the cucumber mixture and stir. Cover and refrigerate. Allow the salad to marinate 1 to 2 hours before serving.

★
PICKLED RED ONIONS

Pickles and barbecue are a classic combination, but this zippy relish takes a bit more chefing than just opening a jar. The payoff is in the punchy flavor. I also like the color contrast of dark, smoky barbecue and the delightfully eerie, translucent red glow of these pickles.

SERVES 10 TO 12

4 large red onions, thinly sliced

3 cups cider vinegar

$^3/_4$ cup sugar

1 tablespoon Morton kosher salt

2 whole cloves or $^1/_4$ teaspoon ground allspice

4 whole allspice berries

Place the onions in a large glass bowl. Combine the vinegar, sugar, salt, cloves, and allspice in a large nonreactive saucepan and bring the mixture to a rolling boil. Carefully pour the pickling liquid over the onions. Cool to room temperature, stirring occasionally. Pack the pickled onions and liquid in an airtight container or clean glass jars. Refrigerate for at least 3 to 4 hours before serving. Store in the refrigerator for up to five days.

★
ST. PETER
FAMILY CORN AND
TOMATO SALAD

This salad came to me by way of Dan Gill, a barbecue man I hold in high esteem and owner of Something Different Country Store and Deli in Urbanna, Virginia. The recipe is an original from Judy St. Peter, the mother of store manager Angela St. Peter. It's a family favorite and one of the most popular sides at the deli. The dish also has friends in high places. Eric St. Peter was a Navy mess cook during parts of the Clinton and Bush administrations, and this simple salad was such a hit that it was included in The White House Cookbook. Judy St. Peter uses frozen corn—preferably shoepeg—but notes that fresh sweet corn, blanched and cut from the cob, makes the best salad.

SERVES 10 TO 12

2 pounds (32 ounces) frozen shoepeg or white corn, defrosted, or 3 (15-ounce) cans shoepeg or white corn, drained

2 to 3 medium tomatoes, diced

$^1/_2$ medium red onion, finely diced

1 red bell pepper, diced

1 tablespoon mayonnaise

Kosher salt and freshly ground black pepper, to taste

Combine all of the ingredients in a large bowl and toss to combine. Serve at room temperature. Store in the refrigerator for up to three days.

TIP: For an added twist, use smoked tomatoes (page 217).

HOT SIDES

 ## GERMAN POTATO SALAD

This rich warm potato salad embodies one of my favorite sayings: Nothing says excess like excess. I have nothing against traditional mayonnaisey potato salad, but everything is better with bacon. It's probably not the potato salad to serve when it's 103°F outside, but when you discover the glory of firing up your cooker on a chilly fall or winter day, this is the first side dish that should come to mind.

SERVES 6 TO 8

2 pounds large red-skinned potatoes,
   scrubbed and cubed (about 1-inch cubes)

1/2 pound bacon (8 to 10 strips)

1 onion, chopped (about 1 cup)

1/2 teaspoon sugar

1/2 cup cider vinegar

1/3 cup water

1 tablespoon whole-grain mustard

1/2 teaspoon freshly ground black pepper

1/4 cup Italian flat-leaf parsley, stemmed and
   chopped

Place the potatoes and 1 tablespoon salt in a large stockpot, and add cold water to cover potatoes by about 1 inch. Bring to a boil over high heat; then reduce the heat to medium and simmer until potatoes are cooked through, about 10 minutes. A fork or toothpick should slide in easily.

Fry the bacon in batches in a skillet over medium heat until crisp, 5 to 7 minutes. Transfer the bacon to a plate. Pour off all but about 3 tablespoons of the bacon grease from the skillet. Add the onion to the skillet and sauté over medium heat, stirring, until golden-brown, about 5 minutes. Sprinkle in sugar and stir until dissolved. Add vinegar and water to the skillet and simmer 5 minutes. Remove the skillet from the heat and whisk in the mustard and pepper.

Add the still-warm potatoes and parsley to the skillet. Crumble the bacon over the potatoes and gently fold to combine. Taste and reseason with salt and pepper.

The salad should be served warm. If making ahead, cover and refrigerate; then reheat the chilled potato salad at 350°F in a covered ovenproof casserole until it is warmed through. Store in the refrigerator for up to one day.

★
FUNERAL POTATOES

It's a grim moniker for such a crowd-pleasing dish, but the name has more to do with its spur-of-the-moment simplicity: the dish can be thrown together quickly for any unexpected occasion. Based on a recipe from Chicago radio host Spike O'Dell, it's the kind of dish that can be doubled or tripled—even quadrupled—to feed the masses. If you increase the recipe, bake the casserole for an additional 10 or 15 minutes per batch, but do not increase the oven temperature. (The top will scorch.) For quadruple batches, decrease the oven temperature to 325°F and bake for 1 hour and 15 minutes.

SERVES 12

¼ pound (1 stick) unsalted butter, divided

1 (32-ounce) bag frozen Southern-style (diced) hash brown potatoes

½ teaspoon kosher salt

1 teaspoon freshly ground black pepper

1 (15-ounce) can cream of chicken soup

1 cup grated Cheddar cheese

1 cup shredded mozzarella cheese

1 pint sour cream

½ cup chopped or grated onion

2 cups cornflakes, crushed

Preheat the oven to 350°F.

Melt 4 tablespoons butter in a Dutch oven over medium heat. Add the potatoes, salt, and pepper and stir. Add the soup, cheese, sour cream, and onion. Gently fold the potato mixture until the ingredients are mixed, but not mashed. Remove from the heat.

Pour the potatoes into a greased 13 x 9-inch glass baking dish. Melt the remaining 4 tablespoons margarine in a saucepan. Stir in the crushed cornflakes. Sprinkle on top of the potatoes. Bake, uncovered, for 45 minutes. Serve immediately, or cool to room temperature, cover, and refrigerate. Reheat in a 350°F oven.

★
CRUNCHY CRUST MAC AND CHEESE

The toasty, crunchy bits on the top and edges of baked macaroni and cheese are really the whole point of the dish—much like crispy chicken skin. The dilemma? There's usually not enough scrumptious browned surface to go around. This recipe, adapted from one that ran in the New York Times, offers a brilliant solution: baked in a shallow jelly-roll pan, the macaroni and cheese has more surface area exposed to the heat, and produces a higher ratio of cheesy, crusty to molten, cheesy interior. It's the muffin top of macaroni and cheese. If you really want to gild the lily, sprinkle a teaspoon of truffle oil over the macaroni and cheese right when you take it out of the oven. (Careful: a little truffle oil goes a long way and can overpower the dish.)

SERVES 8

4 tablespoons butter, divided

1 pound elbow macaroni, cooked al dente in salted boiling water and drained

12 ounces extra-sharp Cheddar cheese, grated,
1 cup reserved

12 ounces mild Cheddar cheese, grated,
1 cup reserved

2 teaspoons Morton kosher salt

1/2 teaspoon cayenne pepper

2/3 cup half-and-half

Kosher salt and freshly ground pepper, to taste

1 teaspoon truffle oil (optional)

Preheat the oven to 375°F.

Grease a 15 1/2 x 10 1/2 x 1-inch jelly-roll pan with 1 tablespoon of the butter. Toss the cooked, cooled pasta, grated cheese (reserving 1 cup of each type), salt, and cayenne in a large bowl until the ingredients are evenly distributed. Spread the pasta in an even layer in the greased jelly-roll pan. Pour the half-and-half over the pasta. Top with the reserved 2 cups of grated cheese and dot with the remaining 3 tablespoons butter. Bake uncovered for 40 minutes. Increase the heat to 400°F and bake for an additional 15 minutes, or until the top is crunchy, crusty, and golden brown. Season with salt and pepper.

TRIXIE-PEA'S MAC AND CHEESE

When I get a yen for rich, fancy macaroni and cheese, the first recipe that comes to mind is this crowd-pleaser from friend Kristina Meyer (a.k.a. Trixie-Pea). Her version starts with a classic béchamel sauce, but she's added a few twists that push it over the top.

SERVES 8 TO 10

1 pound elbow macaroni, uncooked

1 stick unsalted butter

1 to 2 teaspoons dried crushed red pepper flakes

3 to 5 garlic cloves, peeled and crushed

1/2 cup all-purpose flour

1 cube chicken bouillon or 1 tablespoon powdered bouillon

4 cups whole milk

6 ounces grated Fontina cheese (about 2 cups)

6 ounces grated Gruyere cheese (about 2 cups, 1/4 cup reserved)

6 ounces grated extra-sharp Cheddar cheese (about 2 cups, 1/4 cup reserved)

1 tablespoon Tabasco sauce

2 tablespoons Worcestershire sauce

Kosher salt and freshly ground black pepper, to taste

2 cups panko or regular dry breadcrumbs

Parcook the macaroni until very al dente, about 6 to 8 minutes, or 75 percent of the recommended cooking time. To test, bite through an elbow. It should be hard at the center. Rinse the pasta under cold water to cool and stop the cooking.

Preheat the oven to 400°F.

Melt the butter in a saucepan over medium heat and sauté the red pepper and garlic cloves until fragrant and golden brown, about 3 minutes. Stir in the flour and chicken bouillon and whisk until incorporated with the butter. Increase the heat to medium-high and gradually whisk in the milk. Bring the mixture to a boil and continue whisking until the sauce is thick and smooth, about 10 minutes.

Remove the sauce from the heat and fold in 1 cup of grated cheese at a time (reserving ¼ cup of each type), stirring until cheese is completely melted before adding more. Add the Tabasco, Worcestershire sauce, and salt and pepper. Taste and reseason as needed.

In a large casserole dish, combine the cooked macaroni and the cheese sauce. Stir to blend. Mix the reserved grated cheese with the breadcrumbs, and sprinkle generously over the top. Bake until browned and bubbling, about 15 to 20 minutes.

INGREDIENT FINDER: PANKO

Panko [pahn-koh] are coarse, flaky Japanese breadcrumbs, and many supermarkets carry bags of them in the Asian section or near the regular breadcrumbs. Panko make a fantastic, crispy-crunchy—and yet *light*—coating or topping for just about any food you want to fry or bake. If you've ever ordered *tonkatsu* (fried pork cutlet) in a Japanese restaurant, you've had panko.

★
BAKED BEANS

When it comes to barbecue, I do not have a sweet tooth. I like a vinegary tang or mouthful of heat in sauces, sides, or rubs, so I lean toward the tangier, hotter barbecue sauce in this recipe for baked beans. If I'm feeling lazy, Original Open Pit Barbecue Sauce (page 166) is my go-to. If you prefer a sweeter touch, use the Classic Barbecue Sauce (page 106) or your sauce of choice. (Read the label and avoid any sauce that contains liquid smoke in the ingredient list.)

SERVES 6 TO 8

6 ounces bacon (6 slices), coarsely chopped

2 small onions, finely diced

5 garlic cloves, peeled and minced

1 pound dried white beans (about 2 cups), such as navy beans, rinsed and picked over

8 cups water

1 cup espresso or strong black coffee

½ cup Tangy Seven-Pepper Sauce (page 137) or your choice of barbecue sauce

2 tablespoons packed brown sugar

2 tablespoons prepared yellow mustard

2 tablespoons mild molasses

1 teaspoon Louisiana-style or Mexican-style hot sauce, such as Texas Pete, Louisiana, or Búfalo

1 teaspoon Morton kosher salt, plus more to taste

1 teaspoon freshly ground black pepper, plus more to taste

Preheat the oven to 300°F.

Cook the bacon in a large Dutch oven over medium heat until it starts to brown and crisp, about 5 minutes. Add the onion and cook, stirring often, until the onion is softened, about 5 minutes. Add the garlic and cook until fragrant, about 30 seconds. Stir in all of the remaining ingredients, increase heat to high, and bring to a boil. Scrape down the sides of the Dutch oven and stir the browned, crusty fond into the beans.

Cover the Dutch oven and place in the oven. Bake, stirring every 30 minutes, until the beans are tender, about 4 hours.

Uncover and bake until the sauce has thickened, about 1½ hours. Taste and reseason the beans with hot sauce, salt and pepper, or 1 tablespoon of barbecue sauce until desired flavor is achieved.

Beans can be served immediately or cooled to room temperature, covered, and refrigerated for up to five days. To reheat, place the beans over low heat on the stove, stirring occasionally, until warmed through.

★
SPICY GRILLED GREEN BEANS

One of the things I appreciate most about barbecue—in addition to its all-around deliciousness—is its conviviality. It attracts like-minded and interesting people, like friend, food photographer, and LTHForum.com contributor Ron "ronnie_suburban" Kaplan, the creator of this recipe. I've enjoyed this dish at many of his backyard barbecues, and this book just wouldn't be complete without it.

SERVES 6 TO 8

1 teaspoon Morton kosher salt

1½ pounds green beans, trimmed

¼ cup oyster sauce

2 tablespoons Sriracha (see Ingredient Finder, page 164)

½ tablespoon *nam pla* (Thai fish sauce)

½ tablespoon hoisin sauce

2 garlic cloves, peeled and minced

1 tablespoon sesame seeds, lightly toasted

Add the salt to a large stockpot of water, and bring to a boil over high heat. Fill a large bowl with ice water. Blanch the green beans in the boiling water until bright and crisp-tender, about 3 to 4 minutes. Drain the green beans and shock in the ice bath to stop cooking and set color. Strain the green beans and place inside a gallon zip-top bag.

Whisk together the oyster sauce, Sriracha, fish sauce, hoisin, and garlic. Pour the marinade over the green beans, seal the bag, and shake to coat. Refrigerate overnight.

Remove the green beans from the bag, reserving 2 tablespoons marinade. Place the green beans in a vegetable grilling basket. Grill over direct heat, turning several times, until green beans are browned and wrinkled, about 3 to 5 minutes. Allow green beans to cool. Toss with reserved marinade, garnish with sesame seeds, and serve. Store in the refrigerator for up to two days.

★
SKILLET CORN BREAD

Basic corn bread doesn't get much easier than this. The only trick to it is pouring the batter into a sizzling-hot oiled skillet. This technique gives the corn bread a crispy, almost caramelized, browned crust.

MAKES 8 LARGE SLICES OR 16 SMALL WEDGES

2 tablespoons canola oil, divided

1 cup yellow cornmeal

2 teaspoons sugar

1 teaspoon kosher salt

2 teaspoons baking powder

1/2 teaspoon baking soda

1 large egg, at room temperature

1 cup buttermilk

Preheat the oven to 425°F.

Swirl 1 tablespoon of the oil in a cast-iron skillet. Set the skillet in the preheating oven while you prepare the corn bread batter.

Whisk the cornmeal, sugar, salt, baking powder, and baking soda together in a mixing bowl and make a small well in the center with the back of a spoon. In a separate bowl, beat the egg. Add the buttermilk and the remaining 1 tablespoon of oil to the beaten egg and whisk. Pour the egg mixture into the well in the cornmeal and stir to combine, but do not overmix.

Remove the skillet from the oven. Swirl the hot oil around the skillet to coat sides. Pour the batter into the hot skillet, circling the stream of batter from the outer edges of the pan toward the middle. Return the skillet to the oven and bake for 11 minutes, or until a toothpick inserted in the center comes out clean. Remove the skillet from the oven and turn the corn bread out onto a cooling rack.

★
NANCY POWERS' BAKED CORN PUDDING

I have had the honor of cooking with Chicago Salvation Army Captains Merrill and Nancy Powers at many holiday dinners, and this dish is a favorite at their meals. Nancy makes enough to feed hundreds of people, and this version of the recipe is easy to double, triple, or quadruple to feed a large crowd.

SERVES 6 TO 8

1/4 pound (1 stick) butter

8 ounces sour cream

1 large egg

1 (8.5-ounce) box Jiffy Corn Muffin mix

1 (15-ounce) can creamed corn

1 (15-ounce) can whole-kernel corn

Preheat the oven to 325°F.

Cream the butter and sour cream with an electric mixer. Stir in the egg. Add the muffin mix and corn and stir until blended.

Pour the mixture into a 2-quart 11 x 8-inch glass baking dish and bake for 1 hour and 15 minutes.

JALAPEÑO-CHEDDAR SKILLET CORN BREAD

This is not your average rustic corn bread. Rich and dense, spiked with green onions and jalapeño, it's more of a savory cheddar and corn cake. I like the look of corn bread wedges and the crisp crust you get by pouring the batter into a hot oiled skillet, but you can also use a regular greased baking pan if you want to serve the corn bread in smaller squares.

MAKES 8 TO 12 WEDGES

1 1/2 cups all-purpose flour

1/2 cup yellow cornmeal

2 tablespoons sugar

1 tablespoon baking powder

1 teaspoon kosher salt

2 large eggs

1 cup whole milk

1/4 pound (1 stick) unsalted butter, melted, 1 tablespoon reserved

4 ounces extra-sharp Cheddar, grated (about 1 cup), divided

2 green onions, chopped, 2 tablespoons reserved

2 jalapeños, stemmed, seeded, and minced

1 (15-ounce) can whole-kernal corn, drained

Preheat the oven to 350°F. Place the skillet in the preheating oven to heat.

Combine the flour, cornmeal, sugar, baking powder, and salt in a mixing bowl. In a separate bowl, gently beat the eggs; then stir in the milk and butter. Gently stir the wet ingredients into the dry; do not overmix. Fold in corn, 1/2 cup of grated cheese, the green onions (reserving 2 tablespoons), and the jalapeños. Let the batter rest on the counter for 10 minutes.

When the batter is ready, remove the skillet from the oven. Swirl reserved 1 tablespoon butter in the skillet to grease. Pour batter into prepared skillet. Cover with remaining grated cheese and green onions. Return skilled to oven and bake for 20 to 25 minutes, or until a toothpick comes out clean. Let cool and cut into wedges. Serve warm or at room temperature.

BARBECUE GARLIC BREAD

You could grill or bake this bread, but if you want to get more work out of those charcoals, throw it on your cooker after the barbecue comes off.

MAKES 1 LOAF

1/4 pound (1 stick) butter

1 tablespoon olive oil

6 garlic cloves, peeled and minced

1 loaf French or Italian bread, split in half lengthwise

1/2 teaspoon Morton kosher salt

1/2 teaspoon dried crushed red pepper flakes

1/4 teaspoon freshly ground black pepper

Melt butter in a small saucepan. Remove from heat and stir in olive oil and garlic. Brush butter mixture over bread. Sprinkle with salt, red pepper flakes, and black pepper. Place bread, crust-side down, on cooking grate. Cook until warm and lightly smoky, about 10 minutes.

APPETIZERS AND EXTRAS

 ## PIMENTO CHEESE

This is a staple snack in the South, not to mention a favorite of Colleen Rush, friend, coauthor, and barbecue gal extrordianaire. For an interesting variation on the classic deviled egg, increase the mayonnaise to 1 cup and use this pimento cheese blend as the filling.

MAKES ABOUT 3 CUPS

8 ounces extra-sharp Cheddar cheese, grated

8 ounces mild Cheddar cheese, grated

1 (8-ounce) jar pimentos, drained

1 (8-ounce) package cream cheese

3/4 cup mayonnaise

2 teaspoons garlic salt

1/2 teaspoon cayenne pepper

1/4 teaspoon freshly ground white pepper

Combine all of the ingredients in the bowl of an electric mixer. Mix on medium speed until blended, about 1 minute. Serve at room temperature.

Cheese can be stored, covered, in the refrigerator for up to one week.

BLACK BEAN SALSA

A simple dish and an arrow in any barbecue cook's quiver, this salsa is easy to make and holds up well at picnics. If I've made it once, I've made it a hundred times over the last ten years. I usually add more jalapeño and garlic, and throw in cayenne or dried crushed red pepper flakes, but the salsa is spot-on without the additions.

Serves 6 to 8

1 (16-ounce) can black beans, drained

1 (16-ounce) can whole-kernel corn, drained

$1/2$ cup chopped red onion

4 green onions, chopped (about $1/2$ cup)

1 tablespoon cumin seeds, lightly toasted

1 large tomato, chopped, or 2 smoked tomatoes (page 217), chopped

2 jalapeños, stemmed, seeded, and chopped

2 garlic cloves, peeled and minced

2 tablespoons olive oil

1 lime, juiced (about 2 tablespoons juice)

$1/2$ cup cilantro, stemmed and chopped

Kosher salt and freshly ground black pepper, to taste

Combine all of the ingredients in a large bowl and stir until well blended. Refrigerate 2 to 3 hours before serving.

ESCALONETS (BACON-WRAPPED DATES)

It's hard to imagine anything that wouldn't be delicious wrapped in bacon, and this popular Spanish tapas is no exception. My long-time friend and king of Lake Tahoe barbecue Andy Bloom often serves these bites at his table. If you're short on time, the wrapped dates can be broiled and crisped in less than ten minutes. But with your newfound smoking savvy, it's just as easy to pop these nuggets directly on the grate of your cooker. Because you want the bacon to crisp, set the dates close to the hottest zone—the perimeter of the grate on the WSM, near the water pan and firebox on the offset, or in the area closest to the water pan on the kettle.

Makes 2 dozen pieces

24 whole almonds, blanched and lightly toasted

24 large dates

8 bacon slices, cut into thirds

4 ounces goat cheese

Preheat the broiler or prepare your cooker for indirect cooking. Make a small vertical slit in the skin of each date and use your finger to hollow out a small space. Loosely pack each date with goat cheese and slip an almond inside. Wrap a section of bacon around each date and secure with a toothpick. Arrange the dates on broiler tray or near the hottest zone on the cooker's grate. Cook until the bacon is crisp, about 8 minutes under the broiler or up to 1 hour on the cooker.

★ DRAGON TURDS

This is a popular snack anywhere you find barbecue guys, but the origin of the recipe is long lost to wood smoke and bourbon. True chile-heads might use habañero peppers instead of jalapeños, but you can also sweeten the bite by mixing chopped dried fig or date into the chorizo. Given the variability of jalapeño size and cooker temperature, it's difficult to nail down an accurate cooking time. They're done when the sausage is fully cooked, so make a few extra and check them periodically for doneness. It could take as little as thirty minutes, or as long as an hour and a half. Wear gloves when handling jalapeños or any hot peppers.

MAKES 25 SERVINGS

25 jalapeños, washed

1 pound fresh chorizo or spicy Italian sausage

1 pound bacon (about 16 strips), cut in half crosswise

5 to 7 dried figs or dates, chopped (optional)

Remove stem and top of each jalapeño and slice it down one side. Remove the seeds and, if you want to reduce the spiciness, remove the white ribs or pith. In a small bowl, stir together chorizo and chopped dates, if using. Stuff each jalapeño with about 1 tablespoon chorizo mixture. Wrap each with bacon and secure with a toothpick. Set the stuffed jalapeños directly on the cooker grate. Smoke until the sausage is cooked through.

★ SPICY SMOKED NUTS

These nuts are what I call cook's treats—little savory snacks that keep the blood sugar up, the palate awake, and the hungry, hardworking guardian of the barbecue happy. There are countless variations to this simple recipe: increase the heat with a teaspoon of cayenne, use habañero-based hot sauce, or add a note of sweet to your heat with a tablespoon of sugar.

MAKES ABOUT 1 POUND

1 pound nuts (not mixed, as they will not cook evenly)

$\frac{1}{4}$ cup Louisiana-style or Mexican-style hot sauce, such as Texas Pete, Louisiana, or Búfalo

In a large bowl, toss the nuts and the hot sauce to thoroughly coat. Perforate a disposable aluminum pie plate (make holes slightly smaller than the nuts). Arrange a single layer of nuts in the plate. On a cooker set up for a low and slow smoke, cook the nuts until crisp and fragrant, about 1 hour. Remove the plate from the cooker and allow the nuts to cool before serving.

Nuts can be stored in an airtight container for up to one week.

SMOKED FRUITS AND VEGETABLES

THE COMBINATION OF WOOD SMOKE AND A LIGHT CHAR ON PRODUCE is almost as good as it is on pork. (I said *almost*.) Low and slow heat concentrates the flavor of a fruit or vegetable and infuses it with a rustic smokiness that complements any type of barbecue. Smoked fruits and vegetables are delicious as is or with a drizzle of olive oil and salt and pepper, or you can incorporate them into any number of terrific appetizers, side dishes, or desserts.

From size and shape to the thickness of the skin, fruits and vegetables have too many variables for exact instructions or cook times. Use these tips to guide you:

MOST FRUITS AND VEGETABLES are easier to smoke whole, but uncut produce requires a longer cook. If you're short on time or want more smoke flavor, halve or quarter the produce.

CONSIDER THE SKIN. A whole fruit or vegetable with a thick peel or impermeable skin will not absorb much smoke. You may need to halve a lime or slice an eggplant to get a full, smoky flavor.

DON'T OIL OR SEASON the produce before smoking. Oil is unnecessary because produce will not stick to the grate, and you should season to taste, post-cook.

FOR MAXIMUM SMOKINESS, put the produce in the cooker when fresh wood chunks are engaging—at the beginning of the cook or after you restock.

SET THE FRUIT or vegetable directly on the grate, near the hot zone on your cooker. Wrapping it in foil or placing it on a tray will block smoke absorption.

GENTLY ROTATE and flip the food once or twice during the cook.

COOK TIMES

THESE ARE BALLPARK TIME ESTIMATES FOR SMOKING produce. It's not a comprehensive list, but you can use it to estimate how much time is needed to smoke any fruit or vegetable that's comparable in the thickness of the skin, the density and the size of the produce in the list. Always rely on your barbecue instincts—not a timer—to tell you when it's done. Times are based on whole produce, unless otherwise specified.

POTATO OR SWEET POTATO:
2 to $2\frac{1}{2}$ hours

CABBAGE: 2 to $2\frac{1}{2}$ hours

TOMATO: 1 to $1\frac{1}{2}$ hours

SQUASH: 2 to $2\frac{1}{2}$ hours

EGGPLANT: $1\frac{1}{2}$ to 2 hours

ONION: 1 to $1\frac{1}{2}$ hours

GARLIC: 1 to $1\frac{1}{2}$ hours

PEPPERS: 1 hour

CITRUS FRUIT, CUT IN HALF: 1 hour

★ SMOKED CABBAGE ★

THIS DISH IS SO EASY, I CAN'T EVEN CALL IT A RECIPE: Remove the outer leaves and core the head of cabbage, making a hollow in the base about the size of a shot glass. Poke one chicken or vegetable bouillon cube into half a stick of softened butter. Insert the butter into the cabbage hollow. Crimp a sheet of aluminum foil into a doughnut. Set the head of cabbage, butter-side up, on the foil. Smoke the cabbage for two to two and a half hours, until it's soft and loses some of its structure—sort of the vegetable equivalent of pulled pork when it's done.

★ SMOKED TOMATO BRUSCHETTA

The ladies love this light, two-bite morsel, and it's a great way to showcase the full range of your smoking skills. You can also broil or sauté the peppers and onion if you run out of room on the cooker grate.

MAKES ABOUT 15 TO 18 PIECES

1 baguette, cut crosswise into 1-inch-thick rounds

2 tablespoons extra-virgin olive oil, divided

1 large garlic clove, peeled

2 smoked tomatoes (page 217), cored and coarsely chopped

2 smoked red bell peppers (page 217), seeded, and diced

1 small smoked onion (page 217), diced

$\frac{1}{2}$ teaspoon Morton kosher salt, plus more to taste

$\frac{1}{4}$ teaspoon dried crushed red pepper flakes

1 tablespoon chopped fresh basil leaves or 1 teaspoon minced fresh thyme

2 teaspoons balsamic vinegar

1 ounce Parmesan cheese

Black pepper, to taste

Broil or grill baguette slices, about 5 inches from heat source, until golden brown on both sides, about 1½ minutes per side. Brush the toasted slices with 1 tablespoon oil and rub them with the garlic clove.

In a medium bowl, combine tomato, bell pepper, and onion. Season mixture with ½ teaspoon salt and 1 tablespoon oil. Stir in red pepper flakes, basil or thyme, and vinegar. Let the mixture rest at room temperature for 30 minutes to allow the flavors to blend. Taste and reseason with salt and pepper as needed. Ladle a spoonful of the tomato mixture onto each bread slice. With a vegetable peeler, shave a curl of Parmesan cheese over the bruschetta to garnish. Serve at room temperature.

★ SMOKED SALSA

This is my stock recipe for pico de gallo, a simple fresh tomato salsa, with a few key alterations. Instead of using white onions, which have more bite, I recommend using the sweeter Vidalia onion to balance the heat and smokiness. And all of the produce, except the cilantro, is smoked—even the lime. Follow the guidelines and times for smoking vegetables (Cook Times, opposite page), but use common sense, too. You'll instinctively know when the lime is ready or if the tomato needs another fifteen minutes.

SERVES 6 TO 8

4 smoked tomatoes, diced

1 smoked Vidalia onion, diced

2 smoked jalapeños, stemmed, seeded, and diced

2 smoked limes, juiced (about $\frac{1}{4}$ cup juice)

2 tablespoons olive oil

$\frac{1}{2}$ cup cilantro, coarsely chopped

Kosher salt and freshly ground black pepper, to taste

2 ears of corn, boiled, kernels cut from the cob (optional)

$\frac{1}{2}$ teaspoon cumin (optional)

Combine tomato, onion, and jalapeño in a medium bowl and stir. Add lime juice, oil, cilantro, salt and pepper, and corn and cumin, if using.

The salsa can be made one day ahead. Cover, refrigerate, and bring to room temperature before serving.

★ CREAMY SMOKED TOMATO SOUP

If you must eat a meal with no pork or other barbecue, this soup is a knockout—particularly when it's served alongside a crusty, oozing grilled cheese sandwich. If you serve the soup chilled, taste before serving and reseason with salt, pepper, and cayenne, as the flavors will be muted from the cold.

SERVES 6 TO 8

1 tablespoon olive oil

2 to 3 medium onions, chopped (about 1 cup)

1 celery rib, chopped (about $\frac{1}{2}$ cup)

1 tablespoon chopped garlic

2 pounds smoked tomatoes, cored and quartered

4 cups chicken stock

2 tablespoons finely chopped parsley

Kosher salt and freshly ground black pepper

Pinch of cayenne pepper

$\frac{1}{4}$ cup heavy cream

Heat oil in a large stockpot. Sauté the onions, celery, and garlic over medium heat until lightly browned, about 5 to 8 minutes. Add the smoked tomatoes and any residual tomato juice. Cook for 3 to 4 minutes, stirring. Add the chicken stock, increase the heat to high, and bring to a boil. Reduce the heat to a simmer and cook for 1 hour and 15 minutes. Using an immersion blender, purée the soup. Stir in the parsley. Taste and season with salt and black pepper and cayenne pepper as needed. Stir in the heavy cream. Serve hot.

SMOKE-ROASTING

LOW AND SLOW IS ALL ABOUT TURNING TOUGH, FATTY CUTS of meat into tender barbecue, and capturing the ephemeral flavor of wood smoke in the meat. But some cuts and types of meat are naturally tender, and don't require a long, indirect cook. Enter: hot smoke-roasting. With a slight reconfiguration of your cooker, this technique allows you to roast meat at a higher temperature and impart a kiss of smoke flavor to your food. By opening all of the vents and removing the water pan, you can make the temperature in the cooker run closer to 350°F—comparable to oven-roasting, only with the bonus, unique flavor that comes from cooking with wood and charcoal.

In keeping with the progressive methodology of this program, I recommend starting small with the Buttermilk-Brined Hot Wings (page 223). Once you get the hang of controlling the fire at the higher temperature, you can use this technique to cook duck, whole chickens, lamb, prime rib, and other meats.

SMOKE-ROASTING ON A WSM

Open all vents on the cooker. Remove the water pan and the bottom cooking grate. Start a K.I.S.S. Method fire, but halve the amount of unlit charcoal in the setup. (This hotter, faster cook uses less charcoal.) Reassemble the WSM. When the charcoal and wood are fully engaged and no longer billowing white smoke, arrange the food on the grate and close the cooker.

SMOKE-ROASTING ON A KETTLE

Close the bottom vent by one-third. Start a K.I.S.S. Method fire. Set an unglazed firebrick on the grate over the lit charcoal. (Do not use the aluminum loaf pan filled with water in this cook.) When the charcoal and wood are fully engaged and no longer billowing white smoke, arrange the food on the grate and close the cooker.

SMOKE-ROASTING ON AN OFFSET

Open all vents on the cooker. Start a K.I.S.S. Method fire with half the amount of unlit charcoal. (Do not use the aluminum loaf pan filled with water in this cook.) When the charcoal and wood are fully engaged and no longer billowing white smoke, arrange the food on the grate and close the cooker.

SMOKED OYSTERS

This recipe calls for one dozen oysters, but I typically buy two dozen. That accounts for the one-for-the-guests, one-for-the-cook method I employ when making this terrific appetizer.

MAKES 1 DOZEN OYSTERS

1 dozen oysters, rinsed and scrubbed

2 lemons, 1 juiced (about 3 tablespoons juice) and 1 reserved for garnish

Start a KISS Method fire and set up your cooker for smoke-roasting according to instructions for the WSM (page 221), offset (page 221), or kettle (page 221). Shuck the oysters, reserving as much of the liquid in the shells as possible to be used in the Mignonette Sauce. Drizzle a few drops of lemon juice on each oyster. Set the oysters in the half-shell on the grate of your cooker. Allow the oysters to cook until just heated through, about 30 minutes. Serve with wedges of reserved lemon and Classic Cocktail Sauce (page 224) or Mignonette Sauce (page 225).

FIREBRICK

A firebrick is a ceramic block that can withstand extremely high temperatures. Firebricks are used to line kilns, furnaces, fireplaces, and outdoor barbecue pits. In hot smoke-roasting, a firebrick on the cooking grate blocks the direct heat of the charcoal from blasting the food and helps the cooker maintain a steady temperature. A single unglazed firebrick shouldn't cost more than a few bucks, and you can find one at most hardware or home and garden stores.

★
BUTTERMILK-
BRINED HOT WINGS

Although you could easily low and slow cook these wings for a little over an hour, my preferred method is smoke-roasting (page 221), because it produces a crispier skin on the wings. Mmmmm. Crispy skin. You can buy pre-sectioned wings—with the drumette and flat separated and the tip removed—but it's more cost-efficient to buy whole wings and section them yourself. To separate, cut through the joint connecting the drumette to the flat (also called the "fling" in Chicago) and the joint connecting the flat to the tip. Because the slender tips have little meat and slip through the grate, I reserve these pieces and freeze them to use in homemade stock.

SERVES 8 TO 10

⅓ cup kosher salt

⅓ cup brown sugar

⅔ cup Gary Wiviott's Barbecue Rub (page 160)
   or other spicy rub, divided

¼ cup Louisiana-style or Mexican-style hot sauce,
   such as Texas Pete, Louisiana, or Búfalo

¼ cup warm water

5 pounds chicken wings, sectioned

½ gallon buttermilk

Add the salt, brown sugar, ⅓ cup rub, hot sauce, and warm water to a 1-gallon zip-top bag and seal. Shake bag. Add the sectioned chicken wings to bag. Pour the buttermilk into bag, filling to within 1 inch of the zipper. Press the air out of the bag and seal. Place the bag in a large bowl or on a rimmed baking sheet to catch any drips. Allow the chicken wings to brine for 4 to 6 hours in the refrigerator, turning the bag once or twice to redistribute the liquid.

Drain and rinse the wings. Set the wings on a baking sheet and coat with the remaining ⅓ cup rub.

Start a KISS Method fire and set up your cooker for smoke-roasting according to instructions for the WSM (page 221), offset (page 221), or kettle (page 221). Place the wings on the cooking grate. Follow times and instructions for smoke-roasting wings on your cooker:

WSM: At 20 to 25 minutes into the cook, flip the wings. Check the wings for doneness at 45 minutes, and every 5 to 10 minutes afterward.

OFFSET: At 15 minutes into the cook, flip the wings. Check the wings for doneness at 30 minutes, and every 5 minutes afterward.

Serve warm or room temperature.

KETTLE: At 15 minutes into the cook, flip the wings. Check the wings for doneness at 30 minutes, and every 5 minutes afterward.

> **TIP:** I rarely pass up the opportunity to gild the lily when cooking—adding more butter, bacon, or chile pepper makes everything better. But these wings are good enough to eat solo. If serving wings without blue cheese dressing will incite a riot in your house, use really good blue cheese dressing from the refrigerated section in the grocery store, and thin it out with a tablespoon of red wine vinegar.

★ SMOKED SHRIMP

This recipe was inspired by Calumet Fisheries, a fish joint that sits on the bridge at 95th Street and the Calumet River, on the South Side of Chicago. The shabby building camouflages one of the best un-kept secrets of the city: an urban smokehouse that produces some of the finest smoked fish—dare I say?—in the country.

Brining is necessary to keep the shrimp tender and plump, and I recommend cooking the shrimp shell-on to prevent oversmoking the delicate meat. Slitting the shell along the back and deveining the shrimp makes the cooked shrimp easier to peel.

MAKES 2 POUNDS (SERVES 4 TO 6)

$\frac{1}{2}$ cup kosher salt

2 tablespoons sugar

2 cups warm water

2 pounds extra-large (16 to 20 count) shell-on shrimp, deveined

In a large bowl, whisk the salt, sugar and warm water together until dissolved. Add two cubes of ice to cool brine. Place the shrimp in the bowl and fill with cold water to cover. Refrigerate, covered, for 30 minutes.

Rinse the brined shrimp under cold water and pat dry with a paper towel.

Start a KISS Method fire and set up your cooker for smoke-roasting according to instructions for the WSM (page 221), offset (page 221), or kettle (page 221).

WSM: Arrange the shrimp on the grate, grouping toward the center of the grate and away from the hot zone on the outer edges. Smoke-roast the shrimp for 20 minutes and check for doneness.

OFFSET: Arrange the shrimp on the cooking grate, starting one-third of the way down the grate, away from the water pan and firebox opening. Smoke-roast the shrimp for 25 minutes and check for doneness.

KETTLE: Arrange half (1 pound) of the shrimp on the grate and close the lid. Smoke-roast the shrimp for 10 minutes and check for doneness. Repeat with the remaining shrimp.

Remove the shrimp from the cooker and immerse in an ice bath to stop cooking and chill. Serve cold, on a bed of ice, with Classic Cocktail Sauce.

★ CLASSIC COCKTAIL SAUCE

It's sweet, hot, and just a little tart, and the perfect counterpoint to smoked oysters or shrimp.

MAKES $\frac{1}{4}$ CUP

$\frac{1}{4}$ cup ketchup

1 teaspoon fresh horseradish

$\frac{1}{2}$ lemon, juiced (about 1 teaspoon juice)

Pinch of cayenne pepper

Kosher salt and freshly ground black pepper, to taste

Stir all the ingredients together in a small bowl; taste and adjust seasonings as necessary.

★
MIGNONETTE SAUCE

Most recipes do not include the step of simmering and reducing the wine and vinegar, but this is the best-kept secret for a killer mignonette.

Makes about ½ cup

½ cup dry white wine

1 tablespoon champagne vinegar, sherry vinegar, or tarragon vinegar

1 shallot, minced

Kosher salt and freshly ground white pepper, to taste

Reserved oyster liquor (from the Smoked Oyster)

Simmer the wine and the vinegar in a nonreactive saucepan over medium-high heat until reduced by half, about 3 minutes. Remove from heat and add the shallot, salt, pepper, and oyster liquor.

DESSERTS

 ## BANANA PUDDING

Banana pudding is the mashed potato of desserts—a comfort food at its best only when made from scratch. Any fool can make the recipe on the box of vanilla wafers, but don't even think of touching instant pudding for this dessert. The fresh, homemade custard is the pièce de résistance in this recipe. Based on a version in Beth Tartan's North Carolina and Old Salem Cookery, this recipe comes courtesy of Dave Lineback, founder of the Society for the Preservation of Traditional Southern Barbecue.

SERVES 4 TO 6

1/2 cup sugar, plus 6 tablespoons, divided

Pinch of kosher salt

3 tablespoons all-purpose flour

4 eggs, divided (3 yolks separated from whites)

2 cups whole milk

1 (12-ounce) box vanilla wafers

3 to 4 very ripe bananas, sliced

6 tablespoons sugar

Blend 1/2 cup sugar, the salt, and the flour in the top of the double boiler. Heat the water in the bottom section of the double boiler until just barley simmering. Add 1 whole egg and 3 yolks (reserving whites) and beat into the mixture. Slowly whisk in the milk until the custard is smooth. Cook the pudding, stirring, until thickened, about 10 minutes. Remove from heat and allow pudding to cool.

Line the bottom of an 8-inch square glass baking dish with vanilla wafers, top with one-third of the sliced bananas, and cover with one-third of the pudding. (Use more wafers for a drier pudding and fewer for a soupy one.) Continue layering wafers, bananas, and pudding to make three complete layers.

Preheat the oven to 375°F. With an electric mixer, beat the 3 reserved egg whites and 6 tablespoons sugar until stiff peaks form. Spread the meringue over the banana pudding. Bake until the meringue is golden-brown, about 15 minutes.

Refrigerate a minimum of 24 hours before serving.

BLACK BOTTOM PIE

The toughest part about this recipe is choosing between the gingersnap and chocolate crust. (I vote gingersnap.) Like low and slow cookery, this Southern classic only looks complicated. And it only takes one forkful of the rich, rum-laced dueling-custard pie to make it worth every dirty dish in your kitchen.

MAKES 1 (9-INCH) PIE

2 tablespoons water

2 tablespoons rum

1 (.25-ounce) envelope unflavored gelatin

$^2/_3$ cup sugar

1 tablespoon cornstarch

2 cups whole milk

4 egg yolks

$^1/_2$ cup semisweet chocolate morsels

$^1/_2$ cup bittersweet chocolate morsels

1 cup whipping cream

2 tablespoons powdered sugar

Gingersnap Crust or Chocolate Crust (recipes follow)

Chocolate shavings, for garnish

Combine the water and rum in a small bowl and stir to blend. Sprinkle the gelatin over the mixture, stir, and set aside.

Combine the sugar and cornstarch in a saucepan; slowly whisk in the milk and egg yolks. Bring the mixture to a boil over medium heat, whisking constantly. Boil for 1 minute. Stir in the gelatin mixture until dissolved.

Set aside 1 cup of the custard mixture. Pour both types of chocolate morsels into the remaining 1 cup of warm custard mixture and stir until smooth. Pour the chocolate custard into the prepared crust. Chill until set, about 30 minutes. Beat whipping cream with an electric mixer until frothy. Slowly add powdered sugar, beating until soft peaks form.

Fold the whipped cream into the remaining custard mixture, reserving some whipped cream for a garnish. Spoon custard over chilled and set chocolate mixture. Chill pie until it sets, about 2 hours.

Garnish with fresh whipped cream and chocolate shavings.

GINGERSNAP CRUST

MAKES 1 (9-INCH) PIECRUST

Nonstick spray

25 gingersnap cookies (to make about $1^1/_2$ cups crumbs)

2 tablespoons sugar

$2^1/_2$ tablespoons unsalted butter, softened

$^1/_2$ teaspoon Morton kosher salt

Preheat the oven to 350°F. Coat a 9-inch glass pie dish with nonstick spray. Grind the cookies to a fine crumb in a food processor. Combine the cookie crumbs, sugar, softened butter, and salt in a mixing bowl and blend. Press the mixture into the pie dish. Bake at 350°F for 8 to 10 minutes. Cool on a wire rack.

★ CHOCOLATE CRUST

MAKES 1 (9-INCH) PIECRUST

Nonstick spray

6 tablespoons unsalted butter

1 ounce bittersweet chocolate, chopped

30 chocolate wafer cookies
(to make about 1/2 cups crumbs)

1/2 teaspoon Morton kosher salt

Coat a 9-inch glass pie dish with nonstick spray. Melt butter and chocolate in a small saucepan over low heat, stirring occasionally. Grind cookies to a fine crumb in a food processor. Pour the warm chocolate mixture and salt into the food processor and pulse until the crumbs are wet. Press crumb mixture into pie dish. Freeze until firm, about 30 minutes.

★ PECAN PIE

The sweet, smoky flavor of real sugarcane syrup sets this pie apart from the rest. If you can't find true cane syrup, like Steen's, don't even bother. Corn syrup just doesn't cut it.

MAKES 1 (9-INCH) PIE

1/4 cup (1/2 stick) unsalted butter

1/2 cup sugar

1/2 teaspoon kosher salt

2 eggs, beaten

1 1/2 cups cane syrup, such as Steen's

1 teaspoon vanilla extract

2 cups pecans, toasted and coarsely chopped

1 unbaked (9-inch) piecrust

Preheat the oven to 450°F.

Heat water in the bottom section of a double boiler until just barely simmering. Melt the butter in the top of the double boiler. Remove butter from heat. Add the sugar and salt and stir until butter is absorbed. Beat in the eggs, then the cane syrup and vanilla. Return the butter mixture to the double boiler over medium heat. Stir until the mixture is shiny, about 130°F if you have a candy thermometer handy. Remove from heat. Stir in the pecans.

Pour the mixture into the unbaked piecrust. Bake for 10 minutes. Reduce the oven temperature to 350°F and bake until the center is set, about 30 to 35 minutes. Serve the pie warm or at room temperature.

★
TENNESSEE HIGHLANDS BUTTERMILK PIE

Bill Arnold's Blues Hog Barbecue Sauce is the secret behind many a competition barbecue man, triggering a positively Pavlovian response in barbecue judges coast to coast. His buttermilk pie has the same effect on me.

MAKES 1 (9-INCH) PIE

2 large eggs, beaten

1 cup sugar

2 tablespoons butter, melted, at room temperature

2 tablespoons all-purpose flour

$^1/_2$ teaspoon kosher salt

1 cup buttermilk

1 teaspoon vanilla extract

1 tablespoon grated lemon peel

1 (9-inch) unbaked piecrust

$^1/_4$ teaspoon freshly ground nutmeg (optional)

Preheat the oven to 400°F.

Combine the eggs and sugar in a large bowl. Add the remaining ingredients and stir to combine. Pour into the piecrust. Sprinkle with nutmeg, if using. Bake the pie for 10 minutes. Then reduce the heat to 350°F and bake until the pie is firm, about 30 minutes.

★
APPLE CRISP

You can substitute just about any type or combination of fruits in this crisp—peaches, pears, berries, or whatever looks good and is in season.

SERVES 6 TO 8

$^3/_4$ cup all-purpose flour

$^1/_2$ cup brown sugar

1 teaspoon cinnamon

$^1/_2$ teaspoon kosher salt

$^1/_4$ pound (1 stick) unsalted butter,
   cut into $^1/_2$-inch pieces and chilled

5 large Granny Smith apples, peeled,
   cored and sliced (about 5 cups)

1 lemon, juiced (about $^1/_4$ cup juice)

3 tablespoons sugar

Whipping cream, for garnish

Preheat the oven to 350°F.

Place the flour, brown sugar, cinnamon, and salt in a food processor and pulse two times to mix. Add the butter and pulse four or five times until the mixture is combined and has the consistency of wet cornmeal. Refrigerate 10 minutes.

Place the apple slices in a bowl, drizzle with lemon juice, and toss with sugar. Pour into a 12 x 8-inch pan. Cover the apples with the chilled topping. Bake for 40 minutes, or until fruit is bubbling and the topping is golden brown. Serve warm or at room temperature, garnished with whipped cream.

LOUISA CHU'S WHITE PEACH, BLUEBERRY, AND LAVENDER COBBLER

Louisa Chu is a chef of all trades—a graduate of a prestigious culinary school who has cooked at such restaurants as Alain Ducasse and El Bulli. Her inquisitive nature, coupled with a journalism degree, has afforded her a serious case of wanderlust. She has chefed in Alaska for a fishing charter, has judged Iron Chef, and is a correspondent for Gourmet magazine's "Diary of a Foodie."

You will need 8 (8-ounce) ramekins or 8 (8-ounce) wide-mouth canning jars for this recipe.

SERVES 8

FILLING

4 white peaches, halved and pitted

8 ounces blueberries

1/4 teaspoon fresh lavender buds

Softened butter to coat ramekins,
    plus 4 tablespoons butter, melted

Sugar to coat ramekins, plus more for sprinkling

TOPPING

1 cup all-purpose flour

2 teaspoons baking powder

1 cup buttermilk

1 teaspoon freshly grated lemon peel

Preheat the oven to 425°F.

For the filling, combine peaches and blueberries in a bowl. Gently rub the lavender buds between your hands to release essential oils and fragrance, and sprinkle over the fruit.

Coat the inside of the ramekins with butter; then coat with sugar. Divide the blueberries between the 8 ramekins. Place 1 peach half, cut-side up, over the blueberries. (If the peaches are too large to fit, cut into a large dice.)

Place the ramekins on a lined sheet pan and bake until the fruit is soft, about 12 minutes. Remove from the oven.

While the fruit is baking, make the topping: combine the flour and baking powder in a small bowl. In a separate bowl, combine the buttermilk and the lemon peel. Slowly add the dry ingredients to the wet, stirring only until a thick batter forms; do not overmix. Spoon the batter over the fruit. Sprinkle sugar over the batter.

Bake until the batter is golden, about 17 minutes. Serve warm or at room temperature with ice cream.

10.
SMOKIN' LEFTOVERS

★ ★ ★ ★ ★

ONCE WORD GETS OUT about your skills on the cooker, you will be smoking chicken, ribs, and pulled pork more often than you ever imagined for crowds of people who may or may not be deserving of your barbecue benevolence. And as hard as it is to believe, every now and then—even after the hungry descend like a locust plague in your backyard—you may have leftovers from these cooks. Likewise, if you're practicing each cook a few times before you move on to the next lesson—as a good student should—you might grow tired of the same old plate of barbecue. This chapter is devoted to all of the creative and sundry ways you can repurpose those delectable leftovers into different meals.

RITA'S SMOKED CHICKEN WON TON SALAD

Smoky, crunchy, sweet, sour, and delicious on all counts, this recipe is sure to start a feud in my family, as there is much disagreement over which sister in-law was the original creator of the salad. It's very important to let the mixture sit overnight so the chicken really drinks in the dressing. Fry the won tons yourself, or do like I do: buy them fresh from your favorite Chinese restaurant.

SERVES 4 TO 6

¼ cup canola or olive oil

1 tablespoon sesame oil

3 tablespoons rice vinegar or white wine vinegar

4 green onions, chopped

2 tablespoons sugar

1 teaspoon Morton kosher salt

½ teaspoon freshly ground black pepper

3 smoked chicken breasts, shredded

2 tablespoons slivered almonds, toasted

2 tablespoons sesame seeds, toasted

1 head iceberg lettuce, shredded

Sweet and sour sauce, for serving

Chinese hot mustard, for serving

½ pound fried won tons

In a medium bowl, whisk together the oils, vinegar, green onions, sugar, salt, and pepper. Add the shredded chicken and toss. Refrigerate overnight.

Add the almonds and sesame seeds to the bowl, and toss just before serving. Serve the salad on a bed of shredded lettuce with sides of sweet and sour sauce and Chinese hot mustard, and garnish heavily with won tons.

ELLEN'S CHICKEN SANDWICH

There is no bigger fan of my barbecue endeavors than my lovely, sweet bride, but after years of ribs, chicken, and pulled pork, she often prefers a slightly sideways adaptation of traditional barbecue. This sandwich is a tip of the bonnet to her dear Aunt Toni's favorite breakfast—a melty, open-faced sandwich.

MAKES 2 SANDWICHES

½ smoked chicken, shredded

4 slices multigrain bread

4 slices Swiss cheese

Strawberry jelly

Layer the bread with slices of cheese. Broil or bake in a 350°F oven until the cheese is bubbling and the bread is toasty, 5 to 10 minutes. Slather toasted bread with jelly and top each slice with a heap of smoked chicken. Serve warm, open-faced.

★
CHICKEN ENCHILADAS

Enchilada *means "in chile," a reference to the piquant tomatillo sauce used to smother the tortilla-wrapped shredded chicken. Enchiladas suizas refers to enchiladas garnished with sour cream or cheese. Enchiladas montadas, topped with a fried egg, make an excellent brunch dish. Substitute pulled pork for the chicken if you so desire.*

MAKES 16 ENCHILADAS

Vegetable oil for brushing

16 stale corn tortillas

2 cups shredded smoked chicken

2 tablespoons water

$\frac{1}{3}$ cup Mexican *crema* or sour cream

$1\frac{1}{2}$ tablespoons minced onion

2 cups Tomatillo Sauce (recipe follows)

Rings of onion and sliced radish, for garnish

$\frac{1}{2}$ cup crumbled *queso añejo* or shredded
  Monterey Jack cheese, for garnish

Preheat oven to 350°F.

Heat a griddle or skillet over medium heat. Brush the griddle with a light coat of vegetable oil. Place the tortillas on the griddle and heat until softened, about 1 minute per side.

Warm the shredded smoked chicken with 2 tablespoons water in a saucepan over medium-low heat. Add the crema and onion. Remove the chicken filling from the heat and cover.

Spread 1 cup tomatillo sauce in a 9 x 13-inch glass baking dish. Dredge both sides of a tortilla in the sauce. Spoon 2 tablespoons of chicken filling into the tortilla and roll it into a tight tube. Set the enchilada in the baking dish. Repeat with the remaining tortillas and filling. Drizzle the remaining sauce over the enchiladas. Bake, covered tightly with foil, for 15 minutes.

Garnish the enchiladas with onion, radish, and crumbled cheese, and serve.

TIP: Stale tortillas do a better job of absorbing the tomatillo sauce. Leave the bag of tortillas open, on the counter, over-night to dry out.

INGREDIENT FINDER: QUESO AÑEJO

This crumbly Mexican cheese has a sharp, salty flavor and a subtle smokiness that comes from rolling the finished cheese in paprika before aging. It can be found in any Mexican grocery and in some specialty stores.

★ TOMATILLO SAUCE

MAKES 2 CUPS

1 pound (about 8) tomatillos, husked and rinsed well

1 jalapeño, stemmed, halved, and seeded

¼ cup cilantro, coarsely chopped

1 small white onion, diced

2 garlic cloves, peeled

½ teaspoon kosher salt

1 tablespoon canola or vegetable oil

2 cups low-sodium chicken stock

Cook the tomatillos in salted boiling water until tender, about 10 minutes. Drain the tomatillos and pour them into a blender or food processor. Add the jalapeño, cilantro, onion, garlic, and salt and purée.

In a medium saucepan, heat the oil over medium-high heat until it shimmers. Pour in the tomatillo mixture. Cook, stirring, for 3 to 5 minutes, until the sauce darkens slightly. Add the stock and bring the sauce to a boil. Then reduce the heat and simmer the sauce for 10 minutes, until thickened.

★ KIT ANDERSON'S CHICKEN DIP

Describing Kit Anderson as multifaceted barely scratches the surface. An accomplished musician, he and his wife, Janel, opened for mega acts back in the day. He's now a dentist with an altruistic bent and a thriving practice. Kit is also known in serious barbecue circles as the go-to man for food science–related matters, and he is one of the resources I tap for matters of test tubes and lab coats.

MAKES 4 CUPS

1 cup mayonnaise

2 cups diced smoked chicken

1 cup Parmesan cheese

4 garlic cloves, minced

4 canned chipotles, minced

1 (14-ounce) can artichoke hearts, drained and minced

Preheat the oven to 350°F.

Stir together all of the ingredients in a medium bowl. Scrape the mixture into a 9-inch pie plate and bake for 25 minutes. Serve warm with tortilla chips.

★
ASIAN CHICKEN WRAPS

You can use whatever smoked chicken you have on hand for these light and simple wraps, but if you have the choice, choose a chicken smoked with one of the excellent Asian brines or marinades (chapters 3 and 4).

MAKES 8 WRAPS

1 ounce vermicelli rice stick noodles (optional)

2 cups shredded smoked chicken

4 green onions, chopped

$1/2$ cup bean sprouts

$1/4$ cup shredded carrot

$1/4$ cup julienned cucumber

1 teaspoon sesame oil

1 tablespoon canola oil

$1/2$ tablespoon soy sauce

$1/2$ teaspoon kosher salt

$1/2$ teaspoon freshly ground white pepper

$1/4$ cup sesame seeds, toasted

8 round rice paper wraps (plus extras)

Dipping Sauce, for serving (recipe follows)

If using the rice noodles, soak them in hot water for 10 minutes. Drain off the hot water and hold the noodles in a pan of cool water. Drain and dry the noodles when ready to use.

For the filling, combine the chicken, vegetables, oils, soy sauce, salt, pepper, and sesame seeds in a large bowl. Toss until blended.

To assemble the wraps, lay a double thickness of paper towel on a work surface. Fill a shallow baking pan with warm water. Check the rice paper wraps for holes. Soak one wrap in warm water until pliable, 30 seconds to 1 minute, and then carefully transfer it to the paper towels.

Arrange about $1/4$ cup of the filling across the bottom third of the soaked rice paper. If using, lay a few strands of noodles over the filling. Fold the bottom over the filling and roll tightly. Transfer the wrap, seam-side down, to a plate, and cover with dampened paper towels. Repeat to fill remaining wraps and serve them, whole or halved diagonally, with dipping sauce.

DIPPING SAUCE

MAKES ABOUT $1/2$ CUP

$1/4$ cup hoisin sauce

1 green onion, chopped

$1/2$ tablespoon crushed peanuts

$1/2$ teaspoon rice wine vinegar

$1/2$ teaspoon Sriracha

$1/2$ teaspoon freshly ground white pepper

Whisk together all of the ingredients in a small bowl. Serve with Asian Chicken Wraps.

★ JERK CHICKEN

Do not serve this to anyone who whimpers at the sight of a pepper mill. This is serious business. For the best flavor combination, use chicken cooked in Caribbean Marinade (page 66).

SERVES 4 TO 6

4 smoked chicken halves

Jerk Gravy

2 cups low-sodium chicken stock

1 tablespoon canola oil

1 tablespoon rice wine vinegar

3 green onions, chopped

2 jalapeños, stemmed, seeded, and chopped, or 1 habañero (a hotter, traditional jerk substitute), stemmed, seeded, and chopped

4 garlic cloves, peeled and chopped

2 bay leaves

1 teaspoon peeled and grated fresh ginger

1 teaspoon kosher salt

$1/2$ teaspoon nutmeg

$1/2$ teaspoon ground allspice

$1/2$ teaspoon freshly ground black pepper

$1/4$ teaspoon cinnamon

1 tablespoon cornstarch

3 tablespoons cold water

Quarter the chicken halves and set aside.

To make jerk gravy: In a medium saucepan, simmer all of the ingredients, except the cornstarch and cold water, in a medium saucepan over medium heat for 10 minutes. Remove the gravy from the heat and use a pair of tongs to fish out the bay leaves. Purée the mix-

ture with an immersion blender or allow the mixture to cool, pour it into a blender, and purée. Return the gravy to the saucepan and warm over medium heat.

In a small bowl, mix the cornstarch and water. Slowly whisk the cornstarch mixture into the sauce. Cook until the sauce thickens to the desired consistency. Ladle jerk gravy over each serving.

★ PULLED JERK CHICKEN SANDWICH

More proof that there is no limit—other than your imagination—to what you can do with leftover smoked chicken.

SERVES 6

$1/2$ tablespoon canola or olive oil

$1/2$ medium onion, diced

$1/4$ cup diced green bell pepper

$1/4$ cup diced red bell pepper

$1/4$ cup canned, whole-kernel corn, or cut from a cob

2 cups shredded smoked chicken

1 cup Jerk Gravy (see Jerk Chicken)

6 hamburger buns

In a sauté pan, heat the oil over medium-high heat. Sauté the onion in oil until translucent, about 3 minutes. Add the green and red pepper and sauté until softened, about 5 minutes. Add the corn and shredded smoked chicken. Cook over medium heat until slightly warm. Add the jerk gravy and heat through. Serve on toasted hamburger buns.

SMOKED CHICKEN AND CORN CHOWDER

Smoky chicken is the perfect complement to the rich, elemental goodness of corn chowder. Choose corn picked at peak freshness and freeze it on the cob in preparation for chowder-friendly weather. The corncob and corn "milk"—released when the corncob is scraped with the back of a knife—are excellent natural thickeners for the soup.

SERVES 6 TO 8

2 strips bacon

1 tablespoon butter

$\frac{1}{2}$ cup diced sweet onion (such as Vidalia, Maui, or Texas 1015)

$\frac{1}{2}$ cup peeled and diced carrot

$\frac{1}{3}$ cup diced celery

4 cups chicken stock

6 cups whole milk

2 bay leaves

2 cups fresh corn, cut from the cob, corncobs reserved

2 medium Yukon Gold potatoes, peeled and diced

$\frac{1}{3}$ cup diced red bell pepper, 2 tablespoons reserved for garnish

1 teaspoon kosher salt

1 teaspoon freshly ground black pepper

$\frac{1}{8}$ teaspoon turmeric

$\frac{1}{8}$ teaspoon cayenne pepper

2 cups shredded smoked chicken

1 sprig fresh thyme

Render the bacon in a large, heavy-bottomed stockpot over medium heat. Add the butter and onion; sauté until the onion is translucent, about 5 minutes. Add the carrot and celery; sauté 4 to 5 minutes. Add the stock and milk and bay leaves. Scrape the corncobs over the stockpot with the back of a knife to release the corn "milk." Break the corncobs in half and add them to the pot. Bring to a boil, then reduce heat and simmer for 30 minutes.

Remove the corncobs, bay leaves and bacon from the pot. Increase the heat to medium-high. Add potatoes, red pepper, salt, pepper, turmeric, and cayenne. Bring to a boil, then reduce heat and simmer until the potatoes are almost tender, about 10 minutes. Add the chicken, corn, and thyme sprig. Bring back to a boil, then reduce heat and gently simmer for 10 minutes. Remove the thyme.

Serve the soup warm, garnished with diced red bell pepper.

★
CHICKEN TORTILLA SOUP

This soup is labor-intensive, but it's a dish that's highly worthy of your world-class smoked chicken. Bonus points if you can score fresh epazote [eh-pah-ZOH-teh], a fragrant herb that's vaguely reminiscent of cilantro— but also quite distinct. Typically, you'll find it dried (sometimes sold as "wormseed") in Latin markets.

SERVES 6 TO 8

8 (6-inch) corn tortillas, cut into narrow strips

2 tablespoons vegetable oil, divided

2 tablespoons kosher salt

8 cups low-sodium chicken stock

2 medium white onions (about 1 pound), peeled and quartered, divided

4 garlic cloves, peeled, divided

2 tablespoons dried epazote or 2 fresh sprigs, or 5 sprigs cilantro plus 1 sprig oregano

3 medium tomatoes, cored and quartered

½ medium jalapeño, stemmed and seeded

1 chipotle chile in adobo, plus up to 1 tablespoon adobo sauce, divided

1 smoked chicken (about 2 pounds), skinned, boned, and shredded

Garnishes: lime wedges, cilantro leaves, minced jalapeño, diced Hass avocado, crumbled Cotija cheese, Mexican crema, or sour cream

For the tortilla strips, adjust the oven rack to the middle position; heat oven to 450°F. Spread the tortilla strips on a rimmed baking sheet. Drizzle the strips with 1 tablespoon oil and sprinkle them with salt. Toss until evenly coated. Bake until the strips are deep golden brown and crisped, about 10 minutes, shaking the strips halfway through the baking time.

While the tortilla strips bake, bring the stock, 4 onion quarters, 2 garlic cloves, and epazote to a boil over medium-high heat in a stock pot; reduce heat to low, cover, and simmer about 20 minutes. Pour the stock through a strainer and discard the solids.

Purée the tomatoes, the 4 remaining onion quarters, the 2 remaining garlic cloves, the jalapeño, the chipotle chile, and 1 teaspoon of the adobo sauce in a food processor until smooth. Heat the remaining 1 tablespoon of oil in a Dutch oven over high heat until shimmering. Add the tomato-onion purée and a pinch of salt and cook, stirring frequently, until the mixture has darkened, 10 to 15 minutes. Stir the strained stock into the tomato-onion purée and bring to a boil. Then reduce the heat to low and simmer, about 15 minutes. Taste and reseason with salt and additional adobo sauce as needed.

Add the shredded chicken and simmer the soup until heated through, about 5 minutes. To serve, place tortilla strips in the bottom of individual bowls and ladle soup into bowls. Top with garnishes.

★
SMOKY CHICKEN AND SAUSAGE GUMBO

You could use leftover smoked chicken in this soup, but I can justify firing up the smoker exclusively to make this dish. Use the Cajun Marinade (page 63), and while the chicken is smoking, put together the roux and trinity base. ("Trinity" refers to the Cajun "holy trinity" of onion, celery, and bell pepper.) If you can't find andouille, throw some hot links, kielbasa, or spicy Italian sausage on the cooker with the chicken to use as a substitute.

SERVES 6 AS AN APPETIZER OR 4 AS AN ENTRÉE

³/₄ cup peanut or vegetable oil

1 cup all-purpose flour

2 cups chopped onion

1½ cups chopped celery

1½ cups chopped green bell pepper

1 pound smoked sausage (*andouille* or kielbasa), cut into ½-inch slices

1 teaspoon kosher salt

¼ teaspoon cayenne pepper

3 bay leaves

6 cups water or chicken stock

1½ pounds smoked chicken (dark and white meat), skinned, deboned, and cut into 1-inch chunks

1 tablespoon filé powder (optional)

Steamed rice, for serving

French bread, for serving

Heat the oil in a heavy (preferably cast-iron) pot over medium heat for about 2 minutes. Add the flour and blend with a wooden spoon. Break up any lumps with the spoon until the roux has a smooth, paste-like texture. Stir the mixture slowly and constantly until it reaches a color between peanut butter and chocolate brown, 20 to 25 minutes. (Do not leave a cooking roux unattended! A burned roux, no matter how slightly burned, will ruin an entire gumbo. If you burn it, start over.)

Stir the onion, celery, and green pepper into the roux. Cook 5 minutes, or until the vegetables are wilted. Add the sausage, salt, cayenne, and bay leaves. Cook, stirring, 3 to 4 minutes. Add the water or stock and stir to combine. Bring the soup to a boil, then lower the heat to medium-low. Cook, uncovered, for 1 hour, stirring occasionally. Skim off the excess fat that rises to the surface. Add the chicken and simmer for 20 minutes. Remove the bay leaves. Ladle the gumbo over rice in bowls. Sprinkle with filé powder. Serve with crusty, buttered slices of French bread.

INGREDIENT FINDER: FILÉ POWDER

Filé is made from the ground, dried leaves of the sassafras tree. It is used to thicken gumbo, and has a faintly smoky, woody flavor that adds depth and richness to this classic Creole dish. Specialty spice stores like Penzey's and The Spice House carry filé powder, and some supermarkets stock the bottled Zatarain's brand. Because overheating filé changes the texture of the ground herb, it should be stirred in after the soup is removed from the heat, or sprinkled on as an accent—like salt or pepper.

COLD SESAME CHICKEN NOODLES

My favorite brother, Lory, spent a few years in New York City during his medical residency, and I am convinced that he wouldn't have lived to practice medicine without ready access to the inexpensive and ubiquitous "peanut butter" cold sesame noodles offered at Chinese restaurants across the city. This recipe, inspired by the dish that spared him starvation, is a family favorite. For an unusual twist, substitute shredded Asian pear for the bean sprouts.

Serves 4 to 6

1 pound spaghetti or lo mein noodles

$^1/_2$ cup chunky peanut butter or $^1/_3$ cup tahini (sesame paste)

$^1/_4$ cup rice wine vinegar

2 tablespoons soy sauce

$^1/_2$ teaspoon minced garlic

$^1/_2$ teaspoon kosher salt

$^1/_2$ teaspoon freshly ground white pepper

$^1/_2$ teaspoon dried crushed red pepper flakes

1 teaspoon sugar

2 cups shredded smoked chicken

$^1/_2$ cup mung bean sprouts, divided

$^1/_4$ cup green onions, finely chopped, divided

2 tablespoons toasted sesame seeds, divided

1 tablespoon sesame oil

Bring 4 quarts of water to a boil. Add the noodles and cook until al dente, about 7 minutes.

Drain the noodles, reserving $^1/_4$ cup cooking water. Do not rinse the noodles. Set them aside to cool.

In a large bowl, whisk together the peanut butter and reserved cooking water until the mixture forms a smooth paste. Add the rice wine vinegar, soy sauce, garlic, salt, white pepper, crushed red pepper, and sugar. Mix thoroughly; if the sauce is too thick, add up to 1 tablespoon warm water. Add smoked chicken, $^1/_4$ cup bean sprouts, 2 tablespoons green onions, and 1 tablespoon sesame seeds.

Add warm noodles to peanut butter sauce and stir to coat. If the mixture is too thick, add up to 1 tablespoon of warm water.

Garnish with reserved bean sprouts, green onions, and sesame seeds and a drizzle of sesame oil.

★ SPARE RIB FRIED RICE

As unlikely as it seems, you may become weary of eating ribs while you practice the rib cooks over and over. Mother Nature practically designed ribs to be eaten hot off the cooker and right off the bone, but if by chance you have a half rack or so left over from a cook, there's no better way to use them than in this delicious fried rice. The beauty of fried rice is that it is infinitely variable. Use whatever vegetables you have on hand, or even substitute chopped pulled pork for spare ribs.

SERVES 4 TO 6

3 tablespoons canola oil, divided

2 large eggs, whisked with 1 tablespoon water

4 garlic cloves, peeled and minced

1 tablespoon fermented black beans (Chinese style)

2 jalapeños, stemmed, seeded, and diced (optional)

1/2 pound mushrooms, sliced

2 carrots, shredded

1/4 cup oyster sauce

1/4 cup water

1 tablespoon soy sauce

2 cups cubed smoked spare rib meat, stripped from bone

1/2 teaspoon freshly ground white pepper

6 cups cooked rice, cooled (day-old is best)

5 green onions, chopped, 1 tablespoon reserved for garnish

1/2 cup sugar snap peas

1 teaspoon sesame oil

Heat a wok over medium-high heat. Add 1 tablespoon oil. Pour in the eggs to make a thin, lightly-cooked omelet. Remove and set aside.

Wipe the wok clean with a paper towel. Return it to medium-high heat. Add 1 tablespoon oil, garlic, fermented black beans, and jalapeño, if using. Sauté until aromatic, about 1 minute, then add mushroom, carrot, oyster sauce, water, and soy sauce. Reduce heat and gently simmer the mixture until the water is mostly evaporated. Make a well in the center and pour in 1 tablespoon oil, the spare rib meat, and the white pepper. Increase heat to high and sauté, stirring vigorously to mix ingredients. Break the rice into clumps, add to the mixture, and stir until heated through. Add the green onion, sugar snap peas, and omelet. Stir until thoroughly mixed and heated through. Taste for seasoning and add oyster sauce or white pepper as needed. Transfer to a large bowl and garnish with a sprinkle of sesame oil and the reserved green onion.

★ SOUTHERN GREENS AND SMOKY BONES

These Southern-style greens get an extra hit of pork and heat from leftover spare ribs. Fair warning: you may find yourself running an extra smoker just to satisfy your greens craving.

SERVES 4 TO 6

2 pounds assorted greens (mustard, turnip, or collard greens)

1 tablespoon vegetable oil

1 onion, chopped

4 garlic cloves, minced

2 jalapeños, stemmed, seeded, and minced

$\frac{1}{2}$ rack smoked spare ribs, cut into individual bones and halved

2 cups water

1 teaspoon kosher salt

$\frac{1}{2}$ teaspoon freshly ground black pepper

$\frac{1}{2}$ teaspoon dried crushed red pepper flakes

Rinse the greens in cold water multiple times to remove any soil or grit. Greens should be pristinely clean. Trim tough stems. Roll a stack of leaves into a tube and cut it crosswise into 1-inch strips. Heat the oil and sauté the onion, garlic, and jalapeño in a large pot set over medium heat until fragrant, about 3 minutes. Add the spare ribs. Sauté until the rib meat starts to caramelize, about 4 to 5 minutes. Pour in the water and bring to a simmer. Add the greens in several batches, allowing each batch of greens to cook down before adding more. Add salt, pepper, and red pepper flakes. Cover and gently simmer for 1 hour.

Transfer the greens and bones to a serving bowl. Serve with the pot liquor, corn bread (page 212), and a sprinkle of Bob in Georgia's Eastern North Carolina Dip (page 193) for accent.

★ PULLED PORK TACOS

Minimalist tacos are happily consumed all across Mexico and are simple to make. They're not only delicious, but also perfect for a quick lunch or snack. Americanize to your heart's content with sour cream, Smoked Salsa (page 219), and shredded cheese.

SERVES 4

$\frac{1}{2}$ cup cilantro, chopped

$\frac{1}{4}$ cup minced white onion

1 lime, juiced (about 2 tablespoons juice)

Kosher salt, to taste

Freshly ground black pepper, to taste

3 teaspoons vegetable oil, divided

1 pound smoked pulled pork

$\frac{1}{4}$ cup chicken or vegetable stock

8 (6-inch) corn or flour tortillas

Cholula Hot Sauce, to taste

Combine the cilantro, onion, lime juice, and salt and pepper in a small bowl; set aside.

Heat 1 teaspoon oil in a sauté pan over medium heat. Add the pork and stock and heat until meat is warmed.

Place a griddle or skillet over low heat to warm. Brush with the remaining oil, as needed, and warm the tortillas in batches.

Top each tortilla with $\frac{1}{8}$ cup of the heated pulled pork and garnish with the cilantro mixture and hot sauce.

★
SPICY SMOKED CHILI

I am not a chili purist of the Texas variety. As a native son of Milwaukee, I consider beer and chiles the only standard ingredients, and the occasional bean finds its way into my bowl of red. To shake things up even more, I often use pulled pork for an interesting variation on traditional ground beef.

SERVES 8

1 medium onion, chopped

2 jalapeños, stemmed, seeded, and minced

4 garlic cloves, minced

1 tablespoon vegetable oil

2 pounds pulled pork

2 tablespoons Toasted Mexican Pepper Blend (page 18)

1 teaspoon toasted and ground whole cumin

2 teaspoons kosher salt

1 teaspoon freshly ground black pepper

1 teaspoon dried crushed red pepper flakes

6 cups water or vegetable stock

1 (14.5-ounce) can crushed tomatoes

2 (12-ounce) bottles Pilsner beer

In a stockpot, sauté the onion, jalapeño, and garlic in oil over medium heat until onion is translucent. Add the pulled pork, pepper blend, cumin, salt, black pepper, and crushed red pepper. Stir until the spices and meat are thoroughly mixed. Add the water or stock, tomatoes, and 1 bottle of beer. Gently simmer for 45 minutes over medium heat.

Drink the remaining bottle of beer.

Serve with additional beer, grated cheese, chopped onion, jalapeño, crackers, or corn bread (page 212).

★
PULLED PORK PIZZA

The possibilities are infinite in what you can put on a pizza, but pulled pork as the star topping is a good place to start. Likewise shredded smoked chicken or even rib meat. This pizza uses pre-made pizza crust for a no-time-flat meal or snack, but don't let me stop you from using a homemade crust.

MAKES 1 (12-INCH) PIZZA

3 teaspoons olive oil, divided

1/2 cup sliced mushrooms

1/4 cup thinly sliced onion

1/2 teaspoon kosher salt

1/2 teaspoon freshly ground black pepper

1/4 teaspoon dried crushed red pepper flakes

1/4 cup barbecue sauce

1 (12-inch) prepared pizza crust

1/2 cup shredded pulled pork

1/2 cup shredded pepper Jack or Colby Jack cheese

Preheat the oven to 400°F.

Heat 2 teaspoons of oil in a skillet over medium heat. Sauté the mushroom and onion until the onion is translucent, about 5 minutes. Add the salt, pepper, and crushed red pepper flakes, stirring.

Spread the barbecue sauce on the crust. Top

with the pulled pork, the cheese, and the mushroom and onion mixture. Brush the edge of the crust with the remaining oil.

Bake the pizza for 10 minutes, or until the crust is crisped, the pork is heated through, and the cheese is melted.

★
CREAMED PULLED PORK ON TOAST

My brother-in-law Nick, an avid deer hunter, outdoorsman, and retired Chicago policeman, makes a mean biscuits and gravy, which this recipe is based on. Also known as S.O.S., this take on the dish works equally well with leftover shredded smoked chicken. It may seem counterintuitive to throw the pork in before making the white gravy, but I like to crisp up the meat a little to give it some texture. Just be sure to vigorously whisk the mixture to work out the lumps and get the gravy smooth.

For Nick's Hunting Camp Biscuits and Gravy, substitute 1 pound crispy, cooked breakfast sausage for the shredded pork or chicken, omit the butter, and double the black pepper.

SERVES 4 TO 6

4 tablespoons butter, divided

1 pound pulled pork, shredded

1 teaspoon kosher salt

1 tablespoon freshly ground black pepper

1 teaspoon dried crushed red pepper flakes (optional)

4 cups whole milk

4 tablespoons all-purpose flour

Toast or biscuits, for serving

Texas Pete hot sauce, for serving

Melt 1 tablespoon butter in a large sauté pan. Add the pork, salt, black pepper, and crushed red pepper, if using. Add the remaining 3 tablespoons butter and milk, and stir. When the butter is melted, sprinkle the flour into the pan. Whisk continuously until the flour and liquid combine into a smooth paste. Cook until the sauce is thickened, about 10 minutes. Serve hot, ladled over buttered toast or fresh biscuits, with Texas Pete hot sauce.

★
PULLED PORK HASH

I love a big, belly-warming plate of salty, spicy corned beef hash served with the perfect over-easy egg winking at me. The only thing better is substituting pulled pork, with the added dimension of wood smoke taking it over the top and beyond.

SERVES 4

2 tablespoons butter

$1/2$ cup diced onion

$1/4$ cup diced green bell pepper

2 jalapeños, seeded, stemmed, and diced (optional)

2 cups shredded pulled pork

2 cups cubed cooked potatoes

1 teaspoon kosher salt

$1/2$ teaspoon freshly ground black pepper

$1/2$ teaspoon dried crushed red pepper flakes
   (optional

8 eggs

Hot sauce to taste

Melt the butter in a large skillet over medium heat. Add the onion, green pepper, and jalapeño. Sauté until the onion is translucent, about 5 minutes. Add the pork and potatoes. Season with salt, pepper, and red pepper. Gently fold the hash to mix, but avoid mashing the potatoes.

Cook the hash without disturbing for 10 minutes, or until the bottom crisps. Carefully flip the hash in the skillet and crisp the other side. Serve with eggs over easy and your favorite hot sauce.

INDEX

C

M

N

O